WEYERHAEUSER ENVIRONMENTAL BOOKS

Paul S. Sutter, Editor

WEYERHAEUSER ENVIRONMENTAL BOOKS explore human relationships
with natural environments in all their variety and complexity. They seek to
cast new light on the ways that natural systems affect human communities,
the ways that people affect the environments of which they are a part, and
the ways that different cultural conceptions of nature profoundly shape our
sense of the world around us. A complete list of the books in the series appears
at the end of this book.

FOOTPRINTS
OF WAR

Militarized Landscapes in Vietnam

DAVID BIGGS

UNIVERSITY OF WASHINGTON PRESS
Seattle

Footprints of War is published with the assistance of a grant from the Weyerhaeuser Environmental Books Endowment, established by the Weyerhaeuser Company Foundation, members of the Weyerhaeuser family, and Janet and Jack Creighton.

22 21 20 19 18   5 4 3 2 1

UNIVERSITY OF WASHINGTON PRESS
www.washington.edu/uwpress

COVER PHOTOGRAPH: Firebase Spear, 1971. US National Archives and Records Administration.

LIBRARY OF CONGRESS CATALOGING-IN-PUBLICATION DATA
Names: Biggs, David A., author.
Title: Footprints of war : militarized landscapes in Vietnam / David Biggs.
Description: Seattle : University of Washington Press, [2018] | Series: Weyerhaeuser environmental books | Includes bibliographical references and index. |
Identifiers: LCCN 2018003967 (print) | LCCN 2018004835 (ebook) | ISBN 9780295743875 (ebook) | ISBN 9780295743868 (hardcover ; alk. paper)
Subjects: LCSH: Vietnam, Central—History, Military—20th century. | Vietnam, Central—Environmental conditions. | War—Environmental aspects—Vietnam, Central. | Indochinese War, 1946-1954—Environmental aspects—Vietnam, Central. | Vietnam War, 1961-1975—Environmental aspects—Vietnam, Central.
Classification: LCC DS559.92.C44 (ebook) | LCC DS559.92.C44 B54 2018 (print) | DDC 304.2/8095974—dc23
LC record available at https://lccn.loc.gov/2018003967

To my beloved travel companions
Hồng Anh, Xuân Anh, Kiên, and Vinh

CONTENTS

Plates follow page 124

FOREWORD

War Is in the Land

PAUL S. SUTTER

In November of 1986, a happy discovery was made on the northeastern edge of Denver, Colorado: a communal roost of bald eagles. The bald eagle is the national bird of the United States, and today it is thriving. In the 1980s, however, it was an endangered species whose population had been decimated by the spraying of DDT, which biomagnified through the food chain, making eagles' eggs brittle and inhibiting their capacity to reproduce. The postwar age of chemical wonders had brought America's national symbol to the brink of extinction. The US Environmental Protection Agency (EPA) banned DDT for use in the United States in 1972, but bald eagles were still relatively rare in the 1980s. The discovery of these roosts in a stand of mature cottonwood trees was thus an important indicator of slow but steady bald eagle recovery. But there was something unusual, even deeply ironic, about where these eagles had landed. A US Army contractor discovered them within the bounds of the Rocky Mountain Arsenal, long the chief manufacturing facility for chemical weapons and other military chemicals in the United States and, by the 1980s, one of the most desperately polluted places on earth.

The Rocky Mountain Arsenal was a central place in the global history of American military chemicals and their human and environmental impacts. Its existence dates to World War II, when, in the wake of the Pearl Harbor attack, the US Army sought out a site in the inland West to manufacture chemical weapons. In May of 1942, the army selected thirty square miles of land in Adams County, Colorado, just northeast of Denver, removed the farm families who had occupied the site, and rapidly built a facility that produced mustard gas, chlorine agent, lewisite, and napalm. Only the napalm was used during World War II, most notably in the fire-bombing of Japanese cities. At the end of the war, the arsenal was put on standby status, but Cold War realities soon brought it back into service, this time for the production of the powerful nerve agent sarin. During the immediate postwar years, the liquid wastes from chemical manufacturing processes were dumped into unlined holding ponds, where concentrated toxics leached into and spread through the soils and waters of the site. By the late 1950s, signs of contamination were already evident, but chemical production continued. In 1959, after the Soviet Union's successful launch of Sputnik, the US Army added a rocket fuel blending facility, and with the lunar program of the 1960s, chemical rocket propellants became a major production priority. The Shell Chemical Company was also producing pesticides and herbicides on the arsenal grounds from 1952 to 1982. During the 1960s the army shifted to deep-well injection as a purportedly safer method of waste disposal. Then, in 1968, even as napalm and other military chemicals were being used in unprecedented quantities during the Vietnam War, President Lyndon Johnson ordered the destruction of obsolete chemical stockpiles. The Rocky Mountain Arsenal became the place to "demilitarize" national supplies of mustard gas and sarin, a program—named, believe it or not, Project Eagle—that would come to define the arsenal's 1970s career. By the end of the 1970s, the arsenal had constructed its first groundwater treatment system to contain and mitigate decades of toxic waste dumping. All chemical production and destruction ceased on the site by the early 1980s, and in 1987, a year after that army contractor discovered those roosting bald eagles, the Rocky Mountain Arsenal joined the EPA's list of Superfund sites.

One can learn all about this history of chemical production and contamination by touring the sparkling new visitor center at the Rocky Mountain Arsenal National Wildlife Refuge. That's right: this place of extraordinary chemical contamination is now a federally protected refuge for wildlife. The 1986 discovery of roosting bald eagles prompted the involvement of the US Fish and Wildlife Service, whose scientists came to recognize that the restricted and contaminated site had allowed wildlife to flourish there. In 1992 President George H. W. Bush signed into law a bill protecting the site as a wildlife refuge, and by 2004, after the EPA certified its cleanup, the army transferred five thousand acres to the Fish and Wildlife Service to formally establish the refuge. In 2010, as a result of continuing cleanup activities, the refuge reached its current size of approximately fifteen thousand acres, complete with a small bison herd, mule deer, burrowing owls, and lots of eagles.

The army still owns a core portion of the property to maintain its waste consolidation areas and operate its groundwater treatment facilities, but most of the refuge is now open to hiking and wildlife viewing.

Over the last several decades, as environmental historians have studied the historical impacts of warfare on the natural world, they have noted that many such sites of intense militarization, from US bases that protect large natural landscapes from development to places such as the Korean Demilitarized Zone, have served unintended but important conservation functions. The Rocky Mountain Arsenal National Wildlife Refuge is one of those sites, and it is tempting to render its story as a redemptive one, a tale of a once-toxic place reverting to its original pristine character. The moral of this particular interpretation is that humans and their bellicosity sinned against the land, but wild animals and other natural processes reclaimed the area in a show of nature's resilience. That's a happy story, but it's not the whole story, for the legacies of war still haunt this place. Alternatively, we might see the arsenal's current status as a wildlife refuge less as a wiping away of the landscape's military legacy than as a reluctant acceptance of its long-term toxicity, for the former Rocky Mountain Arsenal remains too polluted to accommodate human habitation or other intensive forms of human land use. Because of its military past, it will remain a mostly empty space, even as the real estate value of the land around it skyrockets. In that sense, maintaining the site as a wildlife refuge is an inexpensive way of dealing with the ongoing toxic legacies of war. In this reading, the return of wild nature to the site does not erase the footprints of war; it becomes one of them.

Half a world away, in Vietnam, the environmental legacies of war and militarization also remain, sometimes in similarly empty or underdeveloped spaces. This is the story that David Biggs tells in *Footprints of War*, his innovative and visually arresting history of militarized landscapes in central Vietnam. Fans of the Weyerhaeuser Environmental Books series will know Biggs from his first book, the award-winning *Quagmire*, an environmental history of the Mekong River Delta that made that landscape's ecological and deep historical complexity central to the story of American failure in Vietnam. In *Footprints of War*, Biggs shifts his gaze to central Vietnam, the region around the city of Huế, which was home to several American airbases and other military installations—including Phú Bài and, yes, Camp Eagle—during the American War in Vietnam. As Biggs explains, one of the triggers for this book was a fascinating applied environmental history project that he undertook, using US archival records, to help Vietnamese government officials locate potential chemical hotspots that remain throughout central Vietnam. Chemical compounds such as napalm, Agent Orange, and tear gas were central to American military strategy during the Vietnam War, and they were concentrated on American air bases, where they were stored and then loaded onto American airplanes and helicopters for military use. In the search for buried caches of abandoned chemicals or potential toxic plumes in soil and groundwater, Biggs recognized the power of American records, including aerial photographs and satellite imagery, to reveal where such chemicals might be still lurking today. More than that, though, Biggs noticed curious patterns and began asking deeper questions about how war and militarization had repeatedly inscribed and overwritten the landscapes of central Vietnam.

In the United States we often talk about Vietnam as a war rather than as a place. We pay little attention to what came before the American War and even less to what came after. When American forces entered Vietnam, they tended to conceptualize the country as a blank slate and to regard its environment as hostile and impenetrable. The whole place needed to be opened up to the American gaze. That, after all, was what most of those chemicals were for. But what Biggs came to realize was that the American military presence had followed particular historical cues in how it occupied the region, often placing its bases atop formerly militarized spaces or spaces left undeveloped for other historical and cultural reasons. He also observed in his travels that the American withdrawal and abandonment of its occupied spaces left lasting patterns of redevelopment across the landscape, particularly as the creative destruction of modern capitalism has claimed the region in recent decades. Finally, it dawned on him that the very tools he was using to locate sites of potential chemical contamination were also evidence of novel ways of seeing that had been central to the American conduct of war in Vietnam. The ruins and toxic legacies of the United States' involvement in Vietnam constituted only one layer in a complex historical stratigraphy that had shaped the American War in consequential ways and that still shapes the landscape and Vietnamese perceptions of it today.

Footprints of War is not what you might expect from an environmental history of war and militarization, and that is what makes it such an important book. While the environmental impacts of war are always central to Biggs's analysis, this is not at its core a book about the war's impact upon Vietnamese nature. Nor is it a simple history of how the nature of Vietnam—the jungles, the rain, the mud—shaped the American War, at least of the sort we are used to reading. This is a story, or really a series of layered stories, about landscapes, geographies, and terrains, spatial categories in which the natural or non-human environment is ever present but never exists or acts alone. It is a book in which the environment itself is a historical archive that Biggs, a historian of Vietnam first and foremost, sifts through and interprets masterfully. It is a history without fixed baselines for measuring environmental impacts, a history that contextualizes the American War as but one chapter in a long saga of construction, destruction, and ruination. It is, in short, a primer on historical landscape literacy in central Vietnam.

In Biggs's telling, the footprints of war create paths that others follow. They figuratively compact the soil in ways that affect what grows where after war gives way to peace. Sometimes these footprints become fossilized, disappearing below ground as new layers of history cover their presence without quite erasing them. For Biggs, war is not merely a momentary paroxysm; it is also a haunting. When American marines landed in central Vietnam in 1965, they were yet another in a long line of invading forces. They followed in the martial footsteps not only of the French colonialists through their several occupations but also the Japanese occupation during World War II and the Việt Minh occupation in the wake of the French defeat in 1954. Those previous occupations were in turn shaped by a conflict zone that had been held and contested by Việt, Cham, and Chinese peoples for millenia. As American forces moved into the lowlands of central Vietnam, they sought to build homogenous and placeless military enclaves, but the particularities of previous occupations kept intruding. In the conduct of war, the Americans also had to contend with a gradient that linked the coastal plains to the midlands and highlands to the west and with a traditional elevational logic that had long shaped occupation and resistance in the region. Fighting the war on all sides of the conflict became a process of creating networked spaces linked together by various infrastructures—roads, trails, air bases, landing zones—and technologies of viewing and communicating across space. The American War became one of trying to see and not be seen.

Unlike the Rocky Mountain Arsenal, the legacy landscapes of war and militarization in central Vietnam have not become wildlife refuges. The Vietnamese cannot afford to remediate them as Americans have, and they do not have the luxury of leaving these strategic sites to entirely noneconomic uses.

These landscapes have mostly morphed into industrial parks or ecologically sterile timber plantations, though in some cases they have remained military properties. But the important point is that these legacy landscapes have shaped Vietnam's rapidly industrializing present both by providing open spaces for development and limiting the kinds of development that can occur there. An important lesson of *Footprints of War*, then, is that the historical and environmental legacies of militarization check capitalism's creative destruction in the present. Landscapes, like people, hold memories of war that persist even as the obvious physical markers fade from view.

Military historians are fond of talking about certain regions as "graveyards" of empire, places where successive invading forces become repeat casualties of a common historical, cultural, geographical, and environmental myopia. A similar lesson might be drawn for central Vietnam, with its abandoned bases and ruins of war. But that is not the main point of *Footprints of War*. Instead, David Biggs is intent on drawing our attention to the literal and metaphorical graveyards of the Vietnamese people themselves and how they sit in layers and landscape mosaics with these graveyards of empire. Camp Eagle, like other US military bases in central Vietnam, was built amid a traditional Vietnamese burial ground, and today the local people who remain must be actively discouraged from burying their deceased family members there for fear that they will encounter subterranean toxicity. Here is the central metaphor of the book: the American War, like those invasions and occupations that came before it, has left lasting landscape legacies, some of them poisonous, and yet the Vietnamese people insist on reclaiming these grounds the best that they can, rooting themselves in places of deep historical and cultural significance to them. Such are the footprints of war.

ACKNOWLEDGMENTS

This book is not just the compilation of one person's arguments, stories, and notes but instead relies heavily on extensive support networks that directly and indirectly have shaped it. I am reversing the usual order of thanking my loved ones last, especially my beloved wife, Hồng Anh, because she has played multiple, key roles in this project since I first imagined it. Since we met one enchanted June evening long ago, two Americans in Hà Nội, she has been my most ardent champion, tireless critic, best friend, and creative muse. She supplied me with a unique Vietnamese American perspective as I hashed out ideas, and through her globally extended family around the United States and Vietnam, I found a new role as *chú rể David* (groom, son-in-law) or jokingly as *rể Vịt*. Huế in particular and Vietnam in general is a familiar society; building trust and one's identity often begins by identifying to whom and to where one "belongs." From our first honeymoon trip to visit relatives in Huế and tiny Trung Đơn Village in Quảng Trị, members of this extended family received us with unprecedented kindness and frequently offered places to sleep, delicious meals, and sometimes tips for research or feedback as individuals who lived through many events described in this book. Because Hồng Anh, like me, chose to work and live in Vietnam for a spell after growing up in the United States, we had the terrific good fortune to spend much of my research time in Vietnam together and with our children. We led four study abroad trips with California students to Huế University from 2006 to 2015, and on these trips and other research stints, our children accompanied us in guesthouses, at dinners with relatives and in homes nestled on back alleys in Huế. I feel incredibly fortunate to have been able to share this time with them.

Through my in-laws, especially my parents-in-law, Lý Tô and Hồng Thị Như Nguyện, I gained a glimpse, too, of the incredibly transnational nature of Vietnamese experiences, especially of those who migrated from Vietnam but have since returned. Tô and Như Nguyện were students in the United States; they married in Boston in 1972 and nine months later took their infant baby Hồng Anh to visit parents in Huế and Quảng Trị during the 1973 cease-fire. That was Hồng Anh's first overseas trip to Vietnam. Then the war resumed and the bottom fell out; Tô and Như Nguyện, like many others, were cut off from family for some years. Through their stories and those of Uncle Nghiên, Auntie Lạc, and the relatives whom we stayed with, I was able to follow in the most personal terms the struggles of a large Vietnamese family where some relatives migrated to the United States and others stayed. As a father of three children, I still cannot fathom how Tô managed to house anywhere from three to twenty-three relatives in his three-bedroom, split-level home in suburban Boston. He also sent money to Vietnam and sponsored the immigration of his parents, siblings, and father-in-law while holding down a stressful full-time job. While I have done my best to master the Huế dialect and "follow house rules" (*nhập gia tùy tục*), my success and insights are built in no small part from the love and support of my amazing, transnational family. While not a very successful Buddhist, I nevertheless believe in karma and suspect that the goodwill they have generated over the years opened doors and improved my standing by association. I hope to pay it forward.

The research and writing of this book took place in several stages and at many places. The first stop was a postdoctoral fellowship in the History of East Asian Science and Technology at Harvard University in 2009–10. Thanks to this fellowship, I had the good fortune to start research with an amazing cast of characters at American academe's Hogwarts. I owe special thanks to Professor Huệ Tâm Hồ-Tài, who introduced me to visiting celebrities there, wrote letters of recommendation, and warmly welcomed me into her home. Professor Huệ Tâm has helped many Vietnamese and Vietnamese studies scholars over the years, and I especially benefited from her attention in this amazing academic environment. Thanks to my colleagues at the Department of East Asian Languages and Civilizations, especially Professors Shigehisa Kuriyama, Michael Szonyi, James Robson, and Tomoko Kitagawa for their camaraderie and support. Harvard's Center for Geographic Analysis helped me in the initial applied study with support for acquiring satellite imagery pro bono from the GeoEye Foundation and Planet Action. While the imagery only appears in backdrops in this book, it was crucial in helping identify potentially toxic hotspots around Huế in the applied research project.

The University of California, especially my home campus UC–Riverside and my split homes in the Department of History and the School of Public Policy, played a key role in supporting this research. I was fortunate to receive a University of California Office of the President Faculty Development Grant (2010–13) that provided the funds for me to travel over three years to archives in Paris, Vietnam, and Washington, DC. While most universities struggled during the Great Recession, I was extremely fortunate to have these funds to hire research assistants in the French archives and get help in Huế with interviews. In Paris, thanks especially to Dr. Nguyễn Quốc Thanh for her assistance at the Service Historique de la Défense in Vincennes and with French air photography at Fort de l'Est. Even if I could speak French well, I could never have managed the bureaucratic hoops that she did effortlessly to locate archival records and build relationships with French institutions. In Huế I was especially fortunate to work with Dr. Đỗ Nam and Dr. Hồ Đình Duẩn as well as Hoàng Thị Bình Minh, beginning in 2011 and continuing over the years to 2017. Dr. Nam's Office of Science and Technology helped sponsor my field research, while Dr. Duẩn's geographic information system (GIS) research office helped me in producing reference and historical layers in the GIS. Bình Minh assisted me in developing ties with village authorities in Dạ Lê and Phù Bài Villages, which facilitated gathering oral histories. With her help I was able to visit families in those villages and make less awkward return visits. At home at UC–Riverside, members of the Rivera Library interlibrary loan staff have been my perennial heroes! They helped me tap the vast collections of UC's maps and texts at all campuses, getting materials to me efficiently and at no personal cost. Most of the maps featured in the book come from these collections, thanks to additional help from UC's map librarians to obtain scans. Thanks to my department chairs and colleagues, too, for making it possible to arrange leaves and sabbaticals to make time for archives and motorcycle trips in the Vietnamese backcountry.

In 2011 a Fulbright Scholar Fellowship enabled me and my family to live in Huế for five months to carry out much of the local site-based research. Because of my research topic, I was both surprised and grateful to receive a fellowship supported by the US Department of State with additional approvals given by the Vietnamese Ministry of Foreign Affairs and the People's Committee of Thừa Thiên–Huế Province. Fulbright scholars are relatively high profile foreign researchers, and they frequently use this temporary position to contribute to local policy debates. I spoke about the problem of toxic waste left behind at former American bases, and I demonstrated how one could use American historical materials to find some of them. Staff at the US Embassy in Hà Nội with the US Agency for International Development and the US Department of Defense attended my talk and graciously hosted me even if my arguments may have run counter to US positions on war waste in Vietnam. I recognized the great potential for more scholarly engagement with government agencies on this topic, and I hope that this book might in some ways advance environmental dialogues.

I began writing this book in 2013 and continued developing it between teaching, university activities, and family life until mid-2017. A National Endowment for Humanities Fellowship in 2013–14 provided me a critical year to begin the book-writing process. The first part of this book, a dive into early modern and colonial history as well as a grappling with historical GIS data, owes a lot to this fellowship and the time it bought me. Thanks to generous support and leave from UCR's College of Humanities, Arts, and Social Sciences and a writing fellowship from the Rachel Carson Center in Munich, I was able to wrap up the writing in 2016–17. Colleagues in UCR's Southeast Asia Program supported local endeavors and talks on campus; I owe Hendrik Maier special thanks for his constant friendship and his detailed reading of a first rough draft with incisive comments. During this period, many other universities welcomed me and entertained (or endured) guest talks. Thanks to many colleagues and friends who supported me from such glorious venues as the University of Washington (my alma mater!), the Yale Agrarian Studies Program, the University of Wisconsin, Cornell University, UCLA, UC–Berkeley, and Cal State–Fullerton as well as international workshops at Göttingen, New Delhi, and Takamatsu. Scholarly associations, especially the American Society for Environmental History and the Association for Asian Studies, provided me opportunities to share bits of the research at annual meetings, and I appreciate many friends and colleagues in these societies for their enthusiastic support, especially my historian "comrade" and occasional coauthor Edward Miller. The Vietnam Studies Group, in particular, has been an especially supportive group within AAS, and I thank the many who responded privately to my odd queries on the group's list-serv with insightful responses, pdfs of their work, and primary source materials.

At UCR my students have provided an endless source of inspiration with their boundless enthusiasm and new sets of eyes on the world. Thanks to all who have shared your stories with me, especially those who traveled with Cô Hồng Anh and me to Huế. Your struggles and successes inspire me, and they help me to see places like Huế with new eyes. To Bùi Trúc Linh, a native of Huế who came to UC–Riverside to pursue a PhD, thanks in particular for proofreading the Vietnamese and for teaching me many valuable insights on the particularities of Huế culture.

Finally, as this book heads into press, my last round of thanks goes to the dedicated staff of the University of Washington Press, especially Catherine Cocks and series editor Paul Sutter. The Weyerhaeuser Environmental Books Endowment has allowed UW Press to continue making truly beautiful books. In my case, it afforded the inclusion of many images and a color inset. In an era when academic presses struggle to break even, having a say in everything from color or not to cover design and title is a luxury. To the anonymous reviewers, I thank you for your enthusiastic comments and constructive criticisms. I of course accept all responsibility for mistranslations, missed accent marks, and more substantial errors. Many more individuals are thanked for their contributions in the book's notes, and to any I have missed in total, I hope to make it up at a later meeting.

FOOTPRINTS OF WAR

INTRODUCTION

IN FEBRUARY 1972, WORKING IN THE PERPETUAL DRIZZLE THAT shrouds the central coast of Vietnam each winter, soldiers from the Army of the Republic of Vietnam (ARVN) produced a photographic inventory of two bases newly acquired from the Americans. Just a few weeks before, some thirty thousand US Army and Marine Corps troops removed themselves with thousands of tons of equipment from Phú Bài Combat Base and Camp Eagle. In the peak of fighting during what Vietnamese call the American War, these two bases were round-the-clock military cities. Networks of pipelines supplied diesel and aviation fuel from a makeshift port to the airfield, helipads, power plants, and fuel depots. The helipads supported a fleet of flying UH-1 "Huey" gunships, CH-47 Chinook cargo helicopters, and CH-54 Skycranes that ferried troops and heavy guns to distant firebases near the Laos border. Radio centers near Phú Bài linked the bases with US ships offshore, with top-secret planes carrying radio-listening equipment above, and with commanders in the field. Night and day, the air around these bases buzzed with radio chatter and the whomp-whomp of rotor blades. In December 1971, just before the American troops left, comedian Bob Hope and other entertainers gave a final concert to an audience of more than ten thousand at Camp Eagle's amphitheater, the Eagle Bowl. Two weeks later, the troops were gone; even the stage was gone. Only skeletal frames of lumber and scaffolding remained.

While American media followed this latest wave in Vietnam base closures as a positive end to a tragic war now being overshadowed by Nixon's trip to China, South Vietnam's leaders attempted to retain the attention of the

FIGURE I.1. Demolished troop billets at Phú Bài Combat Base, February 11, 1972. Source: Box 3, RVNAF Base Turnover Inspections, MACV Inspector General Records, Record Group 472, US National Archives and Records Administration, College Park.

world's media attention on these ruined bases. The ARVN produced a visual inventory, noting the missing, vital equipment (figure I.1). ARVN commanders in Huế were furious that the Americans had left these high-tech base cities, operating at full capacity a few months earlier, in tatters. American contractors removed the systems that provided electricity, clean water, and perimeter lighting while fire trucks, communications centers, and air conditioners moved to the few American bases still in operation. The commander of the ARVN's First Division held a press conference, showing reporters these base ruins and the bill that the Americans issued South Vietnam for the remaining buildings, powerlines, and roads. The cost for these "improvements" to the land topped US$4 million, and at the time nobody paid attention to the hastily covered landfills.[1]

The American pullout from Vietnam in 1972–73 revealed many social and environmental scars from one of history's most destructive wars. These

FIGURE I.2. Noncommissioned officers' club, Phú Bài Combat Base, February 10, 1972. Source: Box 3, RVNAF Base Turnover Inspections, Military Assistance Command Vietnam Inspector General Records, Record Group 472, US National Archives and Records Administration, College Park.

extended far beyond ruined bases and bombed-out hills to ruptures in family life and local rites too. Figure 1.2 shows a common though less-remarked feature of many bases that they were frequently sited on village cemeteries. The main subject in the photo is a canteen-like building with concrete picnic tables, an officers' club. Visible just behind the tables is the headstone and lotus-topped pillars of a family tomb. The tomb had been there long before the club or the base. American engineers first bulldozed these tombs when building bases, but local uproar caused them to build around them. Space here on Highway 1 in the narrow central region of Vietnam was limited, so the marines set to work in the village graveyard.

This unfortunate juxtaposition of troops camping in a graveyard is a fitting symbol for the deeply troubling ways that landscapes—military, physical and cultural—figured into the larger struggles of war in Vietnam. Families wishing to tend to these ancestral tombs risked detention at base entries, and those visiting tombs outside base perimeters risked being shot. American troops, traumatized by combat, returned to their bases to sleep amid these tombs. Many websites produced by American veterans feature shots of soldiers standing in or around these old tombs. Some recalled how the concrete walls often provided lifesaving cover from rockets and sniper fire.[2] The marines at Phú Bài even named one landing zone LZ Tombstone, working the graveyard into their gallows humor and operational jargon.

These two images (figures I.1 and I.2) highlight the very different ways that military processes became embedded in the multiple histories of the war, of communities, and of individuals. While the eye is typically drawn in these images to the military ruins, the historical backstory to them reveals new layers that point to the land's deeper, layered past and its multiple meanings. This problem, understanding how military processes become embedded and woven into these multiple landscapes, the footprints of war, is the focus of this book. In places such as Phú Bài, the American military aimed to rewire these landscapes in physical and social terms to achieve the goals of nation building and containment of communist troops. However, the Americans were not the first to attempt to meet these goals here nor were they alone as state-builders in 1965. Communist and noncommunist Vietnamese forces built their own networks in the mountains and here on the coast too. They relied on clandestine hideouts and storage caches to mobilize an underground railroad stretching from coastal villages like Phù Bài to mountain bases. In their propaganda, they highlighted how these ancient village landscapes had long suffered past military occupations, and they linked their revolutionary struggle to ancient Vietnamese resistance movements against such invaders as the Mongols, the Ming, the French, and the Japanese. The removal of the Americans in 1972 revealed the limits of one military's state-building infrastructure in this place and the resiliency of another.

As this environmental history of war in Vietnam is written by an American, my process in choosing Huế, Phú Bài and the mountain valleys of Thừa Thiên–Huế Province as the focus for this story deserves explanation at the outset. Like many children born in the 1970s, I grew up in the shadow of the Vietnam War. My father was not a combat veteran but a nuclear engineer who graduated from the US Naval Academy; before he retired from the military in the mass demobilization of 1973, I lived on military bases. As a civilian kid, I visited military museums and caught pieces of stories from my parents' military friends. In college I became an environmental activist and marched in protest of the 1991 Gulf War. After college I traveled to Vietnam and taught English as a volunteer. In graduate school I studied environmental history and specialized in Vietnamese studies, learning the language and doing research in Vietnamese archives. I found Huế (or maybe it found me) in 2006 while I was leading a student tour on Highway 1, the coastal highway running from Hà Nội south to Sài Gòn. Near Huế's Phú Bài International Airport I noticed dozens of sprawling, empty lots with broken pavement and no houses in an otherwise crowded strip of villages and new factories. When I asked our guide about these spaces, he responded in Vietnamese but then rattled off English place-names—Camp Evans, Camp Hochmuth, and Camp Eagle. The tour guide was, like me, a child of the war. His father was a South Vietnamese soldier, and he grew up on the edge of these bases, but he was quick to note that many older people still remember these names. I was fascinated by this and these spaces. Why were they still empty? What would happen to them now that Vietnam was going through an economic and real estate boom?

That initiated my interest, but the research for this book and the local support necessary for it followed one summer later with a different student program at a July 4 reception hosted by the local chapter of the US-Vietnam Friendship Society in Huế. After the ceremony, I explained to the society's vice chairman, an environmental scientist, that I was an environmental historian and interested in the legacies of the war. Usually, explaining (and defending) environmental history as a serious discipline is a conversation ender, but in this case he listened attentively. He asked if I thought that US military records of old bases might be used to help pinpoint historical waste sites. A geologist with a PhD who had completed his doctorate in the Soviet Union studying at the Baku oil fields in Azerbaijan, he was at that time director of the province's Department of Science and Technology and responsible for toxic waste cleanups in the province, including one involving US military waste near Phù Bài Village. Workers in the village had drained an upstream reservoir to clean it. While scraping away the mud, they uncovered a cache of rusted steel drums. With pickaxes they punctured the drums releasing a powdered concentrate of 2-chlorobenzalmalononitrile, better known as CS or tear gas. The concentrated powder mixed with water and mud, causing skin burns, and some of those who inhaled airborne particles went to the hospital with respiratory injuries and lesions. This find was not uncommon in the province, nor was it the most toxic discovery, but it especially troubled my host (I learned much later) because of the financial and legal conflicts it caused when the military forensics team came from Hà Nội to excavate the drums. Because CS was a war chemical, the Ministry of Defense ran the cleanup but charged the province more than US$75,000.[3] My host hoped to use my environmental history skills to locate other hotspots to avoid future accidents.

This applied environmental history project provided me the opportunity to explore former base sites and surrounding villages with approval from the province, and it led me to deeper questions about the longer-term effects of military conflicts. In American military records, I found a trove of maps, photographs, and detailed textual records that I shared with local officials. The Records of US Forces in Southeast Asia, Record Group 472 (RG472), constitute one of the most detailed public archives of any military occupation in world history. Just the text records of RG472 take up hundreds of mobile shelves, covering an area equivalent to a few football fields. Within this collection I found detailed records of chemical activities at these bases, including operations using tactical herbicides such as Agent Orange and bulk drops of fifty-five-gallon drums containing powdered CS. US records included detailed chemical inventories, flight mission data, and payload information. Air photos and maps from the United States provided an essential visual survey of land features circa 1972. I digitized and georeferenced the historic imagery and maps of Camp Eagle and Phú Bài, then with help from a remote sensing specialist in Huế compared the historic layers with more recent satellite imagery. We produced historic maps showing long-term features, especially bare surfaces around these former chemical sites.[4] We presented our findings and copies of all historical records, and the project concluded.

This work, however, opened a slew of broader questions about history, militarization, and landscape that form the basis for this book. When historians characterize a polluted site, they look for historical and environmental baselines to compare prepollution or premilitary conditions with specific environmental or military events. At Phú Bài I quickly learned that this layer of American military activity was just one of many (figure I.3). Readings at the province library and discussions with village historians yielded a much longer-term view of military occupation and conflict there.

As an example, the Phú Bài airfield was not just a base area for US Marines in 1965 but also a site for many early modern and modern military occupants. Vietnamese and Cham troops fought a Ming dynasty military occupation

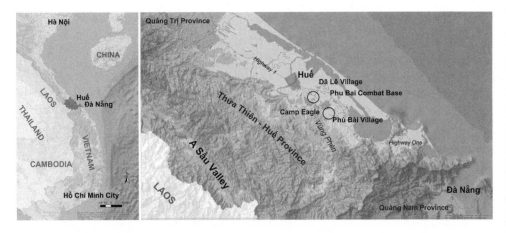

FIGURE I.3. Base areas and villages, Thừa Thiên–Huế Province. Source: VMAP0, ESRI Inc. and Open Street Map. Map by author.

there in the early 1400s. In the late 1600s, the area was an industrial waste zone for iron smelting. Phù Bài Village and its slag fields—the future site of the Phú Bài airfield and bases, had for centuries been a sort of military-industrial village. Its hilly area cut by creeks leaching rust-red soils (Vùng Phèn) contained rich deposits of iron ore, and iron production continued until 1800. Iron smelting left large piles of waste slag and deforested hills.[5] The French colonial government built Huế's airfield in this "abandoned land" in 1924 and opened a leper colony in a valley at the foot of Vùng Phèn (figure I.3). When the Japanese Imperial Army arrived in 1941, it expanded the airfield and closed the leper colony. The Japanese added airplane hangars, a radio tower, and a fuel depot, and they located a camp (possibly for prisoners of war) near the former leper colony. Việt Minh soldiers took the area in August 1945, seizing Japanese weapons and ammunition from bunkers built into Vùng Phèn. The Việt Minh then operated an officer training facility near the former camp until 1947, when French infantry units, mainly Senegalese recruits, invaded and set up a Camp Oasis on the ruins of the Việt Minh training camp. Two years later Việt Minh artillery strikes and nighttime raids forced them out. In 1954 South Vietnamese army units took over the area and, with American assistance, expanded runways at the airfield and erected new facilities around former Camp Oasis. US Marines arrived in 1965, and American base construction accelerated after the Tết Offensive in 1968. The ARVN took over the bases in

1972 and the People's Army of Vietnam (PAVN) took over the area in 1975. It ceded much of the land to the province in 2000, but PAVN and local forces (similar to a national guard) still occupy some areas.

These discoveries during my search for premilitary baselines led to a fundamental shift in my approach to studying the relationship of war to landscape. Instead of following the environmental impacts of one military organization in this dynamic historical landscape, I instead chose to focus on the longer history of this long-militarized landscape through multiple layers of military construction and destruction. This longer historical approach to the militarized landscape is important for *placing* the American War in a deeper, multilayered historical and environmental context. Even since my initial queries in 2006, the concrete ruins and empty lots of the old bases have rapidly disappeared as new layers of industrial concrete or green carpets of forest plantations spread. The Phú Bài Combat Base was reborn in 2000 as Phú Bài Industrial Park, and now television assembly plants and logistics facilities occupy the footprints of US Army truck depots and infantry barracks. Even firebases and battlegrounds in the hills, especially near the former demilitarized zone (DMZ), are regreening, fading into thousands of hectares of acacia and new urban nodes sprouting along new highways running west to Laos and connecting to Thailand. New power lines and water pipes have finally replaced the gutted grids of infrastructure abandoned in 1972. In today's industrial park, women from rural areas live communally after long days on the assembly line. They rest in dorms located just steps from where barracks in the late 1960s housed young Americans resting from missions in the hills. Today's industrial parks are in many ways like the old bases running in reverse. People and raw materials travel from the hills to the industrial zones and exports cross the Pacific to ports such as Long Beach, California. These long-abandoned, abiotic landscapes have revived their industrial ecosystems.

Written from this vantage point of Vietnam's early twenty-first-century economic boom, this history follows the central region's deep history of conflict, its footprints of war, to consider how repeat instances of military conflict shaped the everyday fabric of life and memories in these lands. Its use of the term footprint as a metaphor is deliberate as footprints are deceptively complex as physical traces of past disruptions. While the term commonly suggests an impression or impact on something, a footprint is very much contingent on the relative resistance of the land or surface receiving the event, and the duration of a footprint's trace depends on many post-incident factors. Finally, footprints require visual perspectives to record them. They are innately spatial; and in cases like the empty former base areas along Highway 1 they continue to figure into present-day, development debates.

While the postwar transition from bases to industrial parks in Vietnam is relatively new, the challenges of postwar economic development are not. The base-to-industrial-park transition in Vietnam may suggest an ironic reversal of Karl Liebknecht's famous quote, "capitalism is war," but military theorists have long considered military occupation as a means of opening new markets and capital-intensive opportunities.[6] Base closures and property transfers after the Cold War are but the latest example of postconflict transitions to new urban and industrial landscapes. This transition from bases to cities has been a central feature of urbanization in world history for centuries. The Romans under Emperor Claudius (41–54 CE) invaded Britain and built the empire's largest base in the islands around a bridge crossing the mudflats of the Thames River. Walls followed the bridge, and the medieval city of London spread from those walls along what is now London Bridge.[7] In Vietnam, the ancient capital Hà Nội and its bustling mercantile streets grew up around the Chinese Tang dynasty's walled garrison at Đại La (791 CE).[8]

Philosophers of war from Sun Tzu to Carl von Clausewitz and even the Austrian economist Joseph Schumpeter have long argued that military actions produce a kind of *creative destruction*, empty footprints that permit new spaces for development. Military occupation, they argued, cleared the surface so that new industries and social relations might form. Today Schumpeter is widely cited for coining the phrase *creative destruction* with respect to business cycles and the future of capitalism, but the idea was popular decades earlier. Schumpeter writes about business cycles, not war, but he arrives at the same conclusion that "creative destruction is an essential fact about capitalism."[9] Schumpeter actually borrowed the term from an earlier generation of German historians and economists writing in Prussia before and after the Great War. Economic historian Werner Sombart in *War and Capitalism* (1913) noted how the devastating religious wars in seventeenth-century Europe decimated forests yet enabled a new energy regime, built on coal, and new industries, built on coke and iron. He developed his view of creative destruction in turn from philosopher Friedrich Nietzsche, who drew from Hindu scripture in the Bhagavad Gita, focusing on the often violent processes through which culture is renewed and regenerated.[10] Even after the atomic bombings and the Vietnam War, this idea continues to figure into wars in the present. Advisers of President George W. Bush argued in 2003 for a "shock doctrine" that would obliterate Iraq's existing economy and permit construction of a new free market economy in the wake of "shock and awe."[11]

Debates over these transitions from spaces of war to postwar ruins and postwar renewal form a central theme in this book, and the environmental history of these debates points to the troubling ecological limits of such an idea as creative destruction. Since the detonation of the first atomic bombs in 1945, when physicist Robert Oppenheimer also famously alluded to the Bhagavad Gita, the creative destruction optimists met a new form of environmentalist resistance. What happens when destruction is incomplete and hazards from war ruins persist for many years after conflicts end?[12] The half-life of uranium-235 isotopes released in nuclear explosions tops seven hundred million years, and many of the chemicals used in warfare in the 1960s are persistent pollutants with severe ecological and human health impacts. As local and state governments grapple with the implications of building on former military sites potentially contaminated with these types of toxic waste, the logic of creative destruction breaks down. Bulldozers may scrape clear the rubble on the surface, but who is legally and ethically responsible for cleaning up what may still lie invisible below?[13]

MILITARIZATION AND LANDSCAPE

Because this book proposes a deeper historical treatment of military conflict and landscapes, the terms militarization and landscape require some unpacking. I use militarization in the broadest sense to describe not only acts of military-directed violence, construction, destruction, and land appropriation but also broader social processes where military organizations and demands reconfigured everyday life.[14] Militarized landscapes likewise refer to lands that are not just physically connected to military processes but also tied in cultural and political ways—for example, the communities growing up around a base. Resource frontiers such as Vùng Phèn and even rice fields were touched by demands of military requisitioning just as village sons were conscripted into various armies. Militarization is a deliberately broad term intended to spur readers to broaden their perspective on the reach of military activity beyond bases and camps into village life and cultural practices.

This book's use of the term *landscape*, too, is a choice intended to identify places defined broadly by a mix of ecological and social factors. As a concept born out of the European Enlightenment, the term is a nexus for *views* of land that describe physical, cultural, and historical elements in time.[15] Landscapes are often measurable, physical spaces, depicted in paintings, photographs, and maps, but they can also be cultural spaces where natural and built features take on social meaning. By virtue of its *visibility* (the *scape* in landscape), a landscape can simultaneously exist in physical, cultural, and representational terms. It comprises physical elements such as buildings, soils, plants, and trees, but it also contains many cultural elements: the trails, monuments, and named features that American writer J. B. Jackson called the "vernacular landscape."[16] Despite the best efforts of military engineers to construct globally homogenous spaces, bases protected by minefields and barbed wire, the bases inevitably became entangled in these living, vernacular places—consider the marines' bar in the cemetery.

Where most histories of war in Vietnam use the territory of the state as a relatively empty spatial frame for events, this book begins with a set of densely layered landscapes in Thừa Thiên–Huế Province to examine how a succession of state-builders and military forces attempted to fold these spaces into their competing programs. These landscapes can be roughly divided into three elevational zones: the narrow strip of coastal plains, a wider belt of hills (10–200 m), and an interior region of highlands (200–2,000 m) that form the mountainous border with Laos. The history of militarization from the 1400s to today roughly follows this direction of expansion from the coast into the mountains. This elevational logic is not my own invention but rather follows a traditional perspective used in Vietnam and many lowland societies in Southeast Asia. In central Vietnam, these basic ecopolitical boundaries are divided into lowland (*hạ*), midland (*trung*), and highland (*thượng*) domains. This book excavates this layered history of militarization in each of these elevational domains, beginning at coastal villages in the lowlands and on the streets of Huế before moving to key tactical zones in the hills, then following resistance fighters and foreign soldiers to the headwaters of the Perfume River and the mountainous A Sầu Valley (see figure I.3). It uses spaces in all three of these elevational domains as focal points to examine how different military actors constructed militarized landscapes and how those landscapes figured into broader visions of competing states.

As a history of competing state *visions*, it also relies heavily on visual media, considering how competing military organizations used aerial and cartographic technologies, including maps, airplanes, cameras, radio, and geomantic notions of mountain ridges and rivers, to tie these spaces into larger political networks. Guerrilla forces worked especially hard to "rewire" colonial spaces of roads and outposts into a new revolutionary territory defined by trails, rivers, mountain ridges, hidden radio transmitters, and kilometers of wire and plastic pipelines designed to avoid detection from above. Counterinsurgency experts likewise tried to tap into village life and traditions to modernize rural communities and bring them into a global system of commerce and ideas. The landscape-centered perspective permits a more multifaceted reflection on the natures and visions of these different military occupants.[17]

Finally, with respect to theories of landscape and space, this book considers the generative role that ancient conflict zones and former militarized places played on successive military conflicts. Spaces of past wars, from industrial waste zones to deforested hills and abandoned military camps, often guided new military developments.[18] Environmental factors (food, shelter, vegetation, historic landmarks) and persistent spatial politics (abandoned lands, disputed territories) shaped successive military experiences. American military engineers did not have a blank check to site bases anywhere. They moved into abandoned French camps, into contested "wastelands" covered in tombs, and even into the evacuated camps of Việt Minh soldiers in the mountains. Even the most powerful military in the world in 1965 had to follow some basic rules conforming to the spatial history and logic of this landscape.

My choice of the former imperial capital Huế to center this study is not just due to fortuitous meetings with officials but also an acknowledgment of the especially rich historical, literary, and cultural traditions of this region. During the war and even after, Huế has symbolized the hybrid heart of Vietnam for its blending of northern and southern influences and its legendarily stubborn, antimodern vibe. The region's heritage as an imperial capital and its importance in the twentieth century as a scene of some of the most intense battles is important; however, the contemporary attention to war's legacies in rituals, art, and literature is equally important. Beyond the tombs, cemeteries, and war monuments are many spaces in between, sublayers of ancient remains, a "wilderness" haunted not only by traces of chemicals or munitions but also of ghosts from these contested pasts. Many people even today in Huế pay attention to this ethereal wilderness of "wandering souls" (*linh hồn lang thang*) and the more lethal wilderness of buried waste and munitions. Digging below the top few meters of soil, whether in the city or the countryside, one takes on a number of risks—being maimed by unexploded ordnance, finding human remains, or perhaps being exposed to toxic residues. Vietnamese popular culture is filled with stories of these material and ghostly "hauntings," and virtually everyone knows a family in which someone has been touched by one form of these encounters.[19] In villages near the bases and especially on the streets of Huế, on every full moon (*ngày rằm*) people set up altars in their front yards or sidewalks with incense and plates of food to feed and placate wandering souls. This happens once a year across much of East Asia during the ghost festival, which takes place on the full moon of the seventh lunar month, but in Huế it happens every month.

A narrow strip of coastline that divided Vietnam into separate, warring regimes, the Huế area is in some ways unique as a cultural contact zone too. As a borderland, it fostered decades of reflections by local residents and foreigners on the "two Vietnams." War correspondent and political scientist Bernard Fall described French failures to expand control there in 1953–54 in his book *Street without Joy*. The title took its name from what French troops called Highway 1, just north of Huế, for its frequent ambushes: *la rue sans joie*.[20] During the Second Indochina War, Huế and its embattled hills attracted scores of journalistic and literary works.

Although many focused on particular battle sites, some examined rural life and insurgent life in the mountain bases. North Vietnamese war correspondent Trần Mai Nam's *The Narrow Strip of Land*, published in English in 1969, provides a communist partisan's perspective on the area as he journeyed along the Hồ Chí Minh Trail through the treacherous bombed-out hills to villages on the coast.[21] The 1968 Tết Offensive devastated Huế and by many accounts turned the tide of the Second Indochina War. South Vietnamese artists such as Nhã Ca and the singer-poet Trịnh Công Sơn attempted to put into stories and songs what was too horrible to account for in numbers and news reports.[22] Proximity to Huế, even in the last years of the conflict, afforded such American social scientists as anthropologist James Trullinger rare opportunities to conduct interviews in villages. His book *Village at War* offers a fascinating perspective into villager responses to military bases, multiple episodes of violence, and political change.[23] This collection of

Vietnamese and foreign artistic and scholarly works around Huế provides a rich backdrop for the comparisons and reflections used in this book. Besides this literature, I also draw on years of travel to historic military sites and formal and informal interviews in villages such as Phù Bài (Thủy Châu Commune) and Dạ Lê (Thủy Phương Commune). Given the extremely limited access to post-1975 government records, my visits to the Thừa Thiên–Huế Province Library were essential for turning up local village histories and stories about postwar recovery.

Archives, especially military archives, form an essential part of this research, and in some senses they, too, are like landscapes in that they are often devilishly layered with their own spatial and historical logics. French military records from the Nord Annam–Huế Secteur are meticulously organized and documented at the Chateau de Vincennes near Paris, and they include a rich array of textual, visual, and cartographic sources. Outside Paris in nineteenth-century "caves" extending under the brick walls of Fort de l'Est, the French air force keeps equally pristine collections of aerial photography shot over Indochina from 1947 to 1954. American military records on Vietnam, housed for the most part in the National Archives at College Park, are comparatively sprawling. The vastness of these collections is both a blessing and a curse. It invites in-depth particularistic studies of individual units or battles, but it discourages cross-sectional thematic studies, which would be complicated by the sheer volume of records. There are also large online collections of digitized American records, including the Vietnam Archives at Texas Tech University; the CIA's CREST database featuring declassified documents; and George Washington University's National Security Archive.[24]

Compared with this relative abundance of foreign records, a relative absence of communist and People's Army records presents a major challenge for comparative analyses. Primary records of Vietnamese forces, including the People's Army, various noncommunist armies, and the National Liberation Front (NLF), are practically nonexistent for public researchers. My research approach here has been to mine the rather formulaic sets of published regiment histories, district party committee histories, and province-level histories. Such histories for the most part deny researchers a fine-grained view, but they nonetheless yield some checks on American and French records with respect to accounts of key battles as well as background on unit histories. Foreign military archives also include caches of captured documents, so with careful sifting and some luck, one can locate valuable nuggets.

Civilian records are invaluable, too, in characterizing state responses (and conflicts) with militaries. Given the many regimes that governed Huế from the 1800s to the 1970s, these records are scattered at repositories across Vietnam and beyond. The colonial records of the Résident Supérieur de l'Annam and the 1949–54 Central Vietnam Governing Committee (Phủ Thủ Hiến Trung Việt) are located in the mountain town Đà Lạt at the Vietnamese National Archives Center No. 4. They provide a localized view of affairs close to Huế before the division of Vietnam in 1954. Republic of Vietnam (RVN) state records, located at the Vietnamese National Archives Center No. 2 in Hồ Chí Minh City, provide a post-1954 view of deep regional tensions that festered between Huế and Sài Gòn and erupted with Buddhist- and student-led protests in the 1960s. Finally, American civilian agency records, especially those of the US State Department, offer insights into the ways that the RVN's most powerful ally viewed and framed "the Vietnam situation" as protests and later the Tết Offensive put central Vietnam in the spotlight.

MILITARIZED LANDSCAPES ON PAPER, CELLULOID, AND SCREENS

Considering the visual element that is fundamental to the study of landscape, the many maps, aerial photographs, and satellite images produced during the modern conflicts in Vietnam have resulted in a largely untapped visual and cartographic resource for historians. The timeframe for the Indochina wars in Vietnam, 1945–75, fits perfectly in an incredible arc of technological innovations that included the development of aerial photography (1918–40), high-altitude photography (1940–75), satellite photography (1959–72) and satellite-based, multiband scanning (1972–). The visual products of military geoint—geospatial intelligence—in Vietnam remained largely classified until the early 2000s, but now most are public. As with any set of state or military records, photographic records also follow unique logics (and politics) of organization and pose unique material and interpretive challenges. In the case of US military photos over Vietnam, researchers must locate specific rolls of film using indexes and then wait for the film to be delivered from a privately operated cold-storage facility located in former salt mines near Saint Louis, Missouri. Almost daily, a plane delivers requested historical film, secret and public, to the Washington area. Once the film is at the National Archives in College Park, Maryland, researchers must use 1960s-era photo interpreter

FIGURE I.4. Frame 07, A Shau Special Forces Base, 1961, with original negative film can. Source: Mission J5921, Defense Mapping Agency, Record Group 373, US National Archives and Records Administration, College Park.

machines and either scan or rephotograph the images (figure I.4). That researchers from anywhere in the world can come to College Park and handle original negatives from 1940s to 1960s military air photography is remarkable. The bird's-eye view in figure I.4, depicting a US Special Forces base in the mountainous A Sâu Valley, suggests the aesthetic richness of these views while also providing clues on past land use and the work of military photographers.

Incorporating these high-altitude views into a study also invites new modes of critical analysis into how these aerial views were constructed and how they may have shaped the perceptions of military actors, especially foreign ones, who did not venture out much on the ground. From the introduction of air photography in the 1930s to intense American use of aerial images in the 1960s, the aerial view was fundamental to state-centered ideas of frontiers and American understandings of insurgency.[25] This aerial platform and its bird's-eye logic was of course repeatedly challenged, especially by insurgent groups. Communist forces in central Vietnam may not have flown airplanes and helicopters before 1975, but they developed and maintained their own networks of radio communications and countered aerial surveillance and bombing with camouflage. They read maps, too, but they deliberately used alternative methods of knowing landscapes—especially travel by landmarks—to avoid detection. This ground-based platform, designed to evade aerial surveillance, was equally important.

Finally, this book draws from the initial applied environmental history project by not only reflecting on these visual sources but also digitizing them into a historical GIS to produce visual studies and comparisons at specific places discussed in the book. Selections of map overlays and air photographs figure centrally in the later chapters, and one set of color plates contains figures produced from multiple map layers designed to answer questions about land use, the extent of military-related actions, and the historical persistence of many military features. A companion website featuring products of this historical GIS work allows readers to explore these layers in detail.[26]

A HISTORY IN LAYERS AND WARS

The following chapters are organized chronologically beginning with the early modern Vietnamese settlement of the coast in the 1400s and continuing through the years of French colonization (1884–1945) before turning to focus on the modern wars. The first chapter, "Subterrains," is, at the risk of offending historians of early modern Vietnam and those more interested in modern warfare, a sketch that is necessary for identifying key military and environmental elements of the coast's longue durée history. It is inspired in some ways by historian Fernand Braudel's studies of the Mediterranean, in particular his attention to elevation and views shaped by a sojourn teaching in Algeria in the 1920s that helped him see how the terrains from Algiers to the Atlas Mountains linked Algerian and French histories in a common Mediterranean framework.[27] This chapter doesn't go so far, but it does attempt to rough out a longer environmental history to better explain Vietnamese attitudes toward hills, mountainous interiors, and periods of unrest that usually began with seaborne invasions. Chapter 2, "Terraforming," follows colonial military and political rule around Huế from 1885 to 1945. It begins with the invasion of colonial troops in 1885 and examines colonial debates about degraded lands as well as the birth of anticolonial movements in the 1930s. Like the previous chapter, chapter 2 is not explicitly focused on military conflict; rather it considers how distant events from the two world wars and the

Russian and Chinese revolutions influenced a new generation of nationalists and militants living in the central coast, including many future leaders of Vietnam's communist and noncommunist governments. It follows Vietnamese radicals and French reformers and their visions to "terraform" an impoverished rural landscape to achieve various postdepression, postcolonial, and postwar visions.

The last four chapters of this book turn from these earlier layers to a thirty-year period that includes some of the most intense episodes of military destruction in world history. Chapter 3, "Resistance," begins with the postwar moment of summer 1945, focusing on the development of Việt Minh military logics to rewire the historic landscapes and build new national networks through the hills and mountains. It follows the development of three military occupations that grew out of the ruins of colonial rule: the Việt Minh insurgency, the French military invasion, and a noncommunist Vietnamese army formation. Chapter 4, "Ruins," explores the challenges—environmental and political—left in the aftermath of the 1954 Geneva Accords. Thousands of Việt Minh soldiers evacuated large areas of territory while a noncommunist Vietnamese National Army struggled to extend sovereign claims to the former insurgent zones. This chapter also traces the escalation of American support for counterinsurgency, especially its construction of base facilities and deployment of special forces into the former Việt Minh zones. Chapter 5, "Creative Destruction," is a long chapter that examines the arc of American military involvement from 1964 to 1973. Chapter 6, "Postwar" is a postconflict epilogue comprised of a series of stories generated from personal interviews and site visits.

ONE

SUBTERRAINS

WHEN AMERICANS AND OTHER FOREIGN VISITORS TO VIETNAM DIS-
cuss vestiges of the wars there, they are generally concerned with a relatively
thin layer of modern artifacts near the surface: concrete ruins, rusted metal
debris, human remains, dog tags, unexploded ordnance, perhaps chemicals.
Most Vietnamese war experts, too, focus on deciphering meaning from this
near-surface layer.[1] However, for many people living on the central coast
today, there is a sense that today's communities sit directly on top of more
ancient layers, too, like so many European towns built on Roman ruins.
Beneath the surface of many villages along Highway 1 is a subterrain of ruins
dating back several centuries, if not even further to the pre-Việt past. Village
communal houses (đình), temples, family shrines (lăng họ), and museums
frequently incorporate elements derived from pre-Vietnamese layers. In some
cases, modern excavations even lead to monumental discoveries. In 2001, for
example, workers excavating sand along the coast unearthed a triad of Cham
brick towers dated to the eighth century (figure 1.1). While the find of the
towers was a surprise to researchers, it was not particularly shocking to many
local residents. Local knowledge of Cham sacred sites and Cham occupants
is frequently cited in histories of families, villages, and religious sites. This
ancient cultural layer continues to inform the rich cultural life around Huế
today. This pre-Việt history continues to figure into many of the region's most
famous tourist sites. One of the most photographed sites, Thiên Mụ (Heavenly
Lady) Pagoda (c. 1601), was deliberately sited on the ruins of a popular Cham
temple at a geomantic hotspot, a high point of land at a fork between two

FIGURE 1.1. Eighth-century ruins of Phú Diên Tower. This tower, built in the style of Cham temples at Mỹ Sơn, was discovered inside a sand dune about fifteen kilometers from Huế in 2001. Photo by author, 2014.

rivers. The Vietnamese government at the time did this to shore up ethnic Cham support. The Nguyễn ruler reputedly ordered construction of the pagoda after a dream in which he was visited by the Cham deity Pô Nagar.[2] Even the spatial logic of the region's roads and the layout of its villages is tied in some senses to this pre-Việt past. Many villages that have been recognized in Vietnamese decrees since the late 1300s were built on or near Cham settlements. Village histories frequently note local Cham ruins, too, and archeological digs continue to turn up such ancient and prehistoric artifacts as Đông Sơn jewelry, Chinese porcelain, and Sa Huỳnh burial jars under existing villages.

While the main focus of this book concerns modern militarization in the nineteenth and twentieth centuries, a brief exploration of the region's ancient and early modern past serves to dispel presentist notions that the landscapes of the central coast were especially peaceful or pristine before such baseline dates as 1960 or even 1800 CE. Military conflict in this region over centuries produced deeply inscribed pathways into the region's narrow coastal spaces, which are divided by mountain passes and rivers. As modern armies beginning with colonial troops introduced more severe levels of ecological destruction, they also navigated historical subterrains of ancient trade routes, village shrines, and family tombs built to resist the destructive effects of military occupation. As village histories and the tombs attest, many inhabitants in the region traced their history to ancestors who migrated to the area to flee wars elsewhere or who claimed land there as a reward for military service. This chapter takes a deeper historical view of warfare on the central coast and considers how repeat conflicts shaped local physical and cultural landscapes. The slow-changing facts of the region's geology and multiple experiences of war and military governance produced patterns of settlement and communities in which military service and a military economy became embedded in village work and family life.

THE ANCIENT CONFLICT ZONE

The geologic facts of the central coast and larger patterns in global trade produced a zone prone to conflict as ancient Việt, Chinese, and Cham peoples repeatedly crossed the area. Its narrow coastal plains are backed by steep, forested mountains, and its coast is easily penetrated via lagoons and navigable rivers leading to shipping lanes just offshore. The forested highland interior in the Southeast Asian massif once formed a kind of terrestrial sea, too, a highlands trading zone of dense forests and swidden plateaus populated by various ethnolinguistic groups.[3] One can appreciate that for people occupying the coastal zone, there were rewards and hazards for those who ventured too far into either of these "seas." For those who went uphill, benefits from trade in forest products included the highly prized eaglewood (Aquilaria spp.), as well as elephant ivory and metal ore. Enrichment required transporting these goods via rivers to traders on the coast, so villages in between often played a vital mediating role.[4] There were obvious risks for those going seaward too. Wealth in coastal villages attracted raids from naval marauders. Survival often required protective walls, military patrols, or in the worst cases, retreat into the hills.

These hill-to-sea and north-south exchanges shaped the communities on this narrow coastal strip over several millenia. Prehistoric archeological sites near Huế in present-day Hương Xuân Commune show ancient layers with mixed artifacts derived from cultural centers north and south. It is one of the northernmost jar-burial sites associated with the pre-Cham Sa Huỳnh culture. Besides over two hundred burial jars and jade and shell ornaments associated with Sa Huỳnh culture, the site also includes metallic rings associated with the bronze workshops of the Đông Sơn culture centered in the Việt ancestral homeland of the Red River delta. The presence of Đông Sơn objects in graves at a Sa Huỳnh site indicates an active north-south trade.[5] Sites like this on the coastal plain also include objects associated with the interior trade for forest products. Local historians draw upon linguistic evidence to suggest that prehistoric inhabitants in this area may have first been Katuic speakers who, according to some legends, moved upriver to headwaters as Cham settlements expanded.[6]

After the Han Empire conquered the Red River Delta in 111 BCE, the central coast entered Chinese historical accounts as a frontier zone beyond the Sino-Việt domains. Three mountain passes, Ngang, Lao Bảo, and Hải Vân, formed natural gateways that separated this zone from the Sino-Việt territories to the north and from Cham polities to the south (figure 1.2). People living in this coastal zone negotiated alliances and trade relations with a mix of Việt, Chinese, and Cham figures.[7] The mountain pass to the northwest of Huế, Lao Bảo, marked another key barrier separating the coastal region from early kingdoms in the Mekong Valley.[8]

In this regionally isolated strip protected by mountains on three sides, several rebellions in what Chinese historians called Rinan (Nhật Nam) were recorded in 39, 100, and 137 CE.[9] The people leading these rebellions were elite children of mixed Chinese and Việt or Cham ancestry.[10] Historic records identify one such elite, Khu Liên (Kalinga), who destroyed a Chinese outpost near present-day Huế in 190 CE and then proclaimed himself king of the coast, calling it Lâm Ấp (Lin-yi), with a center near Huế.[11] Over the next several centuries, the territory of Lâm Ấp experienced more raids and rebellions. The coastal area from Ngang Pass to Hải Vân Pass, including Thừa Thiên–Huế, was frequently invaded by Chinese ships, and inhabitants were captured as soldiers, servants, laborers, and prisoners.[12] Only near the end of this long era of Chinese imperial occupation (circa eighth century) did Cham rulers further south near present-day Hội An manage to establish more permanent infrastructure and monuments. The Cham brick towers discovered in the dunes in 2001 (figure 1.1) reflected these closer cultural and trade links between the Huế area and Cham sites near present-day Đà Nẵng and the pilgrimage site Mỹ Sơn.

In mainland Southeast Asia, the end of the Tang dynasty in China in the tenth century corresponds with the start of a golden age for the three

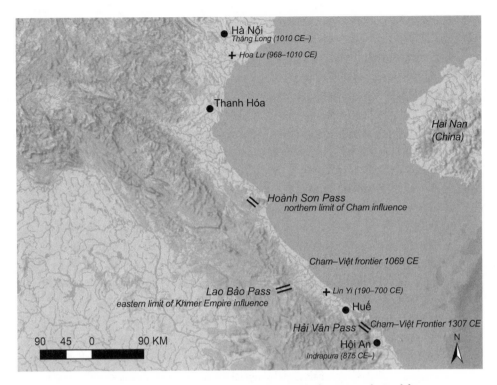

Hà Nội
Thăng Long (1010 CE–)
✝ Hoa Lư (968–1010 CE)

Thanh Hóa

Hai Nan
(China)

Hoành Sơn Pass
northern limit of Cham influence

Cham–Việt frontier 1069 CE

Lao Bảo Pass ═══   ✝ Lin Yi (190–700 CE)
eastern limit of Khmer Empire influence   Huế

Hải Vân Pass ⟍⟍ Cham–Việt Frontier 1307 CE
Hội An ●
Indrapura (875 CE–)

90 45 0   90 KM

N

FIGURE 1.2. Ancient sites and frontiers. Source: Map information derived from Jean Boisselier, *La statuaire du Champa: Recherches sur les cultes et l'iconographie* (Paris: l'École Française d'Extrême-Orient, 1963). Base maps courtesy of ESRI Inc. Map by author.

independent kingdoms of Đại Việt, Champa, and Angkor. During this early independent era, however, the central coast remained a contested frontier zone dividing the three kingdoms beyond the mountain passes. Việt and Cham rulers made repeated claims to the territory lying beyond their core areas. Communities on the central coast from the tenth to fourteenth centuries thus developed as culturally mixed spaces. They were rest stops for Cham fleets heading north and Đại Việt fleets heading south. Vietnamese sources identify one peace-making effort in 1306 CE that became a basis for successive royal claims to the Huế region. The Cham king at the time (Chế Mân, Jaya Simhavarman III) ceded his territorial claims to the Vietnamese emperor (Trần Anh Tông) as a wedding present for Tông's daughter Princess Huyền Trân (Parameswari).[13] This rare matrimonial union was recorded in chronicles as a decisive effort to resolve ancient differences after Việt and Cham armies had fought together to repel repeat Mongol invasions. However, the peace deal crumbled only one year later when the Cham king died and the princess refused to die with him.

EARLY MODERN MILITARY COLONIES

The Vietnamese military's more permanent presence south of Ngang Pass developed in the 1400s largely as a result of Đại Việt's adoption of Ming dynasty military technology, especially firearms and cannons. During the early years of the Ming dynasty (1368–1400), it appeared as though Cham navies might defeat the Việts in the Red River delta and once and for all take control of the coast. Then in 1400 the Trần dynasty fell to a modernizing usurper (Hồ Quý Ly), and the Ming dynasty invaded Đại Việt in response. The Ming army occupied Thăng Long (Hà Nội) and the central coast for twenty years before a rebellion led by a commoner living near Ngang Pass reunited the kingdom and inaugurated the Lê dynasty in 1427. Historian Sun Lai Chen notes that this occupation by Ming riflemen and the guerilla-style rebellion helped produce the first Southeast Asian army capable of large-scale manufacture and use of firearms. After defeating Chinese forces on the battlefield, the Lê dynasty military turned its ship-based cannons and firearm-yielding infantrymen southward to wage war on Champa.[14] In 1470–71 the Vietnamese fleet sailed to Vijaya and sacked it. This decisive victory moved the Việt border south to the Hải Vân Pass.

Even though the central coast was freed from its long history of Việt-Cham wars, the region was governed as a quasi-military state from the late 1400s until the early 1700s. The Việt lords who ruled this coastal realm built a regional variant of Vietnamese society that at times was at odds with the ancient capital in Thăng Long. Similar in some ways to Braudel's *longue durée* view of landscape and history on the Algerian coast, this region's long history of conflict shaped its politics in this early modern era too. Those who governed it spent much of their time on the water for commerce and defense. The Nguyễn lords who ruled it blended aspects of the older, Cham-influenced mercantile lifestyle with military rule.[15] Historians of Nguyễn Cochinchina, this southern domain recognized by the Lê emperor in 1558 with its center near Huế, suggest that Vietnamese and their descendants who settled here blended older, non-Việt customs and produced a distinctly regional language, economy, and martial culture. Naval power remained key to the Nguyễn family. (The name Thừa Thiên–Huế used today is derived in part from the military fighting units organized into boats [*thuyền*] in this period.)[16]

The author of *Ô Châu Cận Lục* (1555), one of the first Vietnamese geographies dedicated to the central coast, remarks derisively on this mixed culture. In one coastal village north of present-day Đồng Hới, he found, people who still spoke Cham, while in another village near Huế he described girls dressing in Cham silk rather than Vietnamese tunics. People followed many Cham religious rites and adopted Cham artistic traditions too.[17] Historian Hồ Trung Tú's social history of the lands around Đà Nẵng suggests a similarly complex interweaving of Cham customs and political alliances south of Hải Vân Pass. As the Nguyễn navy expanded further south into Cham territory in the 1500s, people frequently rebelled. At Ba Đồn (near present-day Quy Nhơn), a rival Vietnamese clan banned together with Cham communities to oust the Nguyễn governor and declare independence. A Nguyễn general put down the insurrection and declared martial rule, his troops operating checkpoints to limit Cham movement in and out of the former Cham capital.[18]

The Nguyễn lords' expansion of trade along the coast from 1558 coincided with large investments in military fortifications to protect trade and local military governors. The family's roughly two-hundred-year rule to 1775 coincided with a boom in sea-based trade at the Nguyễn seaport Hội An (formerly Indrapura) and a persistent emphasis on military readiness. Following the revolution in gunpowder technology in the 1400s, the Nguyễn lords continued to push for the latest advances in cannons and firearms. They traded Ming-era know-how for Portuguese in the 1600s.[19] They employed these weapons in a fifty-year civil war with a Vietnamese clan in the north, the Trịnh lords. Ngang Pass again was a frontier dividing the warring factions.

Even after the Nguyễn-Trịnh war ended in 1673, villages on the central coast retained their martial customs and resisted efforts by the devoutly Buddhist Nguyễn lords to spread their preferred state religion. The region retained its reputation as the Ô Châu Terrible Lands (Ô Châu ác địa).[20] The founder of the clan, Nguyễn Hoàng, had begun the family's preference for Mahayana Buddhism as the state religion when he commissioned the Heavenly Lady Pagoda in 1601. Building it on the ruins of a much older temple to the Cham goddess Pô Nagar, this benevolent gesture was also a strategic attempt to win over Cham-heritage residents. The Nguyễn lords even gave official recognition for the Cham deity, renaming her Thiên-Y-A-Na while opening Buddhist monasteries and temples in the vicinity.[21]

However, this wave of temple constructions and measures to pacify Cham peoples did little to "civilize" villagers in the "terrible lands." Lord Nguyễn Phúc Chu even brought in a celebrity, Zen Buddhist monk Thích Đại Sán (Thạch Liêm, 釋大汕) from Jiangxi Province (China), to help him reform the local sangha (Buddhist clergy). Not unlike Jesuit travelers of his day, Thích Đại Sán traveled the roads and waterways of Ô Châu keeping notes from his encounters in a travel diary. He often remarked on the people he met in the coastal villages, people he found wholly unfit for a civilizing mission but unparalleled in guerrilla warfare:

> In some remote lands due to the isolation of high mountains and unfathomable seas, the greatest king could not send his troops to wipe out local conflicts. Also, his rites and rules could not be announced here; residents gathered naturally, they formed their own martial groups together, accustomed to uncivilized and old-fashioned habits. They did not know anything about the greatest king's rites. They only know using power to conquer other groups; therefore, they were in wars frequently, but in war stratagems, it was necessary to use miraculous craftiness to gain the victory. As a result, residents were interested in discussion of martial-military matters, and they ignored moral-cultural values.[22]

The Zen master returned to China after one year, disappointed by the lack of political and religious will to reform in Ô Châu.

Portuguese trade with the Nguyễn lords in the 1600s played a key role in spurring Nguyễn military readiness too. The Portuguese trade in weapons flourished in Southeast Asia through the 1600s, and it was vital to the Nguyễn during their civil war with the Trịnh. Christoforo Borri, a Jesuit priest and scientist who resided in the ports Hội An and Quy Nhơn from 1617 to 1624, described the Nguyễn lords' hundred-galley navy and their imposing coastal batteries featuring hundreds of cannons. In his letters to Rome, he noted how Nguyễn troops became so expert in shore-based cannons that they excelled beyond the assault capacities of European ships. In one instance, a Portuguese ship fired a warning shot at the shore to test the defenses. Việt gunners responded by walking a series of cannon shots in a line ending just before the hull of the ship and then passing over it. This strong military presence in the ports protected trade with Portugal as well as with Japan and China. It kept hard currency and especially weapons circulating on the central coast. Japanese merchants brought finely crafted steel swords that, like Portuguese cannons, served as models for local smiths.[23] The Nguyễn army in the 1600s was one of the strongest in Southeast Asia, but this constant military readiness took a heavy toll on the central coast's villages and landscapes.

MILITARIZATION AND VILLAGE LIFE ON THE INNER ROAD

The process of Vietnamese settlement along the central coast from the 1400s onward involved not only responding to calls for military service or industrial materials but also a more personal ambition, staking a family's claim to land that was already settled. The fertile village lands where Vietnamese troops landed were a beachhead not only for Đại Việt but also for Vietnamese families.[24] These families facilitated the state's territorial expansion as well as the creation of a new genealogical foothold in the frontier lands. Over several generations, these individuals and their descendants turned homesteads and farms into a kind of family-centered sacred land often marked by tombs and shrines. Genealogical histories even today pay special deference to these founding ancestors (*thủy tổ*) and founding sites where old family shrines continue to serve as focal points for annual gatherings of descendants. A geneaology website dedicated to Võ-Vũ Descendants, for example, documents the family's origins with a Vũ Hồn who migrated from China to establish the family at Mộ Trạch Village in Hải Dương Province near the Red River delta.[25] Members of the Võ family then moved south to Thần Phù Village near Huế in the late 1300s (figure 1.3). They settled on a spit of land extending into the lagoon with a tidal estuary ideal for rice cultivation. The family website features a recent video segment produced by Thừa Thiên–Huế TV documenting the annual return of descendants for a village festival.[26]

While official and family records in Thần Phù are not clear on the exact date of this village's formation or whether the Võ family founder was a soldier, records in nearby Thanh Thủy Thượng Village are more precise (figure 1.3). Records from an ancestral shrine and accompanying genealogy of the Cham-heritage Phạm family note that the founding ancestor, Phạm Bá Tùng (b. 1399), joined Lê Lợi's army in 1418 to fight the Ming occupation and then participated in southern campaigns against Cham armies around Thuận Hóa (Huế) as a commander (*chỉ huy sứ*). A website organized by his descendants suggests that after a final campaign in 1446, he retired from military service and established his family's presence in the village before his death in 1470.[27] Perhaps it was deliberate on the part of the emperor or simply practical, but grants to found villages were extended to multiple families at a time. At Thần Phù, the Võ founders were accompanied by two other families, the Hồ and Lê. Three more families staked further claims sanctioned by the Nguyễn government in the 1600s.[28] Phạm Bá Tùng was the seventh of thirteen founding ancestors in Thanh Thủy Thượng. Service to the state often continued in successive generations, too, and it not only applied to men but sometimes to women. Phạm Bá Tùng's daughter, Ngọc Chân, at age eighteen became a consort of Emperor Lê Thánh Tông in 1471. The family celebrates her at a shrine beside that of her father.[29]

This beachhead pattern of Vietnamese settlement and land titling on the central coast produced distinctive village groupings along an inside coastline that became the economic backbone of the Nguyễn domain (figure 1.4). Protected by shallow lagoons and backed by mountains, it was sufficiently protected that commerce and communications could thrive. This narrow strip of plains corresponds with the path of present-day Highway 1, and it gave the region its common name, Đàng Trong (Inner Road).[30] While many historians have detailed the Vietnamese southward expansion (*nam tiến*) along this road, eastern and western expansions from these founding settlements were just as important. Descendants from these villages often pioneered new lower (*hạ*) satellites in the estuaries or upper (*thượng*) hamlets in the hills (figure 1.4). As scholars of ancient Champa and Sa Huỳnh culture have long suggested, this upland-lowland, east-west relationship was likely *not* a Vietnamese invention but rather followed older Cham (or Cham-Katuic) patterns connecting a rice-based estuarine economy with cottage industries in the hills and valuable forest products in the highlands.[31]

In the twenty-first century, most of these founder-satellite relationships have been forgotten as village names have changed; however, many commune boundaries and a few of the old names retaining *hạ* and *thượng* suffixes survive. The first colonial topographic map series published circa 1909 recorded many of the old names, showing more of these historic relationships. Figure 1.3 is a composite of three maps that show the 1909 topographic map with a selection of village names and family shrines highlighted. The dark gray

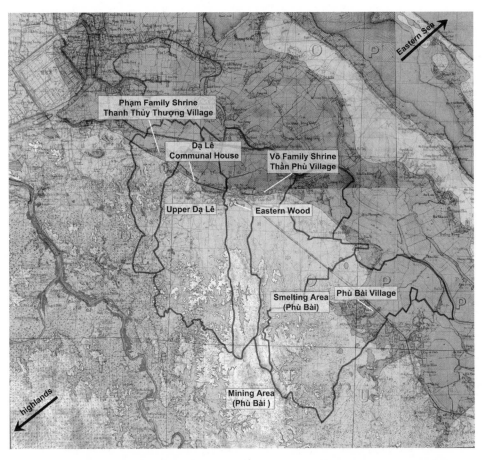

FIGURE 1.3. Founding villages on the inner coast. Source: Topographic map, Société Géographique d'Indochine, 1909, republished 1943; elevation data and commune boundaries provided by Thừa Thiên–Huế Province, 2011. Map by author.

shaded areas indicate elevations from sea level to three meters above sea level, and the light gray areas show elevations from three meters to fifty meters. Areas in white depict hills above fifty meters. The third layer shows modern commune boundaries that in many cases retain the hills-to-estuary orientation. Key sites in these founding villages such as communal houses (đình), family shrines (*lăng họ*, and even rest stops (such as Eastern Wood, or Đông Lâm) were most densely clustered along this isocline at about three meters above sea level. The Inner Road followed this isocline, too, with its north-south paths bisecting the original village domains.

Descendants of the founding families and new arrivals expanded village domains outward, but the Nguyễn government pressed for publicly controlled land ownership to ensure continued loyalty, army conscripts, and revenues. As these villages expanded in the 1600s, the central government remained deeply resistant to recognizing privately held land. A rare set of documents from Dạ Lê Village suggests that public fields (công điền) made up the overwheming majority of village land. It notes the village's founding in 1460, its split into four separate villages in 1515, and a petition in 1671 for new land concessions in the hilly upland section. Nguyễn Đình Nghị, descendant of a founder, petitioned the Nguyễn government for permission to open up 862 acres (mẫu) of new rice paddy and 245 acres of fields in the upper section. This award was an especially large grant for a single individual, perhaps reflecting a high official status with the court. The state awarded him the land, but it required that he keep 90 percent of it as public field. These common properties were not heriditary. Instead, the state, via the village council at Dạ Lê Communal House, determined future tenants. If Mr. Nghi left the village, died, or fell behind in his taxes, the council could reassign these lands to others. This arrangement was, especially in the 1600s and 1700s, a highly effective tool for ensuring continued civil and military service while it prevented families from establishing private estates.

There is a popular proverb in Vietnam that "royal edicts submit to village custom" (phép vua thua lệ làng); however, this proverb should not be misconstrued to mean that village life existed separate from the state. Especially around the Nguyễn capital at Phú Xuân (Huế), the government and its military were deeply integrated into village life. The state depended on taxes, especially in-kind payments of rice and other materials for the army. Village lands formed a critical intermediary landscape for state-village negotiations. Processes of field maintenance, improvement, and abandonment depended on the willingness of cultivators to meet state requirements for rents or taxes. As the ranks of military and civil officers expanded in the late 1600s, the need for resources and land to reward loyal soldiers became more acute. During times of war, many people fled, died in military service, or took shelter in abandoned lands. After each regime change, one of the first campaigns of the new emperor was to resurvey village lands. Military service enabled access to one category of public land specific to veterans' families, called salary fields (lương điền). Drawn from a village's stock of public fields, these constituted a type of payment for military service or welfare for families who had lost men in wars. Typically wives and ineligible relatives tended these fields. Thus the concentration of public lands was closely tied to military recruitment and social welfare for war widows.[32]

Besides this public-private rice economy, most villages developed a single village-wide industry, such as boat building or tool making, that figured into tax obligations and military preparedness. A few villages paid all of their taxes in such essential industrial materials as iron and enjoyed exemptions from military service. Phù Bài Village,[33] by virtue of iron ore deposits in its upland hills, became one of the most important industrial villages on the central coast. Men, women, and children there worked in five family guilds that controlled the iron-making process from stripping ore in the hills to producing charcoal and running the furnaces.Family genealogies tracked with guild identities. Each guild possessed its own communal house, too, thus partitioning land management and cultural affairs by work. Phù Bài Village possessed a relatively large area of rice fields in its lower domain, but it paid most of its taxes in iron.[34]

Iron smelting and associated village industries were ecologically consumptive. Mining was dangerous work, stripping hills with deep pits that filled with rain and frequently collapsed. The village's smelting kilns ran continuously, especially during rainy winter months. By the early 1700s, Phù Bài produced on average thirty metric tons of iron per year for its tax obligation and roughly equivalent amounts for private trade.[35] This produced in turn many hundreds of tons of waste slag annually and consumed thousands of tons of wood for the charcoal fuels. Even in villages without such industries, upland areas were important for supporting an informal economy tied to grazing and wood collection. Geographer Nguyễn Đình Đầu notes that approximately 43 percent of the territory in Dạ Lê District by 1806 was recorded as "hilly, fallow," meaning it was deforested and not farmed.[36] These lands were nonetheless important for such communal activities as burials. For these communal lands, the government required fixed amounts of goods produced from them such as bamboo matting (tấm nạp), wooden furniture, and wooden boats. Despite the general trend of deforestation in this period, some villages maintained small areas of woods. Thần Phù Village kept several hills forested as a rest stop for travelers called the Eastern Wood. Royal officials, merchants, and others stopped here on the journey from the capital. The last independent Vietnamese monarch, Emperor Tự Đức, reputedly composed poems celebrating it.[37]

ECOLOGICAL POVERTY AND WAR, 1750–1802

This era of early modern industrial activity, expansion, and relative peace on the central coast ended abruptly in a devastating civil war, the Tây Sơn Rebellion (1771–1802), that exposed the ecological and political limits of Nguyễn authority. The rebellion drew widespread support especially from those living in upland settlements who chafed at the taxes they considered onerous given the ecological poverty in deforested lands. In the estuary fields, too, villages had expanded to the limit, forming a continuous patchwork of fields and canals across the estuaries. Trade and expansion south to the Mekong delta helped keep the capital's growing population supplied with food. By 1773 in Thừa Thiên–Huế, the population topped 128,000 people while just 158,181 acres of land (approximately 0.6 hectare per person) were in cultivation. The hills at this time were mostly bare of trees, so imported rice and timber were essential to the capital region's economy.[38]

When a tax rebellion in the southern territories cut off the regime's access to imports, the central coast fell into a panic. Famine set in and land taxes rose as the Nguyễn government struggled to survive.[39] The rebellion quickly drew supporters and overthrew Nguyễn governors, especially in the former Cham ports. Famines broke out along the Inner Road, and hungry villagers gleaned the hills, leaving vistas of scrub and eroded ravines in their wake. Many villagers voted with their feet, resettling elsewhere or joining the rebels. The Tây Sơn army established its base of operations near a former Cham center, Quy Nhơn. As the Nguyễn government fell apart, their northern rivals from Thăng Long invaded in 1775, throwing the old land and tax systems into chaos.[40]

The thirty-year period of devastating warfare and famine that ensued along the Inner Road played a pivotal role in emptying surrounding hillsides and ravaging village life. Outbreaks of famine from the mid-1760s led to the abandonment of thousands of acres of unsustainable farms, especially upland plots. Fewer fields in production meant less tax revenue, and fewer people in rural communities meant fewer military recruits.[41] Nguyễn demands for military conscripts in the first years of fighting sapped essential labor from the fields. By 1773 villagers had abandoned more than 112,000 acres of fields in Thuận Hóa.[42] In 1775 the year of the Trịnh army's march into Phú Xuân, a military observer described terrible scenes of corpses stacked along streets and recounted tales of families eating one another to survive. A French missionary in the area noted that during the worst years, rice was more valuable than gold.[43] The military victors in Huế inherited this responsibility for feeding people, restoring infrastructure, and winning wars.[44] However, with farm laborers conscripted in the army and the same degraded environment, little changed. In 1786 the rebel Tây Sơn troops invaded Huế and engaged in a scorched-earth policy that destroyed many cultural landmarks. They razed churches and pagodas, melting bronze bells and statues for cannons.[45]

NATIONAL SURVIVAL, MOVING INLAND

This early modern era came to a violent close when a new military force, a Vietnamese navy featuring several French warships, launched a seaborne assault on Huế on June 12, 1801. This victory ushered in a new phase of Vietnamese rule with European military advisers. Loyalists of the old Nguyễn government, led by the surviving heir Nguyễn Ánh, incorporated European weapons, tactics, and cartographic practices in their years-long effort to defeat the Tây Sơn. As with earlier adoptions of Ming firearms and Portuguese weapons, their adoption of European warcraft helped the Nguyễn forces develop a new imperial government that finally stretched from the northern border with China to the southern tip of the Mekong delta. However, the Nguyễn dynasty (r. 1802–1945) continued to face the same environmental and land-based political challenges as had the regimes before them. Gradually, and especially under the reign of the second emperor Minh Mạng (r. 1820–41), this new government produced something of a neotraditional system that blended modern elements of military architecture and maps with Chinese as the language of the court and Confucianism as the state religion. On the central coast, this government's rule effectively ended in 1883 when a French naval fleet invaded, sacking the same coastal defenses that had fallen in 1801 to the Nguyễns.

A closer inspection of the Nguyễn dynasty's military government and struggles over demilitarization and land policies in the 1830s is instructive for foreshadowing the deep tensions that divided Vietnamese elites and commoners over land use and militarism in the twentieth century. The first era of Nguyễn imperial rule was one in which military officers managed much of the government's administration. This era began on the central coast in 1801 with naval assaults that brought French military officers into key positions of the new government. These assaults bear some description for they indicate the scale of destruction accompanying these battles. A Frenchman, twenty-four-year-old Laurent Barisy, accompanied the Nguyễn fleet as an arms dealer and described them in his letters.[46] In the siege of the Tây Sơn port at Quy Nhơn, the Nguyễn fleet destroyed ninety Tây Sơn vessels and allegedly killed fifty thousand sailors and people on shore. Nguyễn Ánh lost four thousand of his own soldiers in the attack.[47] The fleet then sailed north and attacked Đà Nẵng before preparing its invasion of Huế. On June 12, 1801, the fleet reached the inlet to the Perfume River at Thuận An, a coastal defense about fifteen kilometers from Huế. The Nguyễn flotilla attacked the coastal forts and the Tây Sơn fleet guarding the inlet. They broke through the defenses, and three days later, after heavy bloodshed, Nguyễn Ánh and his officers (including three French captains) walked the palace grounds that his parents had fled. In the ensuing days, he and the Vietnamese commanders commenced sentencing enemy commanders while simultaneously raising recruits for one final assault on the northern capital at Thăng Long.[48] After that assault, Nguyễn Ánh returned to Phú Xuân in 1802 and was crowned Emperor Gia Long.

While many royal armies in Southeast Asia had employed European weapons and mercenaries since the 1500s, this Nguyễn campaign was one of the first to feature European officers commanding European ships under a Vietnamese flag. It marked a critical turn in naval technologies as European vessels expanded in size and replaced Chinese and Southeast Asian ships in much of the region's long-haul trade. The French naval officers each commanded a thirty-six-cannon frigate with three hundred sailors. In the naval assault on Quy Nhơn in 1801, the French officers served as Nguyễn Ánh's naval escort and supported the Vietnamese generals who led the landings. Once on the throne, Emperor Gia Long reorganized his military—and in some ways his government—along European military lines. He rewarded the French officers who served him, giving them official titles with salaries, grand houses, and security details, and he turned to his Việt generals to insure domestic security, appointing them as military governors. He also followed in the tradition of his ancestors by insisting on military rule. In Huế, French officer Jean-Baptiste Chaigneau served as a chief diplomat, receiving delegations of European visitors there.[49] At the northern and southern regional commands (present-day Hà Nội and Sài Gòn), Vietnamese generals governed as viceroys in French-style military fortresses. Sài Gòn's rice granaries and port remained vital to the kingdom, so Emperor Gia Long named his most trusted general, Lê Văn Duyệt, to govern there. Duyệt in turn pursued further military expansions into Khmer territory, establishing a garrison near the Khmer court at Phnom Penh.

Despite the creation of a new imperial government and its European-influenced military, the ecological poverty that had worsened during the Tây Sơn Rebellion continued. On the central coast, provincial military governments faced droughts, typhoons, infrastructure collapse, and more rebellions. Governors continued to complain about abandoned land, and the imperial government resumed high taxes and conscription demands.[50] At a former Cham port, Quảng Ngãi, local protests coalesced into a series of full-scale battles where non-Việt, ostensibly highlander groups fought the Nguyễn forces, taking over some strongholds for a time. They had started this resistance in the 1750s and resumed it in 1803. These rebellions simmered into the 1850s. One estimate of this highlander army in 1844 figured several thousand soldiers manning a perimeter of hilltop forts around Quảng Ngãi.[51] While military campaigns in the kingdom's mountainous and southern frontiers may have advanced state aims to cultivate (*giáo hóa*) non-Việt peoples, the old troubles of abandoned fields and low productivity undermined the appeal of integration into a modern Vietnamese state.

Even in relatively wealthy villages such as Phù Bài, decades of war and environmental degradation left the old, guild-centered life in ruins. The surrounding coastal hills remained deforested and eroded with upland fields and mining areas largely untended. Without essential charcoal, iron production at Phù Bài ceased. The district administration even revoked the village's two-hundred-year exemption from military service. In 1808 Gia Long requested five hundred soldiers from the village, sapping essential laborers from iron working and agriculture.[52] When the government completed new land registers of the village, they described the majority of formerly titled public fields in the hills as "idle wasteland" (*hoang nhàn, thổ phụ*).[53]

Beside the political problems associated with abandoned fields, the spread of cholera in coastal communities added a new, frightening challenge from the sea. As European ships circulating between India and China made port calls in Vietnam, they unwittingly spread the bacteria (*Vibrio cholerae*) in their bilge water and via sick sailors who went (and often died) ashore. Cholera outbreaks ravaged Việt ports during each of the global pandemics. Populations near stagnant water were especially vulnerable; this may help to explain why the Vietnamese government restricted foreigners to the seaport in Đà

Nẵng and prevented most from traveling the road to Huế. In just one year (1820), over two hundred thousand people in the kingdom died from the disease. An outbreak in 1849–50 killed almost six hundred thousand people, and more outbreaks followed in the 1850s and 1860s.[54] This terrifying disease was an imperial one, spreading from seaports along shipping lanes to people living on the water's edge.

Considering the growth of European and American navies in the 1800s and troubles emanating from the sea, the decision of the second Nguyễn emperor, Minh Mạng (r. 1820–41), to abruptly cut ties with France and demilitarize his government signaled an important shift in tactics.[55] Minh Mạng attempted to move away from his father's system of military government while directly addressing the persistent problem of abandoned lands through an agressive new land policy. These moves triggered a devastating insurrection in Sài Gòn and brought foreign condemnation for the execution of Catholic priests, but at least in landscape terms, Emperor Minh Mạng attempted to remedy the social causes of poor lands and to integrate the highland frontiers.[56] In the growing capital at Huế, no work of architecture better symbolized this emperor's neotraditional transition than did the new palace. Construction of Huế's fortifications started under his father in 1804; and the influence of famed military architect Sébastien Vauban is highly evident in the ramparts and walls. Inside the walls, however, Minh Mạng constructed a royal palace that followed a deliberately chosen model: the Ming dynasty's Forbidden City in Beijing. One of the most ornate elements in the palace, the Noon Gate, was completed in 1833. Its tiled roofs, attention to feng shui, and many figurative elements signaled an intention to reorient the nation's political culture along more traditionally Confucian lines.

As the palace was completed, Minh Mạng initiated one of the most ambitious land reform campaigns in the history of the kingdom. He ordered a comprehensive national land survey that would limit the size of private land holdings and reapportion excess lands through reclassification as public lands. This nineteenth-century land-to-the-tiller program and an accompanying mapping initiative triggered a three-year rebellion in the south that left the southern fortress at Gia Định (Sài Gòn) in ruins. A central cause for the rebellion was Minh Mạng's accompanying cultivation policy. The emperor not only sought to boost agricultural cultivation but he also ordered Chinese and Catholic schools closed and aimed to "cultivate" the many non-Việt ethnic groups to a Confucian and Vietnamese standard.[57]

Maps figured centrally in both of the emperor's reforms, indicating non-Việt places as well as lands open for new tenants. While the kingdom struggled with local resistance in many centers of Khmer, Cham, Chinese, and highlander populations, the mapmaking effort over the years produced a valuable spatial record of the kingdom's natural and cultural geography. The maps progressively expanded Vietnamese territorial claims deeper into the highlands too. Published from 1830 to 1882, these atlases and gazetteers offered a spatial platform for cultivation policies.[58] On the central coast, this new wave of mapmaking extended the court's imperial gaze much deeper inland, beyond the edges of the relatively bare coastal hills to steeper slopes and distant peaks inhabited by highlander groups. Nguyễn atlases and gazetteers detail this expanding westward gaze to the terrestrial "sea" of highland forests. One of the first nationwide atlases, published in 1832, shows a heightened attention to the hills—almost every peak and ridge appears named. The atlas presented a bird's-eye view of Thừa Thiên–Huế Province with the coast at the bottom and the hills and the mountainous frontier at the top. This presentation directed the viewer's gaze inland to the remote peaks (figure 1.4). The Inner Road running from north to south was just a dotted line that bisected the walled capital and district seats such as Hương Thủy (encompassing Phù Bài and Dạ Lê Villages). Another line at the top marked a relatively new feature in Nguyễn maps, a border delineating the kingdom's claims to the upland domain from the terra incognita of the mountains beyond. Considering the map's use of Chinese characters as well as traditional scale and symbolic conventions common to East Asian cartography, it also represents a deliberate stylistic shift away from European cartographic techniques that Vietnamese cartographers had experimented with before 1820.[59]

After Minh Mạng's death in 1841, his successors carried forward these policies but failed, like many of the region's monarchs, to respond to the growing military power of European navies. However, while trouble and colonial wars erupted on the coastline, the Nguyễn monarchs continued to pursue expansion inland, above the hills. French naval forces had escalated attacks on Nguyễn ports beginning in 1847, and in 1859 a French fleet attacked and seized the royal citadel at Sài Gòn. Nguyễn maps and gazetteers produced in the 1860s mostly avoided this once-vital southern region; instead they expanded to include new mountainous realms that had previously fallen outside old mapped areas. A comprehensive historical geography of the kingdom completed in the early 1860s, Đại Nam Nhất Thống Chí, introduced the

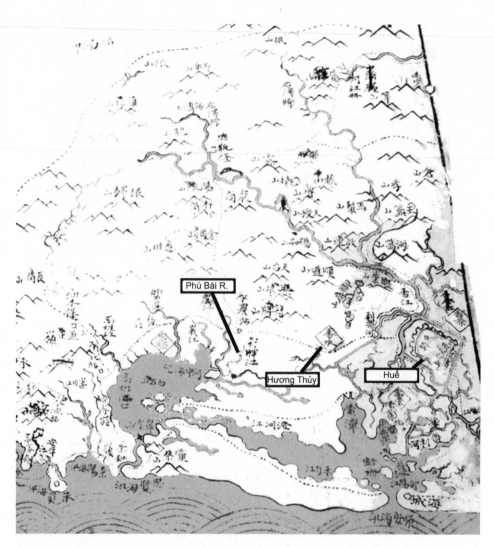

FIGURE 1.4. Map of Thừa Thiên–Huế Province, 1832. Source: *Thông Quốc Duyên Cách Hải Chữ*, 1832, Social Sciences Library of Hồ Chí Minh City, HVN 190. Labels and shading added by author.

terms *động* and *cốc* to signal non-Việt highland slopes.[60] One of the last geographic publications produced before the French navy invaded Huế, it represented one last imperial push to the hills as European forces prepared coastal amphibious assaults. The last geographic volumes published by the Nguyễn even expanded the traditional idea of upper and lower settlements to include this new highlands zone. The final geography of the province was divided into three books describing lowlands, midlands, and highlands.[61]

BARE HILLS AND THE SPATIAL LOGIC
OF COLONIAL CONQUEST

Much has been written about what authors Pierre Brocheux and Daniel Hémery describe as France's "ambiguous colonization" of Indochina in stages from 1858 to 1884; however, little attention has been paid to the role that regional landscapes played in determining the spaces of this colonial expansion.[62] The "idle wastelands" that had long exposed the economic and political weaknesses of the Nguyễn government beckoned to French cartographers and colonial speculators. Here were empty spaces of capitalist possibility with few preexisting claims. Meanwhile the agro-economic engines that sustained the Vietnamese kingdom, the estuarine rice fields and densely settled villages along the Inner Road, presented threats to colonial foot soldiers fearing ambush or disease. When French forces encountered a loyalist rebellion around Huế in 1885, these same bare hills offered new value as a strategic redoubt with clear sightlines and hillocks ideal for artillery.

For a colonizing France anxious to set itself in opposition to the Nguyễn regime, the bare hills represented something different: open space for capitalist enterprises. The ancient lowlands with densely populated villages and exposure to diseases presented multiple threats to French security and health, and the highlands, beyond roads and navigable rivers, were all but inaccessible. Had French planters or scientists been permitted to visit the intervening hills, they might have quickly realized why they were so underpopulated. French interest in this "idle wasteland" began out of unusual circumstances. In 1876 after a series of unequal treaties, the French government presented Emperor Tự Đức with a gift of five outdated French gunships to help the kingdom modernize its fleet.[63] French naval officers traveled from the French camp in Đà Nẵng to deliver the ships and temporarily captain them.[64] This gift of warships and a two-year contract funding a training mission brought a novel reconnaissance opportunity for the French military. Retired naval officer and amateur cartographer Jules-Léon Dutreuil de Rhins took the contract and spent two years captaining the gunship *Le Scorpion* while exploring the countryside around Huế. His detailed attention to Nguyễn coastal defenses informed the French naval assault there in 1883

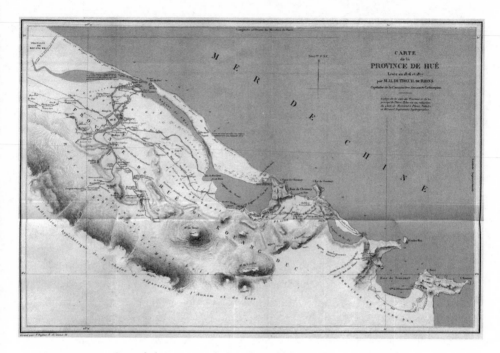

FIGURE 1.5. Carte de la Province de Hué (map of the Hué Province), by J. L. Dutreuil de Rhins, *Le royaume d'Annam et les Annamites: Journal de voyage* (Paris: E. Plon, 1879).

while his gaze from the coastal road into the hills rendered deforested hillsides into verdant spaces for new enterprises. His popular account of the journey, *Le Royaume d'Annam et les Annamites*, included two of the first detailed maps of the Hué area for Western readers. The maps and the travel diary hewed close to the genre of the day, functioning as both entertainment and promotional literature for colonization. He wrote that the lower reaches were "almost entirely deforested, uncultivated, [and] mediate between the mountain and the plain." He described this area as ideal for "cash crops: sugar cane, coffee, tobacco, cotton, mulberry, cinnamon, pepper, etc.," and he added that "the climate of this province is much healthier than Lower Cochinchina or the Tonkin Delta." In light of the cholera epidemics raging in the delta regions, he believed that "Europeans could acclimatize, directing industrial and agricultural establishments and really do the work of colonization."[65] He addressed two vital concerns for the prospective European colonizer: potential for cash crops and the possibility of "acclimatizing" to this tropical locale.

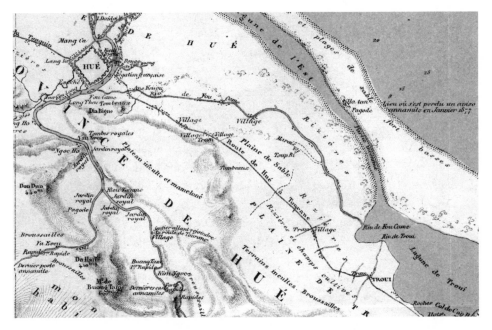

FIGURE 1.6. Detail from Dutreuil de Rhins's map of the Huế Province.

His speculative geography also included many disparaging comments on the "disease-prone" coastal communities that suffered from the political repression of "rapacious mandarins." Dutreuil du Rhins contributed many other common tropes, too, in particular descriptions of villagers as "lazy" given their apparent lack of interest in cultivating the hills.

While the explorer-author attempted to differentiate spaces in the landscape that might appeal to his European audience, his descriptions and maps in many senses continued the upward logic of the Nguyễn atlases and gazetteers. His maps detailed navigable waterways and the Inner Road but then followed royal tombs and gardens upstream to the kingdom's rear gates where Việt hills (sơn) gave way to lands "inhabited by Moïs [savages]" (figure 1.5).

A closer look at this map in figure 1.6 and the descriptive text reveals a combination of purposeful erasures, elisions, and continuations. Dutreuil du Rhins marked in his maps key imperial sites such as "Annamite rear post" and "trạm" (a district-level administrative station), but he replaced the names of hilltops and hamlets with generic terms such as "uncultivated" and "abandoned," conceptually clearing the hills for French ventures. Through a graduated stippling of pen strokes, he may have intentionally hidden some ecological truths of this terrain, too; torrential rains had rent deep gullies through deforested slopes and left little if any topsoil. Places such as Phù Bài and the Eastern Wood melted into more generic terms—village, uncultivated plain, scrub.

Throughout the book, Dutreuil de Rhins contrasted the fallow hills and crowded villages to produce the specter of a space that might receive France's *mission civilisatrice*. For those readers who might have questioned why the Vietnamese had not taken advantage of their bounty, he blamed the Nguyễn government's corruption: "More than half of the arable land in the province of Hue is still uncultivated, due to different causes that we have already spoken, mainly the laziness of the Annamese [Vietnamese] and their pitiful government. . . . The Annamite, for whom foreign trade is prohibited, has no interest in the rich crops which would cost him too much fatigue, and it is not encouraged to produce cereals beyond the needs of his consumption because the mandarins, cowardly and crawling with their superiors and as hard and rapacious with their inferiors, they soon despoil his reserves."[66] The critique of "indolent poverty" was not unfounded. Rulers in Huế since the 1750s had struggled to fix the problem of abandoned upland settlements, and Minh Mạng had taken drastic measures to reappropriate lands, but to no avail.

Dutreuil du Rhins, however, missed one of the most important spatial facts with respect to the villages along the Inner Road. Far from being bastions of "the lazy," these villages were communities of hardened survivors, families that had clung to ancestral lands, tombs, and homes despite waves of violent warfare. The common people he encountered along the road may have been grandchildren of those who had survived the Nguyễn collapse in 1773, the Tây Sơn's rapacious rule until 1801, and life amid increasing military demands of the Nguyễn emperors. Many traced their ancestry to founding ancestors, soldiers who served Đại Việt's armies in the 1400s and 1500s. The patchwork of fields and village courtyards bounded by hedges and dikes in the narrow plain was a model of resiliency. Over centuries, families negotiated with village councils and state authorities to preserve these landscapes and their lineages.

Finally, despite the French and imperial Vietnamese use of such terms as *fallow*, the hills behind these villages were not bare or abandoned. They had long played important roles in village life as zones for speculative industrial development or commons for less productive ventures. The scrubby trees provided essential fuel wood, and the grass supported grazing livestock.

Given the limited space on the plain, the hills provided an essential perch for tombs. Villagers could sleep easy knowing that the ghosts of their ancestors watched down from the hills.

. . .

Despite Detreuil du Rhins's view on which lands had value and which did not, his travelogue came to several similar conclusions with the Nguyễn government. First, he recognized that the bulk of this region's population survived in a very narrow strip of villages and fields hugging the Inner Road, hemmed in by hills and estuaries. He also recognized that the strip was ancient, an economic backbone of the region and a challenge to colonial-style economic growth. As did the Nguyễn chronicles and maps, Dutreuil du Rhins also imagined potential riches that waited uphill. While he gazed on the hills, the Nguyễn government had set its sights higher. The forested, mountainous "sea" beyond the hills was the last outlet for Vietnamese exploration as French and European fleets dominated the coastal waters. This late nineteenth-century shift in territorial ambitions from the seas to the mountains anticipated the elevational logics that guided a later generation of Vietnamese revolutionaries in the twentieth century.

TWO

TERRAFORMING

COMPARED WITH FRANCE'S PROLONGED MILITARY CAMPAIGNS TO
seize control of Cochinchina (1859–67) and Tonkin (1873, 1883–86), the con-
quest of the central coast was relatively quick and mostly achieved at the
negotiating table. This was due in part to the fact that France had already
overcome royal troops in the north and south and, as in the past, Sài Gòn
provided much-needed rice to the center and north. Like the Tây Sơn army
before them, they invaded a weakened, food-starved region in 1883 that offered
little resistance; however, the colonial conquerors inherited the same challenge as their predecessors. A force of about one thousand French marines
(including several hundred Vietnamese from Cochinchina) landed at Thuận
An Beach on August 20, 1883, and obliterated the royal fort, killing an estimated 2,500 royal troops. Aided with ironclads, electric searchlights, and
Hotchkiss revolving canons, the French fleet blasted its way up the Perfume
River to Huế. It made such a show of force at the coast that the royal government, already in disarray with the death of Emperor Tự Đức a month earlier,
immediately agreed to a treaty.[1] It ceded all of its forts to France and agreed
to call back thousands of troops fighting in the far north of Tonkin near
China's Yunnan Province. French forces continued mopping up this northern resistance for the next year before forcing a revised treaty on the Nguyễn
government in June 1884. This new treaty, ratified by France and the Nguyễn
dynasty, cut all ties between Vietnam and China and established French pro-
tectorates over northern and central Vietnam. A French high resident was
established at Huế with the responsibility of conducting most essential affairs

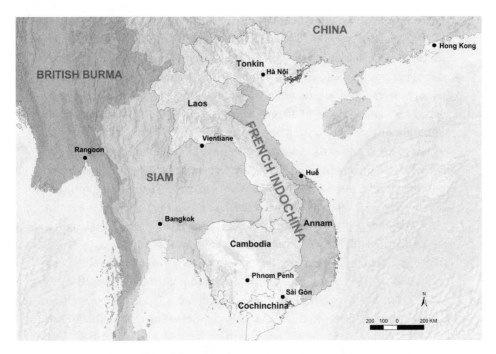

FIGURE 2.1. Protectorate of Annam. Source: Data courtesy of ESRI Inc. Map by author.

for the protectorate of Annam: collection of taxes, adjudicating civil and criminal disputes, and coordinating national defense.[2] (See figure 2.1.)

In a manner in keeping with the 1884 Berlin Conference in which Europeans carved up African lands, French officials drew up boundaries for the protectorate of Annam that bore little relation to conditions on the ground. Annam's northern boundary reached far beyond the natural boundary at Ngang Pass, and its western boundary arced far inland to include remote peaks that had first appeared in Vietnamese atlases only a decade earlier. On the south, it encompassed all of the war-torn former Cham coastline and almost touched Sài Gòn. From a terrain-based point of view, this new state presented the most impossible of territories for any government to manage. The royal road running along the coast was broken in many sections, and there were few roads other than dirt tracks running west into the mountainous interior.

The tiny detachment of French troops and officials posted in Huế and Annam's ports soon realized that this sprawling area was a natural base for insurgency. One year after the treaty was signed and a new king was crowned in July 1885, Emperor Hàm Nghi and a group of advisers ambushed a French delegation. The delegation survived and upon returning to its camp ordered a naval barrage on the palace and surrounding neighborhoods. The king and his supporters fled to the mountains and proclaimed a "Save the King" (*cần vương*) resistance movement. Largely a guerilla movement with secret bases in the mountains communicating from north to south, it drew considerable support from former officials and scholars in many towns on the coast. However, lacking detachments of French troops to attack, the movement's partisans took out their anger on the region's Vietnamese Christian communities, slaughtering over forty thousand.[3] French troops soon reached the central coast, and after a year of fighting to regain the coastal ports, they fought a decisive battle with Nguyễn loyalists at a village near Ngang Pass, Ba Đình. The siege of Ba Đình lasted over two months as over three thousand French troops with artillery pounded encampments of roughly three thousand loyalist forces. In 1887 France enlisted former royal officials such as Hoàng Cao Khải, a former viceroy of Tonkin, to help put down the rebels. The French relied on Mường highlanders, too, who turned over the rebel king.[4]

This violent, rude awakening to the challenges of governing the central coast in many respects tempered French colonial ambitions in the area through the duration of their rule to 1945. The comparatively tiny French population that settled in Annam was almost wholly concentrated within protected coastal ports at Vinh, Huế, Đà Nẵng, Quy Nhơn, and Phan Thiết. French shipping, the coastal highway, and later a railroad preserved their security within the same ancient strip that had protected the domains of the Nguyễn lords. As the 1885 rebellion showed, the majority of Annam's area, its forested highlands and deforested hills, presented a threat to French rule with its inaccessible terrain limiting access from the coast.

Throughout the colonial period to 1945, this militarily weak position and the potential for uprisings in the hills shadowed colonial projects while invigorating would-be nationalists. Military conflicts were extremely few on the central coast before a communist-led uprising in Nghệ An and Hà Tĩnh Provinces broke out in 1930 near the ruins of the 1887 Ba Đình siege. The majority of conflicts on the central coast were internal security or police actions. While minimally violent, some of these actions were nonetheless pivotal. One small action in Huế in 1908 concerned a young man from Nghệ An, Nguyễn Sinh Cung, who attended Annam's prestigious high school for the children of French colonials and indigenous elites, Quốc Học (National Academy).[5] He ran afoul of security police in Huế while interpreting for farmers in a tax protest and eventually fled town and then Indochina before returning three decades later to the Chinese-Vietnamese border as Hồ Chí Minh. Many would-be political and military leaders came from similar experiences on the central coast.

While the central coast was not host to major military encampments during the colonial era, military processes nevertheless played a formative role in shaping the speculative spaces of colonial development and Vietnamese nationalism. With the arrival of surplus airplanes and aerial cameras after World War I, these leftovers from the Great War radically changed views of Annam, particularly its wasted hills and mountain forests. As photographic sources spread through postcards and books, reform-minded colonials in Huế, especially foresters, considered the economic and political costs of colonial clear cuts and these vistas of eroded hills. The spread of newspapers and the *quốc ngữ* (romanized) alphabet in Annam connected Vietnamese audiences with far-off events while textbooks from the 1930s put the old villages of the Inner Road and the hills in new aerial perspectives. The world's conflicts came crashing back to Annam when Japanese planes, ships, and troops arrived in 1941, and new levels of aerial military destruction returned when the US Army Air Force commenced bombing the coast in 1943.

The relatively nonviolent early 1900s in Annam were nonetheless still influenced by military concerns in the colony and militarism globally. Especially during the interwar period (1918–40), colonial leaders struggled with the political and environmental challenges posed by Annam's degraded lands while Vietnamese nationalists drew upon newspapers and such new technologies as radio and aerial imagery to imagine new postcolonial futures. This chapter explores the more latent ways that the postconquest colonial military figured into land politics, and it considers how colonial reformers and nationalists drew on post–World War I military technologies to forge new perspectives on interconnected political and environmental problems with troubled lands.

MILITARY MANEUVERS IN THE HILLS

After years of fighting uprisings in the 1880s and losing massive sums of money on the colonial venture in Indochina, the tactically savvy governor general Paul Doumer in Hà Nội made a decisive move with respect to the central coast. In 1897 he signed an agreement with the Nguyễn emperor that placed all public lands, from the centuries-old public fields to the hilly commons and the highland valleys, under the colony's control. It was a historic moment not because it finally helped the colonial government realize its dreams of terraforming empty slopes into plantations but because it made the problems of these areas, especially their poverty, the business of the French. Doumer recognized the precarious military and economic position for France in this narrow strip of ports and urban quarters around the former imperial capital. The Treaty of Huế in 1884 had protected the monarchy's ability to obtain funds from private fields (*tư điền*), and although it dispossessed the crown of claims to public fields and unincorporated lands, it did not permit the French colonial government to exploit these lands. The treaty limited European businesses to the confines of urban quarters, mainly in Huế and Tourane (Đà Nẵng), and it required sales of public lands to follow Vietnamese customary laws.[6] Only indigenous subjects could buy, sell, and develop these areas. This stipulation was born out of the practical need in 1884 to avoid widening anticolonial sentiment in Annam by preventing what Detreuil du Rhins had imagined: white Europeans running plantations above the old villages. In neighboring Cochinchina, French land auctions and concessions had resulted in sweeping dispossessions as over 3.2 million hectares of land moved into the hands of French nationals by 1902. This did not happen in Huế.[7]

Doumer attempted to remove this legal barrier in 1897 as a response to the costly military campaigns to put down the Save the King rebellion. He signed with Emperor Thành Thái in Huế a decree placing all of Indochina's public lands under colonial law and at the colonial government's disposal. Considering the size of Annam's uncharted forests and the majority of lowland fields classified as public lands in the past, it was an unprecedented land grab. It permitted the Résident Supérieur of Annam (RSA) to manage the economic and civil affairs of this territory stretching from the edges of ancient villages to unexplored, unmapped highland valleys. Even private land sales, while still taking place between Vietnamese owners, would now be governed by French law and subject to colonial taxes.[8] Doumer, famous for consolidating military and political control over Indochina, cut off one of the last main sources of revenue to the royal government. He noted the achievement in a 1902 memoir: "The King abandoned in favor of the Governor General of

Indo-China his prerogative to dispose of assets not already allocated to public service, and as a consequence to concede vacant lands without masters. This provided the means for *colons* to settle in Annam, and we know they will make good use of it."[9] Doumer thus completed the necessary paperwork to open Annam to the full brunt of capitalist enterprises.

There were two problems with this picture, however. First, many of these lands were not—even after the decree—empty of claims, and second, most of the region's eroded slopes did not lend themselves to cash crops. This difficult terrain did not welcome French settlers, and the few who settled in Annam tended to cluster in the ports. A population estimate for all of Annam in 1913 listed just 1,676 French nationals with most living in Huế and Đà Nẵng. The Vietnamese population topped 4.5 million, and highland groups and other Asian groups numbered half a million.[10] Of the land concessions that the RSA did award, many remained "unimproved" and therefore fell back into government hands.

Villagers used what legal claims they could to stymie colonial enterprises, especially in traditional hilly domains. In the hills above Dạ Lê Village in 1900, the RSA awarded one of the first concessions, a 125-hectare tract, to one of its most famous Vietnamese collaborators. Hoàng Cao Khải led the Nguyễn defense of Hà Nội against French attacks in 1883. After defeat, he joined the French and in the next few years helped French troops put down the Save the King insurrection. With the rebellion and its leaders defeated and a collaborationist emperor seated in Huế in 1897, he returned as an adviser to the emperor, steering him into the agreement with Doumer. The RSA awarded Khải a relatively large estate for a Vietnamese national, a sign of his service to the French and also something of an experiment, since few French settlers expressed interest. Khải agreed to improve the property (planting crops) and after five years to start paying taxes on the improved lands.[11]

In the fine print, however, the agreement recognized prior villager and government claims to the land which eventually drove Khải away. The contract required the aging noble to permit villagers access to ancestor tombs during all holidays and death anniversaries, and it reserved the colonial military's access to an "artillery polygon" and firing range.[12] Figure 2.2, an overlay of the land parcel with a 1909 topographic map of the village, provides additional clues as to why Khải may not have kept to the agreement. In one portion, villagers had already established fields and homes, likely in former

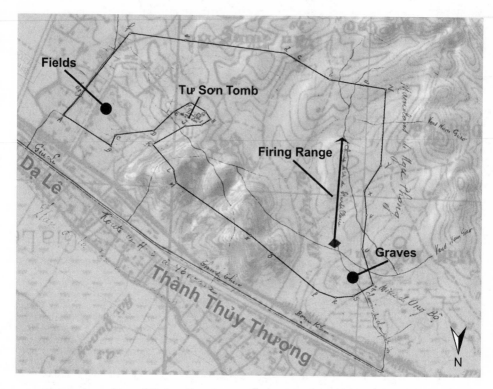

Fields

Tư Sơn Tomb

Firing Range

Graves

N

FIGURE 2.2. Map of Hoàng Cao Khải Land Concession. Source: Land Concession Agreement, October 27, 1900, Folder 220, Résident Supérieur of Annam, Vietnam National Archives Center no. 4; 1909 topographic map, War Office, Indochine 25000e, Deltas de l'Annam, reproduction of 1909 edition by Service Géographique de l'Indochine, Deltas de l'Annam.

public fields. Seizing this land would have engendered personal hostilities as well as problems with village authorities. Khải did not challenge the stipulations or even take the parcel. Instead, he returned north to Tonkin and accepted the position of district chief (*tổng đốc*) in Hà Đông. The plot , like most of Annan, remained "abandoned" but in public hands.[13]

While French expeditionary forces had mostly left Indochina by 1897, such sites as the firing range (*champ de tir*) remained important to the RSA as a symbol of French military hegemony, with hilltop artillery batteries capable of leveling villages below. During the surge in military operations to 1891, the hills around the former capital hosted camps and training grounds for the French Expeditionary Corps. It used sites like this to train an indigenous army of some thirty thousand *tirailleurs* (light infantry) to mop up resistance across the region.[14] Even after the soldiers decamped, many old training grounds continued to host annual training exercises to maintain military readiness. The sounds of live fire drills each year had a calculated political effect, too, reminding people that the destructive power of a modern European military was never far away.

Given the limited entrepreneurial activity in the coastal hills after 1900, these training exercises by colonial military units were some of the most prominent interruptions to traditional land uses in the hills. Their timing and requirements on nearby villages asserted colonial claims in highly disruptive ways. A collection of letters from 1906 to 1913 between residents of Thần Phù Village, the colonial official in Hương Thủy District, the royal court, province officials, the RSA, and the colonial military highlight the political controversy caused by annual exercises. This conflict centered on an annual artillery field school run by the Third Battery of the Colonial Artillery in Tourane. Every year from 1903 until 1914, a group of approximately 15 officers and noncommissioned officers, 50 European artillerymen, 50 indigenous artillerymen, 50 mules, and 6 horses conducted a weeklong fire school (*école à feu*) on the knolls above Thần Phù Village.[15] The location of the fire school in the hills above continued the decimation of what had been the famed Eastern Wood. With the annual fire school running from 1903, the barren hilltops and hillsides became marred by thousands of rounds of artillery shells as students in the fire school practiced their shots.[16]

The exercises lasted just more than a week, but their timing and requirements on the village amounted to an invasion of cultural spaces and spiritual life. They took place during the Lunar New Year (Tết Nguyên Đán) and required villagers to feed the group. The village communal house and pagoda became troop billets while the pagoda yard held the horses and livestock. In 1911 a reform-minded emperor, Duy Tân, used his privy council (*viện cơ mật*) to raise the issue with the RSA, explaining that the days leading up to Tết were some of the most important, sacred days of the year. Villagers visited ancestor tombs in the hills and prepared offerings for their home altars and at the pagoda. Two days before the New Year, families visited the pagoda to make offerings, plant bamboo, and pray. The celebrations ended on the third day of the New Year, and the privy council recommended that the artillery fire school could start after all the rituals had been observed. Careful to recognize the power of the Resident Superior and the colonial government, the privy council nevertheless revealed deep hostility to this move to use military training to assert French power: "Moving the altar to receive the troops and give up the worship service, these are things contrary to the feelings of people and they will generate much resentment on their part."[17] Despite communication from Duy Tân on the villagers' behalf, the RSA and the colonial military continued the training as planned. After the event, however, the French district official caught wind of growing Vietnamese resentment and wrote to his boss, the province administrator, to consider moving the dates.

While villagers in Thần Phù had relatively little power to challenge the colonial military, they nonetheless used their customary rights to push back. They cited traditional claims to visit tombs and family shrines to contest military attempts to permanently seize areas in the hills, tying up French officials in a lengthy exchange of paperwork. After each year's fire school ended, representatives from the village sent a new round of letters to the RSA. They acknowledged their duty to lodge soldiers, but then they attempted to bargain with the government, stating that they should be absolved of labor obligations associated with maintaining the eight kilometers of Highway 1 running through the village. They also requested the government build a permanent barracks for the troops on the hill, perhaps a bid to create jobs and opportunities for local services.[18] After several years of these letter-writing campaigns, the RSA sided with the village in 1911, complaining to Hà Nội that the military school stopped all administrative and judicial business for two weeks.[19]

The dispute, while intensely local, raised larger legal questions about the separation of powers between Indochina's civil and military leaders. Ultimately, General Théophile Pennequin, the commander of Indochina's military, settled it. He proposed a compromise, keeping the same Tết schedule but paying the village for food and lodging.[20] The province chief, facing another Tết with a fire school on the hillside, complained: "Precisely at the moment that Government seems to be to giving the indigenous population the peace and quiet they need, the requirement for less fortunate villages in the area of Huong Thuy for more than a half month to lodge a contingent of more than one hundred men, certainly seems very painful for the people of this region."[21] Despite these letters, colonial troops resumed their holiday bombing in the hills above Thần Phù.

As France mobilized its colonial militaries to support campaigns in Europe during the Great War, military training and camps again expanded in Annam. The expansion of camps on the fringes of the European quarter in Huế in groves around royal tombs drew a new line of criticism from Huế's French residents. Soldiers took to cutting pine groves surrounding former royal gardens that had fallen into neglect. Without local guards since the 1897 edict, the pine groves disappeared as people took advantage of these untended spaces to glean wood. A garden city once surrounded by wooded hilltops, Huế's tree-lined streets and suburban gardens suffered in the early 1900s.

A French priest and historian, Father Léopold Cadière, sounded the alarm in 1916 through a journal he'd founded with senior Vietnamese scholars, *Bulletin des Amis du Vieux Huế*. He had recently visited one of the city's largest gardens, the Nam Giao Pavilion, and found soldiers hacking away at the roots of large pines, gathering sap-rich wood chips to sell as matches. Cadière reacted in shock, writing, "I was stunned, I was angry, I was heartbroken."[22] He went on to explain that these twisted pines with thick trunks were sacred trees. Emperors such as Minh Mạng had planted them, and many had brass plates engraved with the name of the royal patron. Cadière, one of the few Frenchmen who lived in the area before the 1897 decree, noted the rapid decimation of these gardens. He was disgusted that a colonial soldier charged with the protection of Indochina could cut down a tree planted by an emperor.

He took to the pages of his journal to register his alarm. He was careful not to blame the soldiers alone, noting that the pine groves' decimation was not solely the harvesters' fault. The colonial artillery had cleared some hilltops in the 1890s; and a severe typhoon had plowed through the hills in 1904, toppling many large trees. He identified the main source of destruction as repeated hacks of scythes into tree trunks and roots that exposed the trees to storms and disease. He compared walks in the sunbaked, stripped hills of 1916 to those of 1896, when he'd led students to tombs while shaded by black, twisted pines from decades earlier. He recalled that on this past visit, royal soldiers had greeted the group and warned them about fires. He lamented the reversal in affairs in 1916, writing, "today it is the guards themselves who cut the pines. Today is unbridled havoc, devastation beyond measure. We must act."[23]

Despite his plea Annam's forestry department fell short of achieving any reforestation goals. Annam's senior forester in 1918, Henri Guibier, was a friend of Cadière and a member of the *Bulletin des Amis du Vieux Huế*. Like Cadière he wrote books on Annam's forests and later took to the *Bulletin* to articulate views on causes of deforestation and possible solutions. He drew attention to reforestation as essential to mitigate terrible annual flooding in Huế. Forests, he argued, were like sponges, retaining water on the slopes.[24] Guibier railed against the tradition of burning highland forests called swidden (*rẫy*); however, he was careful to articulate the differences between traditional highlander practices and burning for livestock grazing in the coastal hills. Guibier advocated creation of forest preserves in the highlands to study regional biodiversity, but he took special interest in Annam's bare hills.[25] He complained that colonial officials tended to view every type of burning as *rẫy*, assuming this was a sustainable practice and "that excuses everything."[26] Guibier pointed to the hills where he noted that the bulk of inhabitants were not highlanders but ethnic Vietnamese who burned thousands of acres to make permanent grasslands, a sort of "management by clear cut with no reserves, a sort of *sartage*."[27]

Guibier trained his sights on these "idle wastelands" and what he considered "wasteful" behavior, proposing a new, green colonial solution. He presided over tree nurseries set up for pines in 1912, but in the 1920s he turned his attention to newly imported Australian "miracle" species. With support from the RSA, Guibier and the forestry staff opened a string of eucalyptus nurseries. He planted filaos (*Casuarina equisetifolia*) to reforest sandy areas and eucalyptus for the hills.[28] Years later, he took to the pages of the *Bulletin* to trumpet the benefits of this and other colonizing species.

Guibier became the protectorate's chief advocate for a new form of green colonialism taking hold in colonies around the world. His enthusiasm for these exotic species reflected a general interest, especially among foresters during the Great Depression, to expand wood commodity markets through reforestation.[29] Eucalyptus, particularly *Eucalyptus globulus*, were the signature species for white settler colonies too. British foresters in South Africa aimed to "wean" natives away from native species by introducing eucalyptus; in the Nilgiri Hills of Madras, they replaced shifting agriculture traditions of native hill groups with plantation frontiers of eucalyptus.[30] In California Anglo settlers looked to eucalyptus to populate the bare hills of the old rancheros and to line streets in new towns.[31] For Guibier, this botanical "settler" promised finally to do the work of colonizing the hills that Detreuil du Rhins had envisioned in 1876 and Doumer had legalized in 1896. Eucalyptus would colonize the soils and simultaneously kill off native plants by drawing down water tables. This sort of botanical imperialism became the hallmark of colonial terraforming around the world, though it came slow to Annam given the continuing lack of white settlers.

THE AERIAL TURN

The Great War (1914–18) not only spurred new nationalist impulses in colonial territories such as Annam but also brought three important technologies—airplanes, radios, and cameras—that provided colonial officials and nationalists a transformative visual platform that transcended this difficult terrain. The Great War and the failures of the Treaty of Versailles to address the rights of colonized peoples catalyzed a new generation of Vietnamese nationalists hungry for new media and perspectives. A young man from the central coast with a new pseudonym, Nguyễn the Patriot (Hồ Chí Minh), joined French socialists in 1920 and helped form the French Communist Party. Postwar protests in France helped the left gain power in 1924, and many prominent French socialists took on posts as colonial governors where they enacted reforms that popularized vernacular newspapers and textbooks. By the early 1920s, even Huế had become part of this global network, connected by "wireless" communications and air service that compressed time and space. Those lucky enough to ride in old Breguets taking off from dirt fields were exhilarated by views of their homes far below. Aerial perspectives proliferated in the early 1930s, too, via postcards, geography texts, and magazines.

This aerial platform was both enabling and troubling. It opened up new spaces of opportunity for nationalist networks and imaginations at the same time that it revealed the extent of environmental degradation and the territorial limits of colonial "progress" bounded inside the small grids of streets in European city quarters. Aerial technology first reached Indochina's airfields and broadcasting stations around Hà Nội and Sài Gòn in the early 1920s before spreading to Huế and the central coast via a more skeletal presence of dirt fields, airplane sheds, and radio relays. Nevertheless, for budding Vietnamese nationalists in Huế's elite schools and some in the older generation who had returned, it undergirded their territorial ambitions and kept them informed of events across Vietnam and the world beyond.

Colonial military actors, veteran pilots especially, played a central role in this aerial transition. They operated most of the early aviation infrastructure and took most of the pictures. They flew bombing raids on a few occasions and provided aerial reconnaissance for internal security police. This technology was necessarily dual use, justified mainly for its military and surveillance values. French politicians recognized the need to modernize Indochina's military with airplanes, too, to keep up with developments in Siam, Republican China, and Showa Japan. Airfields and airspace in Indochina were primarily military spaces. The Civil Aviation Service of Indochina, founded in 1918, was attached directly to the general government but controlled by a senior French military officer and pilot. The majority of aircraft assigned to Indochina's airfields in the early 1920s were surplus military aircraft, reassigned into four squadrons of eight to ten planes each at Bạch Mai (Hà Nội) and Biên Hòa (near Sài Gòn).[32] While the airplanes and airfields were available for commercial activities, their primary function was defending the colony. In 1924 when an upland minority group in the central highlands killed French and Vietnamese contractors tasked with extending a road, the government responded by sending two planes to bomb the village. The planes landed at a small field near the upland village An Khê. In one day the two planes dropped eight bombs on the village. After more bombing raids, the *garde indigène* regained control of the village and roadwork continued.[33] Five years later, another rebellion broke out in the same region, and planes returned, dropping many more bombs over eight days.[34]

Throughout this early era of aviation, Huế and the central coast played a minor role. The largest airfields—Bạch Mai (Hà Nội), Tông (Sơn Tây), Phú Thọ (Sài Gòn), Tourane (Đà Nẵng), and Biên Hòa (Sài Gòn)—grew as key urban and military centers. The Radiotelegraph Service, established in 1909, expanded its wireless communications after 1919 to commercial communications with two broadcasting centers at the Bạch Mai and Phú Thọ airfields.[35] The Geographic Service of Indochina in 1927 placed aerial photography specialists at Bạch Mai and Biên Hòa to coordinate aerial photographic surveys.[36]

Huế was by all comparisons a minor stop, but as a scenic, royal center of Vietnam it attracted many of Indochina's early air travelers. The RSA opened a landing field at Phú Bài in 1924 after purchasing a stretch of sandy soil north of the Phú Bài River. Acquiring these lands at ten piasters per acre, the provincial government groomed a landing strip out of former wastelands damaged by iron smelting. Locals from Phù Bài Village maintained a few sheds at the airstrip and kept the ground clear for landings.[37] By 1931 the airfield still lacked basic air services such as fuel, radio navigation, and spare parts.[38] The Aéronautique Militaire delivered airmail on a regular basis, but there was only a trickle of letters. The Geographic Service had no personnel in Huế or Tourane, so cartographic-grade aerial photography was limited while the service directed aerial photography missions in Vietnam's two largest deltas.[39] In 1936 the RSA extended a telephone line to the airfield, but it refused requests to relocate Huế's weather and radiotelegraph stations there. (RSA staff preferred to work in Huế's European quarter.) Caretakers at the airfield called in each morning to confirm weather conditions for landings and takeoffs.[40]

While the colonial government had yet to advance aerial land surveys to the central coast, a growing number of oblique shots snapped by pilots over Huế and its environs began to feature in tourist postcards, brochures, and textbooks. Air travel and aerial images played a central role in what historian Christopher Goscha calls the "spatial reworking of Indochina." Citing a popular French travelogue on Indochina published in 1928, *The Five Flowers: Indochina Explained*, he notes a passage where a young Vietnamese passenger on a French aircraft describes his "Indochinese vision": "I thought I was dreaming: I had covered almost two thousand kilometers, crossed ten rivers and a thousand hills. In other words, thanks to a flying-machine, I had just passed over all of Indochina within a *few hours*."[41] Airplanes, trains, telegraph lines, radio broadcasts, and a growing network of paved roads facilitated the creation of this trans-Indochina space. By 1930 Vietnamese geographers had translated a handful of French geographical works into *quốc ngữ*, thus introducing more of this trans-Indochina view to Việt audiences. Radical Vietnamese nationalists such as Nguyễn Ái Quốc (Nguyễn the Patriot; Hồ Chí Minh) adopted this Indochinese framework, too, when he and others formed the Indochinese Communist Party in 1930.[42]

The expansion of commercial travel in the 1930s coupled with advances in photography and printing to produce a new wave of international travel writing. Scores of westerners from academics to wealthy celebrities and self-proclaimed vagabonds visited Huế as a stop on tours of Indochina and Asia. The colony promoted Huế as the seat of "Annamese tradition," characterized by often-repeated scenes of dragon boats on the Perfume River, the royal citadel and palace, and the gardens. The American writer Harry Franck, made famous by his first book, *A Vagabond Journey around the World* (1910), visited Huế in 1924 and produced a pithy, photo-rich account of his visit to Annam in *East of Siam* (1926). Unlike others, however, he advocated an everyman, "vagabond" approach—a forerunner of today's backpackers—choosing to avoid air travel. Franck was also a veteran of the Great War, and his narrated meanderings capture a sense of how the postwar world had become more globally connected.

His opening lines in *East of Siam* capture the various ways that people far beyond the boundaries of the French empire had begun to take notice of this remote place: "Those of us who had the good fortune to take part in that great adventure known as the World War can scarcely have failed to notice, among the many kinds of French colonial troops, some little men in khaki and brass-topped mushroom hats, most of them with black teeth. It was not until five years after the Comedy of Versailles that my perpetual wandering over the face of the globe brought me to the land from which they came—Annam, 'Kingdom of the Eminent South.' There was not only the motive of satisfying, by seeing them at home, the curiosity raised by these little brown men in the French army; as far back as I can remember I had felt inquisitive toward that strangely shaped spot on the map, that slender country which drips like a stalactite of candle-grease down from the southeast corner of China."[43]

Franck eschewed the luxuries of air travel and instead preferred travels by public transport. He traveled by buses along Colonial Route No. 1 and by train on a finished section of the Trans-Indochinois Railway. The book included a map of Indochina, his journey marked in red, and over a hundred "out-of-the-way" photographs snapped by the author, including images taken of the Tết Lunar New Year ceremony at the royal palace, at which he accompanied the Résident Supérieur wearing a formal outfit lent to him by the chief of police.[44]

The Aéronautique Militaire's photos around Huế were few and mainly focused on monuments, but they also offer early aerial views of the land. One such image, featured in a set of air photos prepared by the Aéronautique Militaire for the 1931 Colonial Exposition, shows the newest royal tomb, that of Emperor Khải Định (figure 2.3). As an environmental record, this picture conveys a few key details about surrounding hills too. Rows of Sumatran pines from the nurseries shade the hill and gardens around the new tomb.

FIGURE 2.3. Aerial view of Khải Định's tomb, hills of Hương Thủy District in the background. Source: Aéronautique Militaire, *Souvenir de l'Indochine: Photograph Albums of Indochina*, collection number 2001.R.21, Getty Research Institute, Santa Monica, California, plate 25; reprinted with permission from the Getty Research Institute.

In the background, the image shows hills near Highway 1, all still treeless expanses of grassy, eroded slopes.

For a moment in the mid-1920s, colonial reforms and new developments from airfields to radio stations suggested the possibility of a more peaceful transition to demilitarized life in Annam and Indochina. In 1924 the Cartel of the Left swept France's elections, and in 1925 a prominent figure of the French Left—Alexandre Varenne—who advocated for closer ties with the Soviet Union took the post of governor general in Hà Nội. He was quick to push reforms intended to empower the native population with improvements in native education and health care as well as granting more political freedoms. He ordered a comprehensive inventory of all military property with an intent to convert many areas. In Huế the RSA scrambled to meet the new demands, and it decided against closing the firing ranges.[45] It finally yielded in 1927 by creating a leprosarium in a former military training area in the Vùng Phèn hills near the airfield. However, by converting a former military space into one for people suffering from a communicable disease, the colonial council in effect sidestepped the problem by keeping it as a restricted space.

This fleeting moment of reformism from 1925 to 1927 breathed new political life into Huế, especially for both older and younger nationalists. The Varenne administration opened doors by permitting Vietnamese-language newspapers and loosening censorship. Huế in 1926 became the final home for one of Vietnam's most well-known nationalists, Phan Bội Châu. Apprehended in Shanghai by French secret police, he was convicted as an accessory to murder before Governor General Varenne commuted his sentence to house arrest in Huế.[46] Varenne permitted another famous nationalist, Phan Châu Trinh, to return from France. Trinh intended to visit Huế, but a worsening case of tuberculosis kept him in Sài Gòn. He delivered lectures to packed audiences, making the case for popular democracy. He died the following March, and an estimated seventy thousand people turned out for the funeral. Activists in Huế and across Vietnam used ceremonial eulogies to advocate for more reforms.[47]

One of the most prominent of these older nationalists and newspaper intellectuals was Huỳnh Thúc Kháng. He hailed from the central coast (Quảng Nam Province) as did Trinh and Châu, and he passed the Confucian national exam with a doctorate degree in 1904.[48] Kháng was arrested for his involvement with 1908 antitax movements, and he spent thirteen years at the island penal colony of Côn Đảo until 1921. Upon returning to Huế, Kháng gradually recovered his place in local society, and in 1926 he was elected to preside over a newly formed Indochinese Chamber of People's Representatives. Kháng's attempt at political solutions to reform ended with his resignation in 1928, but during this time he successfully launched one of the central coast's first Vietnamese-language newspapers, *Tiếng Dân* (Voice of the People). First published on August 10, 1927, the paper ran for an unprecedented sixteen years before Kháng closed it in 1943.[49]

VIETNAMESE RADICALISM AND LAND REFORM

Apart from the ouster of Varenne and his supporters in 1927, colonial responses to the Great Depression ended what had otherwise been a collaborative moment while ushering in a new era marked by growing radicalism, violent struggles, and increased attention to poor rural areas. This was especially the case in the hills around Huế. Early supporters of communism in Huế, mostly students, followed the writings of figures such as Nguyễn Ái Quốc (Hồ Chí Minh), and joined local communist organizations with the intent to reach out to the peasantry.[50] In January 1930 young people from the villages south of Huế in Hương Thủy District formed its first party committee, electing a secretary and establishing a government-in-exile. A month later, representatives from similar committees across Vietnam traveled to Canton, China, to form the Indochinese Communist Party.[51]

While RSA authorities repeatedly broke up these local cells and arrested leaders, they could not eradicate the network. On May 1, 1930, members of the Hương Thủy District cell planted a red flag with the words "Vietnam Communist Party" on the summit of Ngự Bình Mountain overlooking Huế. That December these party activists together with high school students at the elite National Academy protested the colonial military's airborne and ground assaults on villagers in the Nghệ-Tĩnh Soviets, a group of breakaway rural districts near Vinh.[52] The colonial police arrested many of the founders of Hương Thủy's party cell as well as students, sending them to the "cradle of the revolution," a penal colony on Côn Đảo island.

As colonial officials struggled to find new ways to respond to this political and agricultural crisis, they used their new aerial platform, especially air photos, to "peer over the village hedge" and suggest new models of social and ecological engineering.[53] By the mid-1930s, geographers in Indochina and around the world had seized upon new views afforded by aerial photography to focus greater attention on the depletion of tropical soils and pressures of overpopulation in densely occupied regions. French geographer Pierre Gourou's 1936 study, *Les paysans du delta tonkinois*, made extensive use of the photographs from the Aéronautique Militaire to suggest how unique cultures and ecologies combined to produce the various agricultural regions in the ancient delta. For colonials, studies like Gourou's marked an important turning point in the ways that military men and social scientists viewed unruly, rural landscapes. They paid greater attention to "local genius" while also advocating large-scale resettlement schemes to transplant these local experts to ecologically different, degraded frontiers.[54]

Aerial photography and aerial perspectives lent themselves to many different social and ecological engineering schemes in the 1930s. They suggested, to colonial reformers and Vietnamese nationalists alike, a detached omniscience from the agricultural traditions and land politics that shaped ancient villages.[55] The wastelands that air photography depicted in the hills of the central coast prompted foresters, politicians, and radicals alike to propose radical regreening strategies. In Huế, Guibier expanded nurseries of eucalyptus while such intellectuals as Kháng took to his newspaper to blend green strategies with views on rural politics.[56] His newspaper, *Tiếng Dân*, and other Vietnamese dailies covered traditional issues important in the countryside such as unfair taxation, famines, and landowner abuses of tenant farmers. One daily, *Ánh Sáng* (Bright light), even went so far as to suggest that a communist defeat of Chinese Nationalist Party troops in 1935 was the direct result of nationalist failures to respond to famine and high taxes in these rural areas.[57] Kháng and other editors evaded the censors by reporting such news from China, but the political point vis-à-vis Vietnam was clear. Rural issues and land were fast becoming a core issue for anticolonialists.

In other essays, Kháng took a more moderate tone on rural development, echoing the terraforming views of Guibier. In one essay titled "Chợ Làng Mới" (New Markets and Villages), Kháng described a "garden city" approach for rural revitalization following the work of Englishman W. R. Hughes in *New Town: A Proposal in Agricultural, Industrial, Educational, Civic, and Social Reconstruction*. The approach was an attempt to build small cities in garden-like environs that addressed the economic, social, and spiritual well-being of rural citizens. (Hughes was a prominent Quaker and an advocate for rural reform.)[58] Kháng applied the book's principles to the famine-prone, impoverished hills around Huế. Playing to his more radical audience, he suggested that a "garden" socialism might take hold, embracing cottage industries, human-scale capitalism, and local craft traditions.[59]

GLOBAL WAR COMES TO THE CENTRAL COAST

This momentary flowering of ideas faded in the late 1930s with the surge of militarism in fascist Italy, Nazi Germany, and Showa Japan. Vietnamese nationalists paid greater attention to the spread of Japan's global military while French voters elected a Popular Front government of communists, socialists, and other leftist groups opposed to fascism. During the Popular Front's rule in Indochina (1936–38), Vietnamese nationalists, especially

Communist Party members, took advantage of relaxed colonial policies to recruit new members and expand the reach of quốc ngữ newspapers. After the Popular Front government dissolved in December 1938, the colonial police in Huế responded harshly, rounding up some sixty journalists and Communist Party members. Most were sentenced to prison, serving terms at Côn Đảo. In July 1939 colonial police finally caught up with the province's party secretary, Nguyễn Chí Thanh, and in April 1940 they sent him to Côn Đảo.[60]

After 1940 new concerns about a second world war took precedent as Japanese armies approached Indochina's borders. After the Nazis' marched into Paris in June 1940 and Japanese troops camped across Indochina's northern border in China, the colonial government signed a treaty with Japan in September that permited Japanese military units to operate in Indochina.[61] The first twenty-five thousand Japanese troops moved to the northern port Hải Phòng and the airfields around Hà Nội in what became a rear base for their campaigns in China.[62] The following July, the troops headed south along the Inner Road, setting up at airfields including Phú Bài in preparation for an offensive to seize all of Southeast Asia. This southward expansion in Indochina provided Japan with military infrastructure useful to the surprise offensive in December 1941. The government of French Indochina accepted the presence of Japanese troops in return for retaining authority over domestic affairs. Japanese military forces, aiming to prevent conflicts in the towns, expanded camps near the airfields and ports while Japanese diplomats, businessmen, and advisers worked in colonial towns.[63]

This unusual wartime agreement between unequal allies inaugurated a new wave of military base construction on the central coast. One company of Japanese troops managed regional air operations at Phú Bài. Across the highway and railway they closed the leper colony and built weapons bunkers and a rice storehouse for shipments to the front.[64] Japan's Ministry of Foreign Affairs and its secret police organization, the Kempeitai, worked with French colonial officials to direct the area's rice and industrial crops to the war effort. A series of diplomatic accords signed between France and Japan delineated annual and regional volumes of rice to be exported.[65] The colonial army, an organization of mostly Vietnamese soldiers with a handful of French officers, remained under arms inside the city; but it was subordinate to Japanese military and police commands.[66]

The Japanese military presence beyond the airfield remained relatively minimal until early 1945 as Allied advances in Europe and Asia caused Japanese military leaders to take a more defensive position around Huế. On March 9 it waged a surprise military coup against the French colonial government, and within a few days they disarmed and imprisoned French officials and military officers, transferring control of the government (at least nominally) to the monarchy in Huế.[67] With this sudden move by the Japanese government, Huế and the royal palace reemerged after more than fifty years as a center of government.

AMERICAN MILITARY VIEWS FROM ABOVE

With a new generation of bomber aircraft and more advanced air photography equipment, the US military began flights over the central coast in late 1943, photographing key Japanese industrial and military sites for bombing runs. This photo reconaissance effort was but one extension of the war effort led by US General Claire Chennault into Southeast Asia. The founder of the First American Volunteer Group or Flying Tigers in Kunming, China, Chennault presided over an expanded military effort in mid-1942 with the creation of the US Army Air Force Twenty-Third Fighter Group. By 1943 it grew into the Fourteenth Air Force. From then until the end of the Pacific War, the Fourteenth Air Force gathered intelligence about Japanese infrastructure and carried out bombing missions.

This US-led photographic effort, turned to destructive ends, finally brought the central coast into the Americans' global mosaic of air photos over strategic areas. By mid-1944 American planes dominated Indochina's airspace while advancing radio and wireless communications to Allied groups on the ground. Air travel and wireless communications transformed the mountain interior into a new battlefield. Intelligence operatives in Kunming combined the photographic intelligence with intercepted Japanese navy and diplomatic wireless messages to expand strategic attacks and develop a more detailed sense of conditions on the ground.[68] This photographic effort fit within a more global reconaissance effort that paralleled the American military's advances through Europe and the Pacific. On photography missions, single pilots flew Lockheed P-38 small bombers outfitted with a large-format camera behind the cockpit. The planes had a range of approximately 1,400 miles; missions to Huế required a 1,300-mile

FIGURE 2.4. Military air photo of Phú Bài airfield and Japanese military camps, October 11, 1943. This image was digitally reproduced by rephotographing the original negative film over a light table, then digitally inverteing the new photograph to produce a positive print. Source: Frame 54, Mission B7735/ON#026656, Record Group 373, Records of the Defense Intelligence Agency, US National Archives and Records Administration, College Park. Digital reproduction by author.

round-trip, stretching the pilots and planes to their limits. Pressurized cabins permitted the pilots to fly high at an altitude of 31,000 feet, well beyond the range of older fighter planes or anti-aircraft guns. The large-format camera (Fairchild K-18) onboard produced high-resolution prints at a relative map scale of 1:16,000 on a large-format, 9-inch by 18-inch negative.[69] Figure 2.4, an image of the Phú Bài airfield and Japanese camps built near the former leprosarium, represents one of the first produced by the United States over Huế on October 11, 1943. The dark area on the right is overexposed, but it neatly details the inner shoreline running along the estuarine rice fields in the lower domains of the villages. Rows of rectangular plots along the coast detail the hedges surrounding village homes. The triangular configuration of lines in the lower center define the airfield, and the parallel highway and railway run through the middle of the image. Compared to colonial photo surveys, these runs covered large areas in just a few frames. The entire series of photos from this mission followed a twenty-kilometer stretch of highway and railroad ending in Huế.

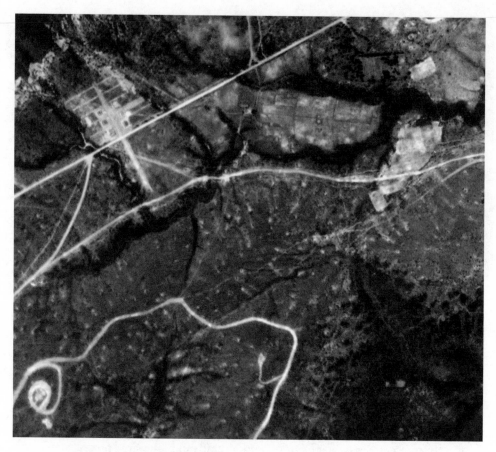

FIGURE 2.5 Excerpt from Frame 54, October 11, 1943, Mission B7735/ON#026656, Record Group 373, Records of the Defense Intelligence Agency, US National Archives and Records Administration, College Park.

While these photos' primary function was to provide the US military with intelligence about Japanese military assets, on closer inspection they indicate stark contrasts between the Japanese military's new roads and buildings and the surrounding poverty of the hills. Figure 2.5, an excerpt of the above frame of the camp in the Vùng Phèn hills, shows white roads connecting bunkers and other buildings across bare hills. A pattern of white dots and streaks in the hills depicts individual family tombs. Every year families from Phù Bài and other villages visited these graves to clean them of weeds, leaving a ring of bare ground that washed down the slope with heavy annual rains. Black

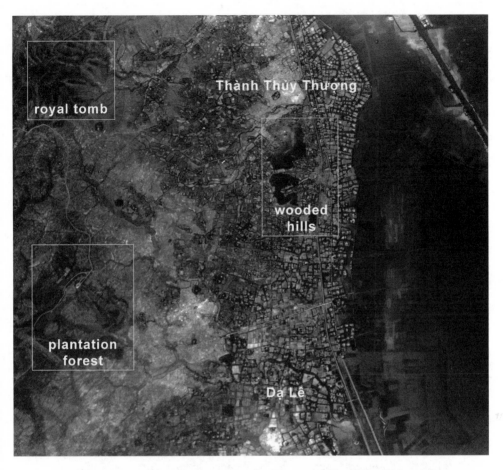

FIGURE 2.6. Excerpt from Frame 59, October 11, 1943, Mission B7735/ON#026656, Record Group 373, Records of the Defense Intelligence Agency, US National Archives and Records Administration, College Park.

blotches indicate the outlines of shrubs and trees; for the most part they hug tight to the streams.

Aside from these photographs, little written record exists either in books or archives to provide more detail about this period of military occupation. Another excerpt from a different shot in the 1943 run (figure 2.6) shows a more promising feature: young forests, in the hills above Dạ Lê and Thanh Thủy Thượng Villages. Here the same pattern of white-marked tombs covers the hills above the villages; however, three patches of woods suggest that village authorities, the royal family, and the colonial forestry department may have achieved some success in regreening. In the area of Emperor Khải Định's tomb, pines cover the hilltops. On three hillocks inside the village of Thanh Thủy Thượng near an old Buddhist monastery, the canopy of an old village wood covers hills that had been on the auction block in the 1900 land concession (see chapter 1). Villagers planted this land as a wood and expanded homesteads around it. Finally, a plantation forest, probably eucalyptus, fills neat geometric outlines of an area along a road connecting the Japanese base area to Huế.

GROUND WAR, GROUND NETWORKS

The lack of American knowledge about conditions on the ground in Vietnam helps to explain why the United States forged closer ties with Hồ Chí Minh and his Việt Minh organization in 1945. In the first years of the American war effort in China, a primarily French network of informants sympathetic to the resistance and the Allies passed intelligence into China. By 1944, however, that network was very much diminished, and it disappeared entirely after the Japanese-led coup overthrowing the French colonial government, police, and military in Indochina in March. Military historian Ronald Spector traces the complex, multilayered communications from January to June 1945 that characterized a developing relationship between the United States, the man from Nghệ An, and the organization he led, the Việt Minh. Contrary to many popular accepted views, the American officials in Kunming and their superiors in Washington had not abandoned support for the French in Indochina; their problem for gathering intelligence on Japanese forces and movements was of a high enough priority that they were willing to overlook Hồ Chí Minh's communist affiliations to achieve short-term strategic objectives of gathering intelligence and retrieving downed pilots.[70]

While American support for the Việt Minh in mid-1945 is remarkable given the later circumstances of the Cold War, the support given to Hồ Chí Minh in 1943 by the Chinese Nationalist commander in the region north of Vietnam played a more substantial role in the development of the Việt Minh from 1945 to 1947. General Zhang Fakui helped free Hồ Chí Minh from imprisonment at his headquarters in Liuzhou (Guangxi Province) in 1943; in September, seeking an effective leader among Vietnamese anti-Japanese organizations, he designated Hồ his liaison for the Chinese Nationalist–supported league for Vietnamese independence, the Đồng Minh Hội.[71] Hồ and his Việt Minh comrades quickly made use of funds and weapons supplied by Zhang to turn the Đồng Minh into an effective guerilla organization and intelligence network with strong support from underground bases in northern Vietnam. Zhang's move permitted the Việt Minh to build an armed resistance and infrastructure that was both anti-Japanese and anti-French. After the Japanese coup in 1945, the US Office of Strategic Services (OSS) had attempted ground operations relying on French officers. The first OSS operation commenced in June, but the group found Vietnamese populations hostile and abandoned the operation. By July OSS agents opted to work with the Việt Minh, finding them to be most effective in intelligence gathering.[72]

The American atomic bombs dropped at Hiroshima and Nagasaki on August 6 and 8, 1945, brought a quicker-than-expected Japanese surrender and caused the Việt Minh to rush not only to Hà Nội but to Japanese military areas and key infrastructure sites like radio stations. In Indochina the rapid and generally nonviolent process by which Việt Minh groups took control over local and national government reflects the depth of the political underground across the country. Historian David Marr draws on OSS records, interviews, and Vietnamese memoirs to provide a province-by-province summary of the Việt Minh's accession, especially in the central Vietnamese provinces. With some exceptions, Việt Minh interactions with foreigners and members of the Japanese-backed government of Emperor Bảo Đại were peaceful. Marr recounts the journey of one member of Bảo Đại's government traveling up the coast to Hà Nội. After being detained at a checkpoint in Vinh, he secured permission from the local Việt Minh official to travel on, remarking that his "captors returned every bit of his baggage, money, and documents."[73]

Local memoirs from Huế and Hương Thủy District describe a similarly well-organized, decisive move to seize control over government, with calculated operations to control key bunkers, granaries, and especially radio sites. On August 15, the same day that the Japanese emperor gave a radio-broadcast speech indicating his intention to surrender, party-led resistance committees met across Vietnam to determine immediate liberation strategies. The committee of the central region, Annam, met in Huế, outlining policies to be carried out by district- and commune-level committees.[74] Four days later, at a colonial blockhouse situated on one of the wooded hills overlooking Thanh Thủy Thượng, village resident Lê Minh became chairman of the District Liberation Committee. From the safety of a concrete observation post built into the hill, Liberation Committee members organized the transfer of authority village-by-village along the main highway. From August 20 to 22, the committees gained control over government, police, and military from Huế south on the highway to the "founding villages" of An Cựu, Thanh Thủy Thượng, Dạ Lê, Thần Phù, and Phù Bài.[75] The rapid transfer of power depended largely on voluntary and often secret commitments of support from Vietnamese administrators and military officers employed in the Japanese-backed government. In Hương Thủy the prerevolution district prefect (*tri huyện*), Võ Thọ, voluntarily threw his support behind the Việt Minh and ordered guards and local officials to do the same. The Vietnamese military commander in charge of a highway post at Thanh Thủy Thượng had secretly promised, before the August Revolution, to transfer all weapons and stand down. He did so, enabling the committee to take possession of military bases and training camps.[76]

In this burst of activity to August 23, the liberation committees and their armed groups moved down the road to the province's strategic prize: the camps and granaries at Vùng Phèn. Besides small weapons and ammunition, the bunkers contained large stores of rice. The Japanese military had hoarded it since late 1944, despite a severe famine that gripped the country and caused over a million deaths. After the Japanese emperor announced his intent to surrender on August 15, Japanese troops at Phú Bài handed their weapons to the Việt Minh and stood aside as they removed the rice.[77]

NATIONAL AIRWAVES

When Hồ Chí Minh delivered his independence speech on September 2, 1945, in Hà Nội to a crowd of several hundred thousand, he was the the first Vietnamese leader to give a live nationwide radio broadcast. The Việt Minh's ascension to power that August was due to victories not only on the ground but also in the air. Hồ Chí Minh was insistent on continuing this aerial presence. He issued an order to establish a national radio station just after arriving in Hà Nội. A Việt Minh communications team, likely trained by OSS radio operators, gathered local radio technicians and the parts to build a transmitter. They took an old Morse code transmitter from the colonial radiotelegraph center at the Bạch Mai airfield, and they converted it to transmit an AM radio signal, locating it at a building near the square where Hồ would give his independence speech. They flipped the transmitter's switch and his

Proclamation of Independence of the Democratic Republic of Vietnam (DRV) went out live on the airwaves.[78]

This historic Vietnamese moment *on* the air signified not only a modern political entrance into the post–World War II world but also the beginning of a military organization that relied on radio as an aerial platform.[79] The radio rebroadcasts on Allied and Japanese stations of the Japanese emperor's declaration of surrender on August 15 spurred local Việt Minh committees into action; OSS agents accompanying Hồ Chí Minh on the journey to Hà Nội used radios to relay news and information to the American military headquarters in Kunming, keeping the Việt Minh informed of the series of events unfolding daily including the atomic bombings at Hiroshima and Nagasaki. The Việt Minh lacked airplanes, but at the independence speech, many Vietnamese in the crowd took the flyover of a squadron of American P-38 bombers as a sign of Allied air support.[80]

While the major events of the August Revolution depict a groundswell of Vietnamese support for independence, they also suggest the fragility of nationalism and diplomacy in a wider world now defined by several air powers, notably the United States and the USSR, that leveraged significant control over much of the planet's airspace. Americans ended the Pacific War by detonating two atomic weapons in the air above Japanese cities; a new ship, the aircraft carrier, helped turn the naval contest in the Pacific to the Americans' favor. The Việt Minh as well as the prerevolution government headed by Emperor Bảo Đại in Huế used radio for communications and information about the war, but their presence in the air was much more tenuous.

• • •

Sixty years of colonial rule in Annam introduced new technologies, ideas, and species that catalyzed new ways of transforming the backcountry and Vietnamese society. But with the global depression and a Japanese military occupation, the "terraformers" had made little progress. In 1944–45 Allied bombing missions destroyed bridges on the highway and railroad, cutting off rice shipments from the south. Japanese troops hoarded rice in preparation for Allied amphibious landings, and many people on the central coast starved. Famine in 1944–45 killed over 1 million people. Detreuil du Rhins's vision of cash crops and Kháng's vision of garden cities had failed to take hold.

Guibier's eucalyptus and filao nurseries propagated new trees, but they had yet to deliver any economic bounty.

Despite the lack of real change on the ground, the arrival of aircraft and radio in the 1930s played a powerful role in shaping futurist ideas and nationalist imaginations. New bird's-eye images of the palace and coastal villages circulated in newspapers and textbooks. A lucky few managed to travel on airplanes, and many more watched them take off and land. Wireless brought world events into the local papers within a day of their occurrence, and radio in the early 1940s connected small audiences with distant events. Emerging nationalists such as Hồ Chí Minh and the provincial party leader Nguyễn Chí Thanh reached followers via underground pamphlets and newspapers. Then, on September 2, 1945, Uncle Hồ spoke to his countrymen in a live, nationwide broadcast. This new aerial perspective offered hope to nationalists while it permitted the few French who had survived in Huế after 1945 to hold on to dreams of imperial networks.

THREE

RESISTANCE

IN JULY 1946 THE CHAIRMAN OF THE PROVINCE'S UNDERGROUND COM-
munist organization, Nguyễn Chí Thanh, said the following as he left the
province to lead a newly formed Việt Minh tactical area covering six provinces in north central Vietnam: "Stick with the people, for we only have the
organization of the people to fight the enemy. Jungles, war zones are necessary, but the deciding factor will be people's organizations that can fight the
enemy in their own villages."[1] Through a deal negotiated by Hồ Chí Minh in
France, French soldiers replaced Chinese Nationalist troops in Huế on March
6. From their arival, they worked with anticommunist Vietnamese to hunt
down people like Thanh who narrowly escaped. In the four months that followed, he established a tactical zone (khu chiến thuật) in the hills for comrades and their families who had escaped the counterrevolutionary sweeps
in Huế. As he prepared to walk west into the mountains, he spoke with his
comrades, reiterating the vital need to maintain personal underground networks inside the cities, bases, and villages. This was a pivotal moment for the
Vietnamese revolution. A radical political organization led by students and
political elites in Annam's schools, coastal villages, and imperial towns had
hastily formed military and political organizations. Anticipating a French
military invasion by sea, they prepared defenses around Huế but set their
sights on the hills. Few of Thanh's comrades had likely ever ventured past the
hills fringing their ancestral villages, and only a handful spoke Katu, Bru,
Lao, or other languages of the people in highland communities along the
trails.[2] Thanh accepted the nomination as chairman of Tactical Interzone IV

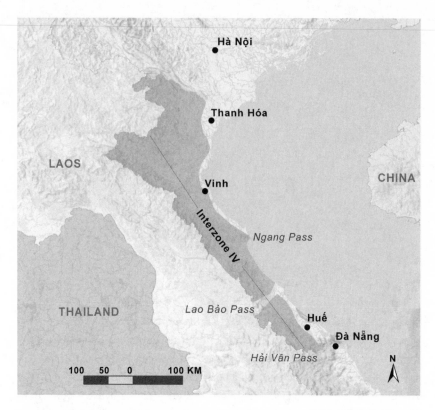

FIGURE 3.1. Interzone IV. Source: Approximate boundaries of Việt Minh–held areas by 1952 derived from Security Classified General Records, 1950–61, MAAG-Vietnam Adjutant General Division, Record Group 472, US National Archives and Records Administration, College Park. Map by author.

(*Liên khu chiến thuật IV*), an area that included a formidable terrain populated by several dozen ethnolinguistic groups from Hải Vân Pass south of Huế past Ngang Pass and north to Thanh Hóa.[3]

While this image of *du thượng* (going to the mountains) has lent itself to many romantic and patriotic portrayals in Vietnamese stories, songs, and films, Thanh's primary aim in this speech was not to glorify those who were volunteering but to remind them that their struggle depended on family ties and clandestine networks on the coast. Many loved ones would stay behind in ancestral villages, facing counterrevolutionary groups sure to label them as sympathizers. The political landscape in Huế was chaotic too. There was no longer an imperial government to provide cover for nationalists. Emperor

Bảo Đại abdicated and joined the Việt Minh in 1945; when the first French troops moved into Huế in March 1946, he left Hà Nội for China and took up residence in Hong Kong.[4] New coalitions of anticommunist nationalists, some affiliated with the former Japanese-backed government and others with the French, worked to root out communist sympathizers.

In terms of militarization, invading French troops violently reoccupied the airfields, cities, and ports while they posted allied Vietnamese soldiers in the hills. Việt Minh military and political units established tactical zones and networks in the mountains, and they fought French forces in the hills and almost to the edges of Highway 1 (see figure 3.1). As the war evolved from an anticolonial struggle in 1947 to a global cold war in the early 1950s, these ancient battlefields along the Inner Road became part of a more global front.

This chapter follows that evolving struggle but with more of a focus on how it played out in the landscapes around Huế than on the larger political history of the war. The unique histories and ecologies of these places shaped Việt Minh and French experiences as wartime victories and defeats produced new heroic and tragic places.

DU THƯỢNG

While the Việt Minh "zone" in Huế and much of Vietnam became associated with hideouts in the mountains, its military origins after 1945 began on the Inner Road. North of the sixteenth parallel, the Chinese Nationalist general in charge of the postwar occupation, General Lu Han, refused to rearm the French. Instead, he permitted Hồ Chí Minh and his Việt Minh government to build a "self-defense" force.[5] Especially in Hà Nội and Huế, Việt Minh military leaders set to work training military officers, building regimental commands, and training infantry soldiers. This twist in the postwar occupation was not without pitfalls, however; communist leaders viewed the plan as an American "imperialist plot" lurking behind the banner of the Allies to arm noncommunist groups. Vietnamese Nationalist Party militias affiliated with the Chinese Nationalist army arrived in Huế with five thousand Chinese soldiers in September 1945. They competed with communists while taking part in the military training. Vietnamese Nationalist Party (Việt Nam Quốc Dân Đảng) partisans used their connections to the Chinese to create shared power arrangements with communist Việt Minh leaders in many villages.[6]

Amid these global arrangements and internal struggles, Việt Minh authority in the narrow territory of central Vietnam was precarious. While Việt Minh leaders were still in control of the civil government following the nation's first popular election on January 6, 1946, they had to contend with many practical difficulties at all levels, especially issues of finance and military preparedness. Hồ Chí Minh urged the new government to fight "three enemies": famine, fire, and foreign invaders. The new government organized "gold weeks" to take contributions from citizens and rapidly build up the coffers. In Dạ Lê two women from poor families donated their wedding earrings and urged other women to contribute. In many rural families, a woman's gold jewelry amounted to her life savings.[7] The government also relied on trading companies and smuggling networks to bring in commerce by sea. In Huế a branch of the Việt Thắng Trading Company managed imports and exports for the Việt Minh primarily via the Chinese port at Beihai. Even before Chinese communists took over the port in 1949, Chinese Nationalist merchants participated in this trade, reselling supplies from the huge stockpiles of World War II weapons. Việt Minh groups used secret radio communications with the seaborne junks to arrange landings and transshipment to the hills.[8]

The power-sharing arrangements between the communist-led Việt Minh and the Vietnamese Nationalist Party frayed after just eight months when a provisional agreement and cease-fire signed by France and Vietnam on March 6, 1946, resulted in the removal of the Chinese and the arrival (in secret) of a small but heavily armed French military detachment in the former French quarter in Huế. French forces under General Philippe Leclerc had violently retaken port cities south of Đà Nẵng and moved up the Mekong River into southern Laos.

The Việt Minh used the opportunity, however, to purge Vietnamese nationalists and began a crash program to build their army.[9] Over eight hundred French soldiers had driven through the Lao Bảo pass and into Huế to occupy the southern bank of the Perfume River and heavily armed posts inside it such as the Morin Hotel, Quốc Học high school, and the former RSA offices. Once settled in the European quarter, they faced across the river the imposing walls of the nineteenth-century citadel with the Việt Minh's red flag with gold star flying overhead.[10] Several hundred more troops, mostly soldiers recruited from French Africa, moved into the airbase and training grounds at Phú Bài. A much larger force gathered offshore and in base compounds near Đà Nẵng.[11]

Việt Minh leaders on the central coast began preparations for a French offensive. They evacuated their newly formed Trần Cao Vân Regiment from Phú Bài into the hills. Only the regiment's Eighteenth Battalion stayed to patrol the perimeter of the base in the hills of Vùng Phèn.[12] French soldiers, mostly European officers commanding colonial African recruits, spent the summer amassing supplies at the airfield and constructing a ring of block-houses with machine guns on the perimeter. They fired on anyone who ventured into the grassy perimeters; one memoir tells the story of a small child who wandered into the perimeter zone and was shredded to pieces by the guns.[13]

Contrary to French and other foreign representations of the Việt Minh as a jungle-based insurgency, the military forces that dug defensive works and prepared for a French invasion strove to maintain an organization deeply embedded in the ancestral villages of the Inner Road. Besides an under-ground network of runners and supporters, the Việt Minh relied on radio to connect its military units and also to broadcast to popular audiences. Radio linked up what historian Christopher Goscha calls an "archipelago space," a network of "forest villages" and provincial military commands as well as listeners. It broadcast from the cities before the French invasion, and after the invasion it broadcast from remote sites, even from stations in China, Laos, Thailand, and Burma.[14] Hồ Chí Minh readily understood the power of radio to project his party's claims to territory that had never—in colonial or pre-colonial times—been fully integrated.[15] While radio broadcasts played edu-cational and patriotic programs, soldiers and partisans worked to educate themselves whether acquiring basic literacy or studying military texts. One newspaper in Huế, *Chiến Sĩ* (Fighter), circulated daily articles on military affairs ranging from practical defensive concerns to more philosophical top-ics such as Sun Tzu's *Art of War*.[16]

The keys to maintaining these logistical and political links between the highlands and the coast were a string of fortified hamlets in the foothills called tactical zones. Each tactical zone was located along one of the smaller east-west rivers running from the highlands to the sea, and most were situ-ated in transitional spaces where bare hills gave way to forests and ethnic-Việt communities gave way to highlander ones. The first bases in Thừa Thiên–Huế Province were at Khe Trái and Hòa Mỹ, villages just west of Huế. Both had the advantage of being located within protected valleys but close enough to reach Huế in a day. The flow of information, persons, and materials followed the rivers and ridge lines through this landscape. In winter 1947 the Việt Minh added two more tactical zones at Dương Hòa and then Nam Đông, hamlets located farther upstream and beyond the reach of French forces (figure 3.2).[17]

Fighting between Việt Minh and French forces began on December 19, 1946, in Hải Phòng, and a destructive French naval invasion at Huế commenced one month later, spurring thousands of young people to retreat from lowland defenses to the tactical zones. In the months leading up to the invasion, the Việt Minh urged its followers to dig tunnels, trenches, and barricades. In the city of Huế and in nearby villages, several thousand youths dug defensive positions with barricades, bomb shelters, and tunnels. Upon receiving word about the fighting at Hải Phòng, Việt Minh units blew all of the bridges to Huế along Highway 1. Việt Minh troops in Huế attacked the eight hundred outnumbered but well-armed French troops in the Morin Hotel and other government buildings in the French quarter, inflicting heavy casualties.[18]

Unlike the naval assault in 1883, this military landing met fierce resistance from the landing beaches to the streets of Huế. Launched just five days before the start of the Lunar New Year, this 1947 Tết offensive resulted in high numbers of civilian casualties and left sections of the town in ruins. French marines, most of them from French Africa, brought naval artillery and heavier weapons against the more lightly armed but dug-in Việt Minh. Việt Minh forces had governed Huế for a time after the August Revolution, and even after the return of French soldiers in 1946, they commanded a military regiment and enjoyed strong support in the villages. Their units engaged French forces invading by sea at two inlets, Tư Hiền and Thuận An (figure 3.2). French forces landed on the beachheads and took high casualties. One group, a few thousand troops with armored cars loaded on American-made military landing craft, unloaded at the banks of the lagoon at Truồi within a few hundred meters of Highway 1. The other group landed at Thuận An beach with armored vehicles to attack Huế from the north. In contrast to the French naval landing in 1883, French forces in 1947 met sustained resistance from the beaches to the city. The southern group required nineteen days to travel thirty kilometers along Highway 1 from Truồi before meeting the other group that reached Huế only two days earlier. From Huế and Phú Bài, French forces spent the next month reoccupying key military installations, finding them emptied with all supplies removed.[19]

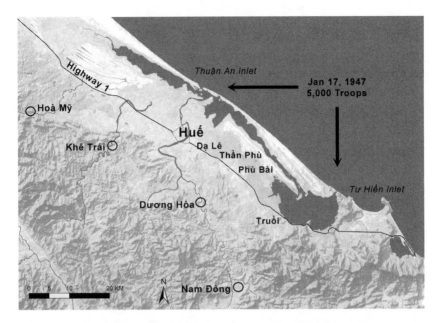

FIGURE 3.2. French invasion routes and tactical zones near Huế, 1947. Source: Shaded relief and landcover layers courtesy of ESRI Inc. Annotations and map production by author.

As the French troops secured positions along Highway 1, they destroyed a number of village communal houses such as at Dạ Lê and Phù Bài and set up command posts at some of the region's most historic sites. One the most symbolic was the Nam Giao Pavilion on the southern edge of Huế. Nam Giao included pine groves and a pavilion that hosted the annual rites the emperor performed to bring prosperity and good harvests to the kingdom. The profaning of the site with French troops and military equipment gave a clear visual sign of the French position vis-à-vis the recently abdicated head of state, Bảo Đại. On the edge of the French quarter in the deforested spaces of Nam Giao, the French military established its Nord Annam–Huế Sector command.[20]

After French forces broke the Việt Minh defense, Việt Minh units retreated to the tactical zones. Over the next several years, this move uphill (*du thượng*) facilitated profound territorial and personal transformations, especially for thousands of Vietnamese youths. The political and military leaders of the Việt Minh had regrouped with their families at Hòa Mỹ for more than a year, since March 1946. The Trần Cao Vân Regiment's three battalions retreated here and formed a company of commandos to operate guerrilla missions into

Huế.[21] After the French invasion, in summer 1947 more army units and larger communities of soldiers and their families continued the exodus, expanding tunnel networks into the mountains and digging bunkers and underground caches. The province committee aniticipated that French occupation forces would force youths in the lowlands to serve with the occupation military, so it built the tactical zones as spaces for removing young men from their mid-teens to late thirties from villages along Highway 1. They established routes of communication—trails and secret codes—to guide youth volunteers into the war zones, opening paths for escape and for guerrilla teams to return.[22]

While most histories focus on the *tactical* elements of these zones, a Hương Thủy District history of the resistance captures some glimpses of the tolls on families in occupied villages whose sons and daughters had "gone uphill." Resistance zones were difficult places to survive, even without enemy attacks. Mosquitoes carried malaria, and Việt Minh field hospitals were lucky to have quinine as a preventive medicine. Young women with limited training as nurses regularly risked search, detention, and torture for carrying medicine from towns such as Huế into rebel areas. One doctor left a prosperous practice in Huế to carry medical supplies to manage a field hospital at the Khe Trái base.[23] The tactical zones fostered deep emotional connections linking people from different lowland villages with each camp. A district history describes this yearning for relatives: "The tactical zone was a place of much longing, excitement for reunions and deep compassion, here was a basis for understanding the preciousness of life. . . . In the afternoon, the people of Phú Vàng and Hương Thủy Districts looked from their homes in the countryside to the tactical zones in the distant mountains, remembering those working there in service, transport, communication, logistics, remembering their first trips into the tactical zones."[24] As the resistance continued for seven years, these emotional ties and the traffic in and out of the region helped forge new trails and webs of local networks through which the Việt Minh national vision extended across more of the central coast's rugged terrain.

By 1948 this web of trails had not only greatly expanded in east-west, lowland-highland directions but had also added many north-south links paralleling the Inner Road in the foothills and highlands. A history of the trails in Bình Trị Thiên notes that by late 1948, the Việt Minh had established three main north-south corridors for nationwide travel. In those early years of the resistance, the trails connecting tactical zones such as Hòa Mỹ were the preferred routes for soldiers moving north to the main battlefronts. In those early years, tactical zones in the highlands were more limited, and paths running along the border with Laos were less used. Finally, a third, coastal network of paths passed through safe houses and hiding areas in lowland villages and cities, a sort of underground railroad that connected to parts of actual railroad in Việt Minh–controlled provinces south of Đà Nẵng.[25]

Going uphill for the Việt Minh also meant going off the map, at least in terms of topographic maps. That "uphill" areas were generally not mapped was partly a reflection of the rugged terrain that had challenged French surveyors on the ground and in the air. The lack of roads, bridges, and buildings in the highlands precluded surveyors from laying geodetic benchmarks that allowed accurate measurements of distance and elevation. The steep irregular slopes, many of them covered in canopies of trees, made the geometric correction (orthorectification) of air photos almost impossible. The lack of good maps of Việt Minh strategic zones and trails meant that French military intelligence teams had more difficulty communicating coordinates for artillery or aerial bombing.

For Việt Minh forces, communicating positions by place-name, ridge, and river helped keep their location more hidden in the grid-space of aerial maps. This *topological* mapping of highland terrain also reflected the fact that most of the thousands of youths who left for the highlands had likely never seen a topographic map, much less read one. The association of tactical zones to mountain-river intersections was an expression of a traditional Vietnamese way of organizing the landscape. Atlases (such as the 1832 atlas discussed in chapter 1) recorded names for mountain peaks and rivers to aid coastal navigation and travel (usually on or along water) into the interior. Gazetteers and province geographies likewise began with a section titled "Mountains and Rivers" (*núi sông*). This traditional juxtaposition of rivers and mountains reflected not only a practical need for helping someone orient themselves but also a long-standing tradition of geomancy or feng shui (*phong thủy*, wind and water). Feng shui is a traditional science used to help individuals orient homes, businesses, and fields in propitious locations with respect to winds, possible floods, and less tangible flows—good air, abundant money, or good health. A core principal is that invisible "dragon lines" run through the spines of mountains and rivers, tracing paths of energy flows (*chi*). Although only a few individuals were experts in geomancy, most people were at least familiar with this system of orienteering.[26]

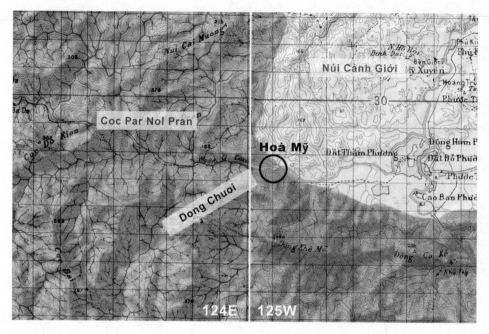

FIGURE 3.3. Excerpts of sheets 124E and 125W, Hòa Mỹ Tactical Zone. Source: US Army Map Service, "Indochine 1:100,000," Series L605, May 1954. Underlying shaded relief, georeferencing, and annotations added by author.

Figure 3.3, an excerpt from two 1952 French map sheets of the Hòa Mỹ area, shows the area's location at a nexus of topographic, environmental, and cultural borders. The finer isoclines in the open hills (white background) are matched with a finer orthography of place-names. Diacritics are included for Vietnamese place-names such as Núi Cảnh Giới (Boundary Mountain). West of Hòa Mỹ, as the elevation and slope increase, the level of detail decreases. Pen widths detailing streams and rivers are wider, less precise, and the names of higher, forested ridges shift to non-Vietnamese place-names such as Coc Par Nol Pran (possibly a Katuic name) and Động Chuối (Banana Ridge, but using the term "động" to denote a non-Việt community). Like the use of mountain peaks and rivers as an aid for surface navigation, use of these non-Việt place-names signed the movement into non-Việt cultural spaces. A recent province history of the tactical zones continues this more familiar style of description, noting that Hòa Mỹ was "situated between the Ô Lâu–Rào Quao Rivers and the forested ridge and foothills of Động Chuối."[27]

FIGURE 3.4. Oblique view of Hòa Mỹ area (*valley center*) and the forested foothills and valley beneath Động Chuối (*left*), 2017. Source: Google Earth with author annotations.

In figure 3.4, a reconstructed oblique view of the Hòa Mỹ base area and the mountains behind it gives a more embodied sense of the space as this terrestrial gateway into Interzone IV. Việt Minh troops and area populations spent months carving tunnels, trenches, and protective barricades along the steep slopes of Động Chuối. This surface view also suggests how Việt Minh control of the highlands presented insurmountable challenges to French forces. The first French military offensive against the Hòa Mỹ base started on May 7, 1948, when three airplanes commenced a bombing attack followed by paratroopers landing along the dirt roads and bare hills. Infantry units, mostly composed of African soldiers, marched in by road from Highway 1. The offensive included a battalion of African soldiers, two battalions of Franco-Vietnamese troops, two artillery battalions, and thirteen armored personnel carriers. It lasted for sixteen days, but the French forces could not push past Hòa Mỹ into the mountains. Việt Minh units remained entrenched in rock bunkers carved into the higher slopes, sending artillery shells down into the valley.[28]

As the French airborne attacks intensified, the Việt Minh moved further into the highlands, forging new networks and, more significantly, integrating

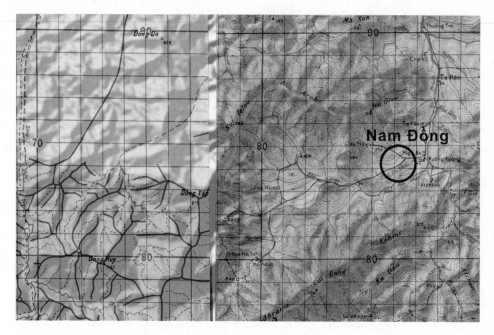

FIGURE 3.5. Nam Đông war zone. Source: US Army Map Service, "Indochine 1:100,000," Series L605, May 1954. Underlying shaded relief courtesy of ESRI Inc. Digitization, georeferencing, and annotations by author.

non-Việt highlanders into their networked nation. Nam Đông tactical zone (figure 3.5), located at the headwaters of the Perfume River (Sông Tả Trạch), was fifty kilometers south of Huế. In spatial and cartographic terms, it lay on the edge of mapped territory; in ethnic terms, it was a different world before 1947. In the old map of Dutreuil du Rhins, this was the blank space on the map, "inhabited by savages." Limited colonial ethnographic essays on the local Katu (Cơ Tu) people described them as headhunters who engaged in "blood raids" against outsiders.[29]

Việt Minh organizing in this valley began after the French amphibious invasion of Truồi in February 1947. Several thousand Việt Minh partisans in coastal Phú Lộc District retreated here from the slopes of Truồi Mountain as French forces broke their defenses. A party history of this mountainous backcountry notes that Việt Minh bases provided vital east-west connections to north-south traffic on the Lao border. Việt Minh development projects here began with expanding rice fields and creating camps at Nam Đông. The official history reports that they aimed to educate their indigenous comrades (in

Vietnamese) who were "100% illiterate." Besides opening literacy classes for the Katu people, the Interzone IV government promptly abolished all of the debts highlanders might have accrued before 1947, thus "liberating" them to support the Việt Minh effort. French forces mounted a large attack on Nam Đông in April 1949, but Việt Minh troops with Katu partisans repelled them. They held the region uncontested for the rest of the conflict.[30]

LAYERED SOVEREIGNTY ON THE INNER ROAD

While Việt Minh partisans in these deeper mountainous zones encountered little military opposition to inland expansion, the situation in lowland villages such as Phù Bài and Dạ Lê was troubled by multiple competing authorities. From August 1945 Việt Minh national guard (*tự vệ*) units helped foster development of the first postcolonial government, confirmed in a popular election in January 1946. Nationalist Party groups played a role in this early state-building process, too, protected by allies in the Nationalist Chinese military occupation. In February 1947 when French expeditionary forces launched the military invasion to reoccupy Huế, they violently attacked Việt Minh military defenses and prominent cultural sites under Việt Minh control. At Phù Bài on February 5, French forces razed the main communal house, ostensibly to prevent Việt Minh troops from sheltering there. Two days later they occupied the communal house and roadside pagodas at Dạ Lê and Thanh Thủy Thượng.[31]

From this violent start to France's military occupation, the French position vis-à-vis allied Vietnamese groups was fraught with problems too. Expeditionary troops aided by allied Vietnamese tracked down Việt Minh political and military leaders who had not escaped to the war zones. Through 1947 and 1948, Franco-Vietnamese forces detained, tortured, and executed these prisoners. The French military command and a hastily assembled Central Vietnam Governing Committee aimed to "pacify" village populations and cut them off from the Việt Minh mountain bases.[32] The pacification strategy, ostensibly led by noncommunist Vietnamese groups, was at all levels undermined by French reluctance to cede sovereign control. Conflicts over the extent of Vietnamese versus French control of internal affairs arose at every level from village disputes to international diplomacy. France sent a new high commissioner of Indochina, Émile Bollaert, to negotiate with Hồ Chí Minh in March 1947. American diplomatic cables from the period remarked extensively on the French "quandary" in relying on former Emperor Bảo Đại as a Vietnamese head of state. The former emperor retained an official title in the Việt Minh government and resided in Hong Kong with an entourage of supporters. Many noncommunist nationalists and Huế-area Catholics, especially South Vietnam's future president Ngô Đình Diệm, expressed strong opposition to the return of the monarch.[33]

Bollaert tabled the Bảo Đại issue and named a prominent Huế Catholic and monarchist, Trần Văn Lý, as head of the Central Vietnam Governing Committee. Lý had been trained as a civil servant in the old colonial system, and he maintained muted nationalist aspirations. Unlike vehemently anti-French Catholics such as Diệm, Lý held a modicum of respect in central Vietnamese political circles and was willing to work under French commanders.[34] As an advisory governor of Central Vietnam (Trung Việt) with limited powers, Lý carried out one of Bollaert's key directives, establishing a national guard with the task of shoring up security in the upper villages to prevent Việt Minh commandos from ambushing convoys on the highway. He directed a hastily assembled network of village and district chiefs in 462 "controlled" villages to recruit youths for this paramilitary force, the Việt Binh Đoàn (VBD). This would-be army built eighty-four forts and dozens of watchtowers along Highway 1. The expeditionary forces called especially European units, camped in heavily fortified bases at Nam Giao Pavilion, at the Morin Hotel in the French quarter, and at airfields such as the one at Phú Bài. They assigned expeditionary troops, French Africans and several battalions of former Nazi soldiers, to camps along the highway; then they ordered the lightly armed, largely untested Việt Binh Đoàn to guard the hilly frontier with the interzone.[35]

This geographical split in military areas, VBD troops in the hills and French forces along Highway 1, produced deep rifts between Vietnamese and foreign troops. French forces were frequently caught in Việt Minh roadside ambushes, where commandos set explosive devices or opened fire on passing trucks. Upon being hit, the French troops retaliated against local villagers, whom they called *nhà quê* (peasants). Việt Minh commandos retreated, in many cases exposing relatives of VBD troops to French reprisal. A common story in such lowland villages as Dạ Lê described a husband or son returning from guard duty at a watch post on the hill to find a member of his family wounded or dead from the fighting. One governing committee report in 1949 concluded: "If the French troops continue their policy of pacification by terror, there will come a day of no return for repairing the Franco-Vietnamese problem. The withdrawal of French troops to their bases seems to be the only possible remedy."[36]

Such reports highlighted a critical weakness in the French approach and counterinsurgency more generally. At the heart of the governing committee's complaint was the issue of *sovereignty* and French *extraterritoriality*, especially in the villages and on the streets of Huế. As in the colonial days, French agents and troops could not be prosecuted by local courts; they operated outside Vietnamese law. The long-feared secret police from the colonial era, the Sûreté Federale (internal security forces), apprehended and interrogated Vietnamese suspects irregardless of their affiliation with the allied government and without the Vietnamese authority's knowledge.[37]

Even after the victory of Mao's Chinese Communist forces in China in October 1949 and the French decision to bring back Emperor Bảo Đại as a head of state, officials in the post-1950 Associated State of Vietnam (ASV) highlighted the vicious bind that they and "ralliers" (people who left the Việt Minh) faced. They had to protect their community from Việt Minh reprisal as well as French military and secret police attacks. The ASV had no legal basis to protect individuals, especially ralliers, from French military attacks or detentions.[38] Even as he returned to Vietnam, Bảo Đại refused to denounce the Việt Minh given the "treason-provoking" behavior of the French. On his return to Vietnam in June 1949, he laid a palm branch at a tomb dedicated to Vietnamese killed by the 1946 French bombardments in Hải Phòng. Members of his entourage openly talked about the Việt Minh guerillas who fought the French there as "our heroes."[39] Even high-level French military leaders such as Army Chief Georges Revers understood this double bind. He advocated giving full independence to Bảo Đại and turning the war over to the Vietnamese national army; however, political opponents leaked his report with these recommendations, and Revers was sacked.[40]

Even on the ground, French military forces were internally divided about the war, often along ethnic and national-origin lines. A handful of European officers commanded mostly African units coming from Senegal, Tunisia, Algeria, and Morocco, all countries undergoing their own independence crises. The overwhelming burden of advancing French military aims in central Vietnam was borne by Africans. On the central coast in the Nord Annam Secteur, only the Second Foreign Legion Regiment, a group that included

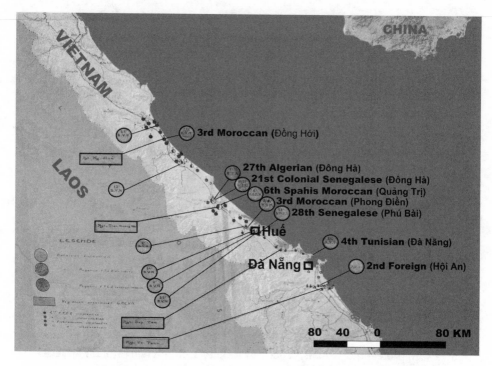

FIGURE 3.6. Franco-Vietnamese military units on the central coast, 1951. Source: Box 3448, Series 10H, Service Historique de la Défense, French Air Force Photo Archives, Fort de l'Est, Paris. Underlying terrain courtesy of ESRI Inc. Georeferencing and annotations by author.

former Nazi soldiers, was made up of mostly Europeans; the unit was stationed south of Đà Nẵng at the southern limit of French control, Hội An. Close to Huế an assortment of European tank squadrons, artillery batteries, communications companies, and combat engineers operated in the vicinity of Nam Giao.[41] Throughout most of the French military occupation on the central coast, the area under Franco-Vietnamese control hugged Highway 1, creating an intensely volatile zone where VBD forces faced attacks from the Việt Minh zones and retaliation from French units behind them (figure 3.6). North and south of this string of highway, the Việt Minh–controlled most of the land from the mountains to the coast.

At a closer scale, the occupied zone did not cover all of the coastal areas, either. A sketch map of Việt Minh zones (plate 1) produced by the French in 1952 shows zones of dunes, swamps and coastal estuaries also under Việt

Minh control. Large coastal and estuary areas just a few kilometers north of Huế were described as "non-controlled," too. French forces were thus limited not only by the *friction* of climbing hills but also that posed by moving across brackish, shallow estuaries and dunes.[42] Isolated by the mountains and long stretches of coastline, the occupied zone was part of a struggling late colonial archipelago state. Supplies reached the French by ship from Đà Nẵng or by air, and the "controlled zone" extended just a few hundred yards from Highway 1 in many places.

For African troops, proximity to Việt Minh zones often carried deeper political challenges, as Việt Minh propaganda highlighted that many of their countrymen in Morocco, Senegal, and especially Algeria were also waging resistance struggles. Resistance supporters circulated missives in Arabic and French aimed to win the hearts and minds of African and Arab "brothers." One flyer obtained by French security services read:

FREEDOM IS MY LIFE—IT IS ALSO MY CHILD'S—O INDEPENDENCE!

ARAB: Know that a jihad has been declared against the France that oppresses us all. Whoever wants to fight for independence knows that he will fight under the Independence banner.

Listen! In the CONBAN [Cao Bằng] region of Vietnam, [Việt Minh] veterans have won a great success in a very short time. From 01/11/49 to 10/12/49 they made 9 operations. Losses on the French side included: 112 killed, 17 wounded, 63 prisoners. The recovered materials included: 1 mortar, 9 machine guns, 7 submachine guns, 181 British and American rifles, a portable radio, etc.

I FIGHT FOR MY COUNTRY AND INDEPENDENCE WHILE YOURS IS BEING SOLD OUT—YOUR SOUL WILL BE LOST[43]

While all sides in the conflict produced propaganda, flyers such as this struck at the heart of French African troops' "motivation" to fight in Indochina. Like the VBD troops, they were caught in the middle of competing military logics.

The actions of African troops in the hills, especially a group of commandos from Morocco, often triggered sectarian conflicts in a region where Vietnamese Catholics were a powerful minority. In an effort to stem the flow of rice, medicine, and information into the mountains, French commanders outsourced this local counterinsurgency campaign to a distinguished unit of Moroccan light infantry unit, the Ninth Tabor. The "goums" had attracted international attention in World War II for breaking the Nazis' southern defenses in the Italian mountains. The word *tabor* came from Turkish for *battalion*, and the word *goum* was a Maghrebi Arabic word meaning *people*.[44] The *goumiers* were troops recruited from different tribes and castes but mostly from Berber-speaking peoples of the Atlas Mountains.[45] The Ninth Tabor set up a headquarters at the Nam Giao Pavilion in early 1952 with the mission to destroy underground Việt Minh networks in the hills. Working outward from Nam Giao, they established fortified posts in villages and along roads by cutting down bamboo hedges, cutting and burning large brush and felling large trees. They established sniper positions on the denuded hills, and they used common tactics of intimidation at checkpoints to interrupt day-to-day movements of people on roads and footpaths.

These actions caused obvious friction with villagers and the VBD, but they also triggered widespread protests as the *goums* targeted religious clergy, detaining them and raiding their churches and pagodas. The French sector commander in Huế justified this tactic with the *goums* as a last-ditch campaign called the Battle of Rice to more strictly regulate movement of rice postharvest. The *goums* were to be the model for training Vietnamese paramilitary groups.[46] The campaign escalated arrests as troops removed stores of rice from religious centers and individual households. Under new draconian rules, villagers on the central coast were permitted to store no more than ten kilograms of rice on their property. All other rice was required to be shipped to a government-controlled silo. Transporting rice in quantities greater than a few kilograms required signed papers from zone military authorities.[47]

If previous episodes of violence had not turned people in the lowlands against the French, the Battle of Rice triggered widespread protests and defections. Most important for the ASV, many prominent Buddhist and Catholic leaders threatened to turn on the French after a series of conflicts, especially with *goum* units near the base at Nam Giao. On an adjacent hill was one of the region's largest Catholic seminaries, Thiên An. Priests there traveled to rural congregations throughout the region, and they frequently traveled across the borders into Việt Minh–controlled areas to conduct services and perform rites, especially last rites. The *goums* not only harassed the priests crossing the frontier but also raided the seminary, removing rice and other foodstuffs donated to feed the poor.

The father superior of the seminary wrote to the ASV government, to Bảo Đại, and to the French sector commander posted at Nam Giao highlighting the dire situation. Catholic and Buddhist congregations were furious that the all-Muslim *goums* were not only taking rice in the seminary and several large Buddhist pagodas but looting the facilities and desecrating them. Both the seminary and the pagodas had traditionally stored rice on their properties to feed large numbers of people on holy days and to provide free food to the poor. The father superior, a man closely allied with such anti-French Catholics as Ngô Đình Diệm, echoed the sentiments of VBD commanders who suggested that this repression of local populations sounded a death knell for the ASV.[48]

Besides these deep disruptions in the cultural lives of people in the central coast, increased raids and use of American-supplied weapons by 1952 had an equally devastating effect on the natural and cultural landscapes of the central coast. Nowhere was this impact more visible to Vietnamese and French as at Nam Giao Pavilion (figure 3.7) The Nord Annam–Huế Sector headquarters was located on the approach to the imperial site next to the Ninth Tabor base. The rectangular plot of the Nam Giao Pavilion was completely denuded of the pines that shaded it. French forces used the level platform for surveillance of the surrounding hills, and they dug bunkers for munitions underneath the concrete platform. While these actions might not have disturbed Huế residents who had grown up with decimated pine groves in the hills, the presence of French and Moroccan camps on top of the surrounding cemetery surely caused some alarm. This cemetery, close to the city and imperial sites, was a burial ground for many elite families.[49]

In the hills south of Huế, the four main military posts followed a logic of terrain—open sites with good views—and a logic of past militarization. Besides the bases at Nam Giao, French forces occupied two of the military areas, Dạ Lê Thượng and Vùng Phèn, left by the Japanese. The French commander at the airfield ordered his Senegalese troops to set up camp across the highway at the base of a mountain with roads connecting to the airport and Dạ Lê Thượng (figure 3.8). The former leprosarium turned POW camp and Việt Minh training area was reborn in 1952 as Camp Oasis. VBD units guarded two key villages, Bang Lang and Dạ Lê Thượng.[50]

At hilltop posts such as Dạ Lê Thượng, the military's clearing of trees and vegetation escalated after 1952 with the arrival of more American aid and mounting French concerns about Việt Minh attacks on Highway 1. French military engineers brought bulldozers and flamethrowers from Nam Giao to village posts for brush-clearing (*débroussement*) campaigns.[51] Concerns for

FIGURE 3.7. Aerial view of Nam Giao Pavilion with zoomed view of graves, 1953. The larger base area in the image was the Huế Sub-Sector Command Headquarters, and the smaller base was a camp for African soldiers, first the Twenty-Eighth Senegalese and then the Ninth Tabor. Source: File TV310, August 13, 1953, Service Historique de la Défense, French Air Force Photo Archives, Fort de l'Est, Paris.

security in this porous frontier meant that all trees, planted or wild, were destroyed. The fledgling tree plantations of 1943 were erased, and whitish blotches of bare clay indicated the locations of VBD posts (figure 3.9). The blackish veins in the image depict streams draining from the hills where low vegetation hugged the banks.

AMERICANS RETURN

New bulldozers in the hills and airplanes overhead signaled the arrival of American aid to Huế, too, a small extension of more profound shifts elsewhere

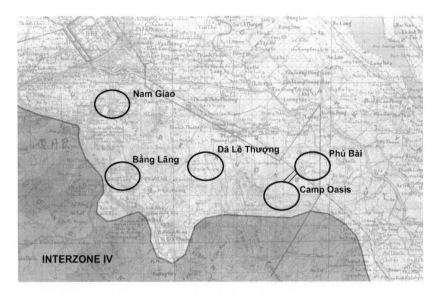

FIGURE 3.8. Detail from map "Military Sub-Sector." Source: File 3368, Series 10H, Service Historique de la Défense, French Air Force Photo Archives, Fort de l'Est, Paris. Shading, circles, and annotation by author.

FIGURE 3.9. Aerial view of Dạ Lê Thượng Post, May 1953. Source: File TV310, Service Historique de la Défense, French Air Force Photo Archives, Fort de l'Est, Paris. Georectification and annotations by author.

in the Indochina War. As in the past, events in China played a crucial role in triggering this American return to military events. Mao Zedong's victory in 1949 put Chinese communist troops at the northern border of Indochina, providing critical rear base support to the Việt Minh. Mao's army gained full control of Hainan Island, too, putting Chinese ships and airplanes within easy striking distance of French positions in Hải Phòng and Hà Nội. The newly established People's Republic of China extended diplomatic recognition to the Democratic Republic of Vietnam in January 1950, and the United States passed legislation soon after to aid France and recognize the Associated State of Vietnam.[52] At the same time that the US Congress authorized increased military intervention in Korea, it created a military assistance advisory group (MAAG) and a special technical and economic mission with offices in Sài Gòn.

This pivotal moment, documented extensively by diplomatic historians, marked a decisive material shift for the French military.[53] The first shipments arrived at Sài Gòn and Hải Phòng in early 1951 and included one hundred fighter planes, fifty bombers and air cargo transports, ground arms for thirty battalions, artillery, naval craft, and almost two thousand jeeps and six-by-six trucks.[54] China responded to the American move by dramatically increasing its military aid to the Việt Minh. By 1952 the PRC had sent 40,000 rifles, 4,000 submachine guns, 450 mortars, 120 recoilless guns, 45–50 anti-aircraft guns, 30–35 field guns, millions of rounds of ammunition, and tens of thousands of grenades.[55] These twin flows of military aid to the French and Việt Minh respectively accelerated in 1953 and 1954 before the Việt Minh's stunning victory over the French forces at Điện Biên Phủ.

With the increase in American aid came a rapidly enlarging group of advisers, diplomats, aid workers, journalists, and spies. Fredrik Logevall's history of the US entry into Vietnam follows two of the period's most prominent Anglophone writers, Englishman Graham Greene and French-raised, American-naturalized doctoral student Bernard Fall. They both wrote from experiences in Indochina from 1952 to 1954 in *The Quiet American* (1955) and *Street without Joy* (1961), respectively.[56] Greene's *The Quiet American* conveyed the notion that nonlethal aid was largely a front for clandestine political actions, and Fall's *Street without Joy* described the precarious position of the French, especially on the central coast.

While American aid piled up at the port in Đà Nẵng, much of it did not reach the Huế area until late in 1953. The primary focus for Americans at the time was a large-scale base construction effort at Đà Nẵng. Đà Nẵng before 1950 had been a sleepy port; however, the Chinese military's expansion to Hainan Island in 1950 caused American planners to abandon construction projects slated for bases near Hà Nội. The airfield and surrounding lands in Đà Nẵng grew into an American town of sorts. The base-building campaign featured new cargo docks, new barracks for American air mechanics and support staff, dozens of munitions bunkers, and improvements to the main runways and several auxiliary airfields.[57]

Another important, indirect effect of the Chinese communist victory was that it pushed a fleet of American military aircraft from China into the wider region. After war ended in 1945, Claire Chennault, the head of the American Flying Tigers squadrons at Kunming, purchased several surplus airplanes to fly aid to the Chinese Nationalists. After the Nationalists' defeat, Chennault sold his small fleet to the US Central Intelligence Agency. Using a shell company called Civil Air Transport (CAT), the CIA bought the lot of airplanes for about US$1 million total and redirected the planes to support activities in Indochina. The old mix of Chinese, American, and European pilots continued flying CAT's scheduled passenger flights via Taiwan as well as military charters to Indochina. This resurrected airline provided Americans and their French allies with quasi-commercial service to such cities as Huế, Đà Lạt, Quảng Trị, and Đà Nẵng. CAT, later made famous in the movie *Air America* (1990), was emblematic of the ad-hoc nature of early American involvement. Most of CAT's pilots and its fleet of DC-3 aircraft had logged thousands of hours in the air over China, Korea, Japan, and Taiwan before arriving at airfields such as Phú Bài.[58]

By 1952 this air-hopping cast of American advisers oversaw the delivery of a relative flood of military equipment to Vietnam. Many US aid workers, like Pyle in Greene's novel *The Quiet American*, worked clandestinely for the CIA. They dropped in from place to place in Indochina along with US military advisers, journalists, and French officials. While novels such as *The Quiet American* portray the American aid workers as naïve and dangerous, archival records from the US mission in Sài Gòn suggest that the Americans' first order of business was simply to figure how to get from one place to another. One of the first Americans to visit Huế was a public health officer, Dr. Clifford H. Jope. Tasked with visiting hospitals on the central coast and the highlands, he found it near impossible to reach half of the towns. He wrote in October 1951 of his repeated frustrations reaching hospitals due to a lack

City	Commercial Service	Field for DC-3	Field for light plane
Donghoi	Fair	Yes	
Quang tri	No	No	Yes
Hue	Good	Yes	
Tourane	Good	Yes	
Faifo	No	No	Yes
Nhatrang	Fair	Yes	
Phan rang	No	No	Yes
Phan thiet	Poor	Yes	
Dalat	Good	Yes	
Djiring	No	No	No
BanMeThuot	Awful	Yes	
Pleiku	No	?Yes	
Kontum	No	?Yes	

FIGURE 3.10. Dr. Clifford H. Jope's listing of airfield conditions and commercial service, October 1951. Source: Box 3, Mission to Vietnam: Office of the Director Subject Files, Entry 1430, Record Group 469, US National Archives and Records Administration, College Park.

of reliable air transport and airfields. Planes frequently canceled stops at Phú Bài, and for more distant locations such as Quảng Trị, access by CAT's larger DC-3 was impossible. Jope asked for a smaller plane to reach remote sites, and he provided the table shown in figure 3.10 to emphasize the poor state of the airfields.

As the war continued to worsen for French forces in 1953, the American presence in the air increased. A steadily increasing supply of planes and pilots meant more air traffic, development of runways, and more support for aerial photography. Surplus American World War II–era photoreconnaissance planes—B-26s with Fairchild K-17 cameras—generated in 1952–53 a new wave of air photography on the central coast.[59] While French military commanders managed the air photography effort, pilot logs in Huế show that the community of pilots and photography technicians included many non-French: Americans, Englishmen, Chinese, Indians, Norwegians, and Swedes. French military commanders tracked their circulation through the military zone and paid special attention to their flights given concerns about planes flying over the interzone.[60]

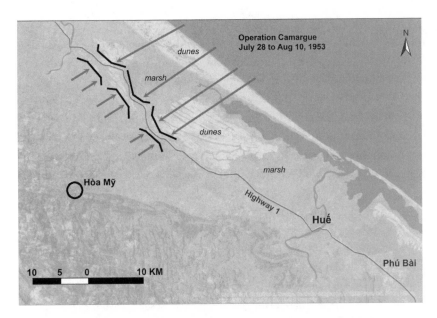

FIGURE 3.11. Operation Camargue. Source: Base layers courtesy of ESRI Inc. Details of operation from Bernard Fall, *Street without Joy* (Harrisburg, PA: Stackpole, 1961), 168.

VISIBILITY AND INVISIBILITY

Despite this influx of eyes in the sky, little changed on the ground with respect to the boundaries of occupied zones along Highway 1. Although the bulldozers cleared hilltops and aerial photography missions helped to map new areas, French forces were unable to clear and hold frontier zones such as Hòa Mỹ or even coastal areas just a few kilometers north of Huế. In 1953 the French command launched an unprecedented airborne assault on the marshes and dunes, using American aircraft and an element of surprise to surround a Việt Minh regiment, the Ninety-Fifth, alleged to be camped there. Bernard J. Fall's account of Operation Camargue, one of the largest French operations in the war, highlighted the continued inability of French and allied forces to even see their opponents. The combined air, land, and sea invasion involved over thirty batallions (approximately fifteen thousand troops) landing on all sides of the area of dunes, backswamps, canals, and arroyos. Mechanized battalions of Spahis (French recruits from Morocco), Algerian infantry, ex-Nazi legionnaires, paratroopers, and amphibious units moved north on Highway 1 to prevent Việt Minh forces from retreating hillward (figure 3.11). Fall reported that the invasion resulted for the Việt Minh in 182 dead and 387 prisoners while costing the French 17 dead and 100 wounded. However, the bulk of the Ninety-Fifth Regiment's forces escaped at night via a maze of canals and established trenches hidden by bamboo hedgerows.[61]

Fall's account of the follow-up occupation of this region by Vietnamese allies highlights the failure of the French forces to *connect* not only with the complex landscape and ecology but also with the relatively invisible social networks binding Vietnamese people living in these zones. Fall recounts a conversation between two French batallion commanders after the operation:

> "Funny," said Major Derrieu from the 6th Spahis, watching some of the new [Vietnamese] administrators in the village of Dong-Qué, they just never seem to succeed in striking the right note with the population. Either they come in and try to apologize for the mess we've just made with our planes or tanks; or they swagger and threaten the farmers as if they were enemy nationals which— let's face it—they are in so many cases. "That may be so," said young Lieutenant Dujardin, standing on the shady side of his M-24 [tank], "but I wouldn't care to be in his shoes tonight, when we pull out. He's going to stay right here in the house which the Commie commander still occupied yesterday, all by himself with the other four guys of his administrative team, with the nearest post three hundred yards away. Hell, I'll bet he won't even sleep here but sleep in the post anyway."[62]

Comparing this observation by French officers to Nguyễn Chí Thanh's quote at the beginning of this chapter about the strength of people fighting in their own territory, what both have in common is a ready apprehension of the centrality of human-based networks before, during, and especially after a major military action.

While French forces were repeatedly successful at violent insertions to occupy stretches of the central Vietnamese countryside, they lacked an ability to structure new village-level organizations in occupied zones. The French command's reluctance to transfer authority to the ASV or military leadership to the VBD highlighted the double bind that noncommunist Vietnamese groups found themselves in, between the French and the Việt Minh.

What led majorities of elected representatives in the deliberative bodies of France and the United States to continue this war was not a lack of knowledge *on the ground* but an overwhelming faith in their global, *aerial perspective.*

For most Americans and French, Indochina was one space among many in a shifting global array of communist, noncommunist, allied, and nonallied spaces. The local concerns of VBD commanders or administrators were subsumed within this larger, air-global set of concerns. Friction within such spaces as the central Vietnamese coast was inevitable, but French and American advocates of counterinsurgency continued to believe that sufficient clearing of these spaces might ultimately open them to new social and spatial possibilities, integration into an expanding global network of commerce.

FOUR

RUINS

THE GENEVA ACCORDS, SIGNED ON JULY 21, 1954, SILENCED MOST OF the guns. Slowly over the summer, combatants and governing bodies regrouped, abandoning forts and tactical zones they had established over nine years of conflict. In central Vietnam the Việt Minh moved to the north while French forces and State of Vietnam militias such as the Việt Binh Đoàn moved south. This period lasted three hundred days and permitted civilians and foreign observers alike the first glimpses of areas that had long been hidden behind battle lines. Evacuating French troops left behind caches of spent and abandoned weapons in urban posts. Most foreigners concentrated on the post-Geneva transition in the larger cities: Hà Nội, Hải Phòng, Đà Nẵng, and Sài Gòn. Very few made it to Huế or to rural areas of central and southern Vietnam.

Despite its proximity south of the new border and demilitarized zone following the seventeenth parallel, Huế and the central coast receded further from the limelight of nationalist performances, the protests and parades taking place on the streets of Hà Nội and Sài Gòn. On the central coast, the Geneva Accords brought a shadowy transition characterized by unchecked movements of soldiers, foreign and Vietnamese, recently released from active duty but not yet allowed to return home. Bands of French African soldiers camped on mountain slopes in former Việt Minh terrain while noncommunist Vietnamese militias competed with one another for control of lowland villages. In the first year of cease-fire until July 1955, the Sài Gòn government continued a breakneck expansion of port, airfield, and military facilities at

Đà Nẵng, but only a trickle of this burst of American-funded military aid reached Huế and the airfield at Phú Bài. The idea that central Vietnam with its ancient delta villages and troubled hills might now be a noncommunist zone bore little relation to facts on the ground.

Before the Geneva Accords, the Việt Minh's interzone governments claimed uncontested authority over large swaths of the central coast and the hilly interior. These areas were subject to ocassional French bombing raids and paratrooper operations, but since 1947, the Việt Minh organization had worked mostly unchallenged to develop new citizens, new soldiers, and new communes. They were the first Vietnamese state-building organization to integrate large areas of the central coast's mountains into their networked nation of trails, clandestine logistics hubs, and radio transmitters. A map produced by American advisers in 1954 titled "The Viet Minh Situation in Indochina" (figure 4.1) shows the extent of these networks.

Unlike some key battle zones of the Indochina War in the north, much of the land in central Vietnam saw little damage until *after* the war's end as tens of thousands of soldiers regrouped north and south. Ironically, it was the nature of the peace, not the war, that brought ecological ruin to many highland areas. The three-hundred-day regroupment meant that large areas of Việt Minh–evacuated hills and mountains were left without a replacement government. Party histories of the period describe life behind Việt Minh lines before the cease-fire as relatively orderly but subject to ambitious land reform, conscription, and literacy programs.[1] The relocation of Việt Minh forces and party leaders north of the DMZ produced a political vacuum in the interzone that all but eliminated nine years of socialist nation building.

Many works by Vietnamese and foreign historians have examined the ebullient fervor with which Hồ Chí Minh and communist leaders in the north engaged in "building state socialism" while Ngô Đình Diệm and American allies in the south forged a Republic of Vietnam.[2] Far from these crash programs in the capitals, however, life in the margins was more chaotic and splintered. In Huế rival militias sparred with the new national army. Diệm's younger brother Ngô Đình Cẩn built a secret police unit and a network of business interests that by 1963 exerted a strong influence over the region's politics and economy. He did all of this without holding any official office. He recruited a secretive network of junior officers from the VBD and from networks of fellow Catholics and local businessmen. Working through the Cần Lao (Workers) Party that supported his brothers Diệm and Nhu, Cẩn's

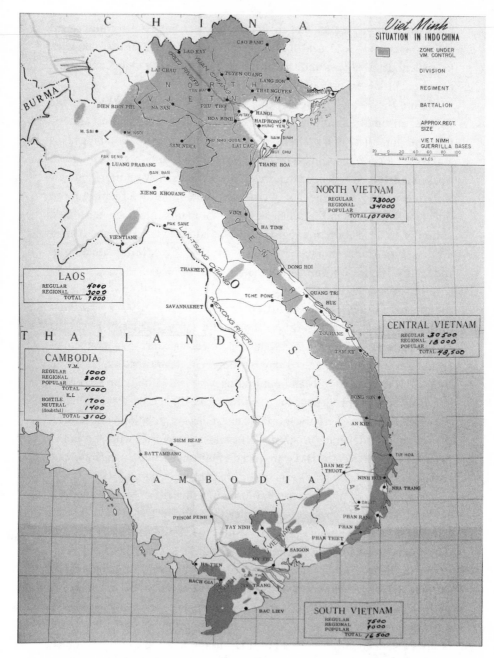

FIGURE 4.1. Việt Minh–controlled areas in 1953–54. Source: Security Classified General Records, 1950–61, MAAG-Vietnam Adjutant General Division, Record Group 472, US National Archives and Records Administration, College Park.

FIGURE 4.2. An attendant at the Nine Bunkers monument opens the gate to Bunker8, a bunker with twenty cells that were reserved for torturing Communist Party operatives, 1956–63. Photo by author, July 2015.

network of spies and police commandos worked in a vaguely titled Special Works Division and pursued alleged communist agents and anyone who might rival the Ngô family.[3] The United States was intimately involved in military construction and training around the Huế area by 1959, but its political influence with Cẩn was nonexistent.

Today in Huế, Cẩn is most famous for his association with a special prison and interrogation center operated by his special police in the hills near Nam Giao. Chín Hầm (Nine Bunkers; figure 4.2) is now a national historical site and a memorial to over one hundred people who were taken by police and tortured there.[4] As a site of well-documented suffering for all of Cẩn's "enemies," the Nine Bunkers serves as a useful lens for exploring the ways a landscape of military and imperial "ruin" left behind after years of fighting and decades of colonial occupation played into this post-1954 period of extrajudicial torture and killing. As anthropologist Ann Stoler and others suggest, the term "ruin" reflects a "privileged site of reflection."[5] Certainly today, with the site's individual prison cells preserved as historic reminders of the abuses of the American-Diệm era (1954–63), these ruins serve a highly constructed state-centered purpose of intentional reflection. Far less clear, however, are the ways that new ruins produced by the evacuation of French military forces in 1956 may have given rise to a man generally described (in communist and noncommunist works alike) as a monster.

Cẩn mobilized a secret police network that quickly established clandestine settlements and outposts atop the ruins of the evacuated tactical zones. All of this he and his supporters did in spaces left behind after the evacuations of Việt Minh and French soldiers and the chaotic arrival of northern refugees and American aid workers. The Geneva-mandated evacuation, the sudden drawdown of French troops, and a flood of American equipment and weapons produced the spaces and opportunities that enabled Cẩn's ascent.

To understand why he chose to work through a special police network and not military or official government channels, one must appreciate the extent to which Vietnamese military commanders were allied either with French or American military networks. Cẩn's deliberate choice to appear in public wearing the traditional áo dài robes worn by mandarins and his refusal to appear in public with American officials suggest a careful attempt to craft an identity not tethered to the colonial past, to socialist networks, or to the growing American military infrastructure. Like so many Vietnamese, Cẩn made do amid the physical and legal debris of a prolonged anticolonial war. While the party-sanctioned biography of Cẩn duly marks out his many crimes against the resistance, one senses at some level a measure of respect even from party authors for the extent that his Special Works Division built a formidable security infrastructure independent of people whom Cẩn viewed as sympathetic to French colonial hangers-on or subservient to American military advisers. As an American consul suggested in his reflections on Cẩn in 1961, the rapid expansion of this homegrown "shadow government" in Huế was in many ways a response with deep local support among Vietnamese who shared a resistance to the legacies of colonial and Cold War destruction.[6]

LEAVING THE INTERZONE

In the weeks after the conclusion of the Geneva Accords in August, the Việt Minh government of Interzone IV worked to remove the troops, political officers, archives, and equipment from its tactical zones south of the seventeenth parallel to portions of the interzone in the north. The Geneva Accords cut Interzone IV in half, and communities in the provinces of Thanh Hóa,

Nghệ An, Hà Tĩnh, and Quảng Bình received thousands of people relocating from south of the DMZ. Beginning in August 1954, the province's party leaders gathered for final goodbyes at Hòa Mỹ, overseeing the removal of personnel and offices to the north. From August 17 to 19 almost three thousand party cadres (cán bộ), military fighters, and civilians left Huế and started the trek north. On August 20 in Quảng Trị, another two thousand persons joined these northbound migrants. By October the northern half of the interzone had received over twenty-six thousand evacuees from Quảng Trị and Huế.[7]

This orderly departure masked what party officials and local supporters recognized as a devastating gutting of Việt Minh government, communications, and security. As it completed the removal of its people and offices, Interzone IV's new leaders issued the following words to party members who chose to stay behind: "Continue solving problems, agree with the provisions [of the Geneva Accords], follow the mission and new way of the Central Committee, fix mistakes, and address shortcomings. Staff at all levels have to see the [new] situation of Trị Thiên and the South. . . . The basic Party organizations must maintain confidentiality and ensure close ties with the masses. The work of reorganizing Party cells, choosing new Party members must be selective and proceed gradually, avoiding any shocks to the Party. Regular retraining of cadres is also needed to strengthen local organizations."[8] In effect, these words did little but soothe. The higher-ups relocating north had no inkling of the violence with which the new southern government would bring to Việt Cộng in the area (Việt Cộng nằm vùng). A party history of the tactical zone at Nam Đông reports that after the removal of most of the province's staff, remaining party members returned to the lowlands, where they were often imprisoned or killed by the Diệm government's "denounce communists, kill communists" (tố cộng, diệt cộng) campaigns. Many cadres stayed in the hills and relied on comrades from the highland groups to help them survive anticommunist purges in and around Huế.[9]

Months after the Việt Minh units departed, bands of French African soldiers moved into the abandoned tactical zones. Heavily armed bands of Senegalese and Moroccan soldiers (including the goums) camped in abandoned Việt Minh areas and declared to South Vietnamese officials that they intended to stay. A memo by the province's police chief noted that the Moroccan soldiers were generally friendly to area persons and were not violent. One group camped at a waterfall below the former tactical zone at Nam Đông. When local people gathering fuelwood approached, the troops gave them bread. The police chief also noted that a French military plane made routine airdrops of food and supplies, suggesting continued military support of this effort.[10]

The consequences of this expansion of French soldiers uphill were not just political but ecological. Without any clear government authority, foreign troops and landless locals attempted to extract anything they could for their camps and to earn money. Peacetime freed them to cut forests without fear of attack. A new forestry chief in Huế attempted to counter the destruction. Nguyễn Hữu Đính wrote that nine years of war had taken a heavy toll on the region's forests, but after August 1954 destruction of the pines "grew like a storm." He estimated that over 1 million trees were cut in the nine months following the cease-fire.[11] Đính and his colleagues implored French military commanders to rein in this forest destruction, comparable as it was to looting in the cities.[12]

CHAOS IN THE OCCUPIED ZONE

For the villages along Highway 1, the social and physical impacts of the Geneva Accords in the months immediately after their signing are poorly understood. State of Vietnam and French military records provide glimpses of the chaos and violence unfolding in such places as Hương Thủy and Dạ Lê. In the villages along Highway 1, Vietnamese military units and paramilitary police associated with a spate of pro-French political parties took advantage of the cessation in hostilities to track down and detain communist rivals. Similar to Ngô Đình Cẩn's shadowy government of Personalist Party members and special police, these paramilitary police did not fully belong to the province or the state.

One of the largest such forces camped near Huế was the Bảo Chính Đoàn (BCD; Primary Security Division). This paramilitary force was made up mainly of northerners; it relocated south of the DMZ from the Red River delta. It enjoyed support from members of the royal family as well as many pro-French Vietnamese in a Greater Viet Party (Đảng Đại Việt). In Huế by September 1954 a fledgling Vietnamese national army shared power with the BCD and VBD, separate paramilitary groups jockeying for control in many lowland villages. Eager to forge a new space for themselves, the BCD agressively pursued alleged communists too.

In one incident of BCD-related violence, the post-Geneva province chief in Huế wrote to the central Vietnam delegate—another provisional governmental position created by the French—about two alleged communists caught by BCD police in Thanh Thủy Thượng Village. Two BCD platoons stopped two individuals without legal identification papers at a checkpoint. As they apprehended them, the two individuals called out to fellow villagers for help. Instantly, over three hundred villagers surrounded the BCD platoons, threatening them with bamboo spikes to let the two neighbors go. The platoons radioed in to a Vietnamese National Army (VNA) post at Dạ Lê for backup, and a company of soldiers soon arrived. They dragged away twenty-one villagers and the two detainees to the district jail.[13]

In these new spaces opened up by mass relocations and large supplies of surplus arms, bitter local contests also erupted between Vietnamese loyal to France and those who resented the French, feeling caught between destructive French military actions and Việt Minh military pressure. The newly formed VNA was divided from the top down, as officers challenged each other and on occasion South Vietnam's leaders. From his first days as prime minister of South Vietnam in August 1954, Ngô Đình Diệm and his brother Nhu built networks of anti-French, Catholic allies to challenge the pro-French commander of the National Army, Nguyễn Văn Hinh. In Sài Gòn, American diplomats and spies assisted Diệm with President Dwight D. Eisenhower promising to directly support the National Army with a "crash program" of aid once it cut off relations with French advisers.[14] Especially in the Ngô family's home lands around Huế, a pro-Diệm network led by Ngô Đình Cẩn worked to draw in significant numbers of lower-ranking officers from the paramilitaries, mounting a grassroots effort of sorts, even within networks in historic villages.

French military intelligence reports from the Huế Sector in August 1954 reported these "anti-French activities" with great alarm. One such report, dated August 3, 1954, describes on the local scale how such campaigns worked. One Sergeant Hiếu accompanied two national guard soldiers from the post at Phú Bài airfield to a meeting at the house of Mr. Ngô Thảo in nearby Phù Bài Village. The sergeant, an intelligence service informant, reported that all attending were Catholic. His recounting of Mr. Thảo's discussion bears reading in full to convey the extreme range of military options being considered and the deep divisions within the anticommunist ranks. He said:

Ngo Dinh Diem will travel shortly to America to ask the armed intervention of that country against the French and the V.M. [Việt Minh] If Ngo Dinh Diem lets the French share Vietnam, it is because he hopes that a US reaction will materialize in the atomic bombing of the V.M. area. France looks, after the division of Vietnam, like a prostitute who offers to everyone, even a leper, for money. It's a treacherous enemy that we must fight before the V.M. who are our countrymen. Our duty, patriotic Catholics, is to effect all anti-French propaganda. This propaganda must emphasize the loss of prestige of France after the Geneva conference.[15]

While diplomats and heads of state negotiated in Sài Gòn, Paris, and Washington, similar conversations broke out in homes, garrisons, and schools across Vietnam. Contrary to popular notions that the Geneva Accords effectively ended French involvement in Vietnam, these struggles revealed the depth of hostilities between Vietnamese and French forces even within the same military organization. Just a few days after this event in Phù Bài, another French military informant reported that an anti-French faction of local forces in central Vietnam led an assault on the army post at Dạ Lê on Highway 1. They took 28 Vietnamese soldiers hostage; only 2 escaped. More importantly, the anti-French faction made away with 17 submachine guns, 14 rifles, 2 cases of grenades, and other equipment.[16]

In some respects, the Geneva Accords prolonged the chaos by stipulating (in Article 2) that the French Union military forces had three hundred days to regroup at bases and camps in the south. Around the bases at Huế, this meant that European French commanders and French African troops remained in control of security at key ports and airfields until May 1955. Phú Bài airfield remained a center for French military commanders during this period, and occasional conflicts with Vietnamese workers and military units highlighted the unusual stresses of post-Geneva life.

As more Americans and military personnel traveled by air to Huế, Phú Bài airfield became a stage for local people, too, to air their grievances directly with Americans. One of the first such incidents took place in September 1954. After an American plane touched down, over two hundred workers mobbed the delegation on the tarmac. After July 1954, the French military stopped paying their salaries. The workers had not been paid for two months, so they protested to the new foreign advisers for their salaries. French military police, afraid for the safety of the Americans, fired tear gas into the crowd and severely injured two women. An investigation into the "politically sensitive" incident involving senior American officials, French troops, and Vietnamese workers blamed delays in establishing new transfers of American funds from Sài Gòn to Huế. The United States had, even before 1954, been indirectly paying for the airport services; it sent payments to the French military commission that in turn paid the Vietnamese.[17]

Besides working out new ways to pay for and operate formerly French-controlled installations, the South Vietnam government began the difficult and necessary work of excavating military materials while attempting to build new military infrastructure. French forces, upon evacuation, hastily buried caches of machinery, munitions, and weapons. In some cases, they dumped weapons in the rivers, and in others they covered bunkers with dirt. Vietnamese officials in Huế recorded scores of caches uncovered after French units evacuated; the hills around Huế were littered with them. One report dated May 25, 1955 lists the details of one such find: a mountainous junk pile of American-made brakes, radiators, pieces of GMC trucks, and totaled jeeps.[18] Vietnamese police and military units, desperate to maintain stocks of ammunition and arms, noted with alarm the systematic destruction of weapons. One report dated March 9, 1955, described French barges loaded with ammunition leaving the beach at Thuận An, either to salvage the munitions or dump them offshore. French troops along Highway 1 moved heavy guns, rifles, carbines, and pistols to dump in the rivers too. Wherever possible, Vietnamese police and troops intercepted them to recover these American-made weapons.[19]

For South Vietnam, salvaging French military waste was critical because the Geneva Accords limited new purchases of weapons. Second, the possibility of unmanaged caches meant that rival groups or Việt Minh cells might recover the weapons themselves. Finally, this military junk produced challenges for American advisers to the Diệm government since most of the abandoned equipment was of American origin, materials lent or given to France through the mutual assistance programs.

AMERICAN AID AND THE GLOBAL AIRSPACE

Besides retrofitting South Vietnam's military, American aid played a profound role in connecting Vietnamese landscapes to a global air network. Where French troops had in 1947 returned to Vietnam by sea and reoccupied

FIGURE 4.3. Shadow of a DC-3/C-47 over rice fields. Source: File 10H3254, Service Historique de la Défense, French Air Force Photo Archives, Fort de l'Est, Paris.

urban strongholds and ports, Americans arrived at airfields and used them as critical nodes for nation building. Their unprecedented emphasis on air spaces was in many respects a byproduct of the boom in aircraft manufacturing during World War II, especially of one plane, the C-47 Skytrain, a militarized version of the DC-3 (figure 4.3). As a plane designed to transport troops, bombs, and cargo, the C-47 played a pivotal role in the American D-day invasion at Normandy, dropping paratroopers behind German lines. Douglas Aircraft's sprawling plants in Southern California produced thousands of planes, as did Allied plants in Britain, Russia, and postwar Japan.[20] After 1945 the US military began selling off planes, and they found homes in the air fleets of American-backed nations such as South Korea or in private military charters such as Chennault's pro–Chinese Nationalist CAT group. The plane became an icon of early Cold War struggles from the Berlin Airlift to the Indochina War.

After the Geneva Accords, DC-3s went into service for a South Vietnamese airline, Air Vietnam, and militarized C-47s helped form the South

Vietnamese air force. More DC-3s and C-47s arrived in 1956, providing many people with opportunities to travel by air across the country and overseas to such destinations such as Manila, Tokyo, Bangkok, and the United States. The planes had become global symbols of American aid from Berlin in the 1948–49 airlift to urban and mountain airfields across Asia. Their low landing speed allowed them to land on shorter runways, and the all-metal construction of the C-47 permitted landings on dirt. They provided a physical air platform for linking up remote airstrips in the central highlands with Sài Gòn and a regional network of affiliated fields in Southeast Asia and Japan. Vietnamese bases and military organizations became linked into the network of air spaces in this military aerial economy and into an American-directed network of offshore contractors, technical experts, and military logistics managers working at key air materials areas in the Philippines and Japan. Given strict limitations on military personnel placed *inside* Vietnam, the United States relied upon this extraterritorial Pacific network to provide training and repair damaged equipment.[21]

On the ground in Vietnam, the American advisory mission was limited by the Geneva Accords to several hundred staff, but with connections to a global military logistics network they managed an unprecedented flow of military materials in and out of Vietnam. In the first years after 1954, the operation was complicated by commitments to France and Vietnam. The United States had supplied the French military in Indochina with airplanes and equipment since 1950, and US military personnel such as airplane mechanics were already deeply rooted in French military operations at bases in Đà Nẵng and Sài Gòn by 1953. After the Geneva Accords, American military aid in Vietnam was bifurcated between the old program for France (in Indochina), the Military Assistance and Advisory Group–Indochina (MAAG-Indochina), and the new MAAG-Vietnam.[22] In 1955–56 MAAG-Indochina facilitated the exit of French forces and their equipment while MAAG-Vietnam worked with abandoned French equipment and salvaged airplanes for the Army of the Republic of Vietnam. Because the Geneva Accords placed strict limitations on military buildup, MAAG-Vietnam had to salvage existing equipment without drawing criticism from international observers sent after the 1954 cease-fire.[23] This simultaneous export and import of military goods brought a flood of activity to the docks at Đà Nẵng and Sài Gòn. In one month, September 1956, MAAG staff signed off on US$230 million of materiel—trucks, ammunition, and aircraft—leaving the docks with French forces. In the same month, they

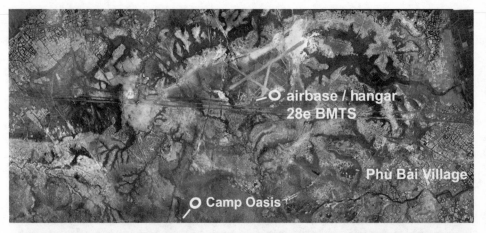

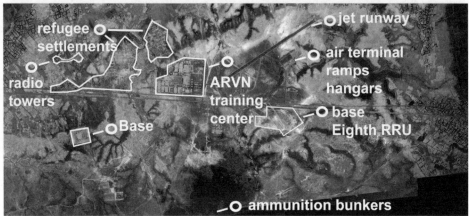

FIGURE 4.4. Comparison of 1952 and 1963 air photographs. Source: File TV279—ELA54—June 4, 1952, French Air Force Photo Archives, Fort de l'Est, Paris; Mission F4634A, ON#69708, Record Group 373, US National Archives and Records Administration, College Park. Digitizing, georeferencing, and annotations by author.

managed the overhauling and import of 25 C-47s for South Vietnam's air force, seven hundred trucks, and several thousand tons of ammunition. While this equipment was heading into the port at Đà Nẵng, over fourteen thousand junked vehicles awaited export for similar repairs.[24]

While MAAG and TERM (Technical Equipment Recovery Mission) staffers in Huế never numbered more than a dozen, they played a pivotal role in 1955–56 in directing the refurbishment of an ARVN division and expanding facilities around Phú Bài. They linked ARVN military units to a global infrastructure of military bases, supply depots, and repair facilities. A comparison of historical air photography from 1952 and 1963 shows the extent of this American-supported construction around Phú Bài (figure 4.4). While Phú Bài was small compared to Đà Nẵng, by 1963 it included radio antenna farms, runways capable of landing jet aircraft, an army base, several refugee settlements, a military administrative compound, and new ammunition bunkers. Airfields like Phú Bài became hubs of this American aerial economy. Longer runways, modern control towers, weather stations, high intensity lights, visual omni-ranges, hangars, and bunkers guided this traffic.

Besides rapidly urbanizing the dunes and bare hills of Vùng Phèn, the American focus on Phú Bài provided an opportunity for Vietnamese officials to move military personnel and the ruins of decades of colonial military occupation from sites inside the city, especially Nam Giao. A Vietnamese adviser for the region took advantage of the American construction to push ARVN military units out of the city. He noted that French officers and the *goums* had camped amid Nam Giao's royal sites and tombs since 1947. By eliminating the military post and opening the site to the public, he hoped to reopen a "historic monument of state culture and religion." He asked the MAAG office in Huế to remove buried piles of artillery shells and his military colleagues to relocate to Phú Bài.[25]

SHADOW GOVERNMENT IN FRENCH AND VIỆT MINH RUINS

If the DC-3 was a symbol of US aerial influence, the Nine Bunkers was a fitting symbol for Cẩn's reign in the cities and villages of the central coast. He held no official office in the RVN, but after the Geneva Accords he quickly assembled a network of anti-French, mostly Catholic loyalists from area businesses and the police who used the family's political party to build a regional empire.[26] As had the communists, he used a political party to connect leaders in military and civil affairs at all levels. His Cần Lao Party allowed him to coordinate loyalists, promote cronies, and punish critics.[27] He formed a special cases unit in the province police and claimed the abandoned bunkers on Ngữ Tây Hill near Nam Giao as a site for extralegal interrogations and torture. He lived nearby with his mother and a former nanny, Mụ Luyến, who people regarded as his mistress, the "first lady of the Advisor of Central Vietnam."[28] Abandoned since the mid-1940s, the bunker complex functioned as a dark space. It held not only communists but any "enemies" of the Cần Lao. Cẩn's special police rounded up such adversaries as "French spies," the manager of the Morin Hotel, and, after a series of protests in 1963, Buddhist clergy and students.[29] While rumors in Huế swirled around the abandoned bunkers, by 1956 Cẩn's network reached far beyond Huế to Đà Nẵng and down much of the coast. In Huế he combined use of the Nine Bunkers prison site with what American intelligence observers feared were "death squads" to engage in targeted assassinations of suspected communists and political rivals.[30] More than his brother Nhu in Sài Gòn, Cẩn was adamant in keeping his special police unit separate from CIA operatives too. Americans at the US consulate in Huế remained largely cut off from the Cần Lao networks.

In such villages as Dạ Lê and Phù Bài, the Cần Lao enforced support by insisting that all members of village councils and police offices be members and therefore subject to regular training courses in Huế. Anthropologist James Trullinger, based on his interviews with residents in 1975, describes in more detail how this new organization coerced locals to participate. Besides swearing allegiance to the Cần Lao, village councilmen serving at the time engaged in common abuses of power such as renting out communal lands in exchange for bribes. Whether they supported the Cần Lao or not, villagers knew that in order to rent land or obtain "public" medical services, they needed to pad the pockets of the village council. Those councilors in turn paid part of these bribes to district and provincial Cần Lao Party officials for the "privilege" of collecting them. Village councilors were also required to ensure the party's success at the ballot box through coercion or ballot box stuffing.[31] Most threatening however, especially to families who had children in their teens, was the requirement that all village youth join the party's Republican Youth, an organization modeled directly after the Hitler Youth with similar brown shirts and militaristic assemblies. Those children who did not attend rallies or assist local military forces were deemed antigovernment or, worse, as "Vietnamese communists in the region."[32]

This pyramid-like corruption scheme resulted in private enrichment and funds traveling up the chain of command, but it rarely returned benefits to the village. Council members in Dạ Lê realized this in 1956 when they attempted to regain control of their village's school from the district military commander. Only the richest residents in the village could afford to send their children to Huế for school, but the village school promised education to all. Residents had built the school from their own funds after the August Revolution in 1945, and the school operated from August 1945 until February 1947, when French soldiers invaded and claimed the school grounds, turning it into a military post. After July 1954, the ARVN continued to occupy the school grounds, keeping the school closed.

The village council—all loyal Cần Lao members—first asked the local military commander and then wrote directly to President Diệm in 1956. They explained their plight and asked him to relocate the military down the highway near Phú Bài. That summer and fall, in a series of exchanges between the village council, the province chief, the central Vietnam regional delegate, and the Ministry of Education, everyone repeatedly agreed that the school grounds should be returned. However, no office volunteered the funds to pay for the school's reconstruction or the creation of a new military post. The province chief finally asked the village to contribute funds to pay for a new miiltary post if they wished to regain the school.[33] This failure of local Cần Lao partisans to bring even the most essential nation-building benefits back to the village highlights the stark limits to development or aid beyond military bases and certain privileged groups.

Besides building its political networks in the lowland villages, Cần Lao partisans also pushed their influence hillward, establishing refugee settlements directly on top of the two largest Việt Minh tactical areas, Hòa Mỹ and Nam Đông. Strictly from a landscape perspective, a development focus on these abandoned sites made sense, as both were logistical hubs located on transportation corridors linking the lowlands to key highland valleys. From a more symbolic perspective, however, these two former tactical zones were critical nodes in the social and logistical networks that the Việt Minh had developed with participation from highland groups. Hòa Mỹ and Nam Đông were "cradles of the revolution" (cái nôi của cách mạng), not just defensive bulwarks. They were centers where many highlanders became literate (in Vietnamese), joined party ranks, and participated in the defense and governance of the interzone.

The Cần Lao's special police thus viewed both of these highland gateways as special targets in their reign of terror. They directed the province's allotment of American bulldozers, road-building equipment, and funds for refugee resettlement to raze the grounds and then repopulate both sites with refugees from the north, most of them Vietnamese Catholics from the Red River delta. This joint sedentarization and gentrification program produced a facade of a refugee settlement at each location while special police and military units hunted for the region's remaining communists. Their violent tactics in the lowlands all but eliminated former Việt Minh political cadres in lowland villages while several hundred Việt and highlander members hid out in the hills. Local party histories describe this moment as one of the darkest in its history. At the signing of the Geneva Accords, some 23,400 persons were party members in Thừa Thiên–Huế; by 1958 the number had dwindled to several hundred.[34]

While the province government in Huế presented these settlements as models for a nationwide agricultural development center (*dinh điền*) scheme, American visitors to both sites expressed deep skepticism. In the southern highlands and the Mekong delta, the US Operations Mission supported the government's refugee program to establish new settlements for thousands of individuals. On the central coast, however, marginalized by Ngô Đình Cẩn, Americans had little contact with these projects and viewed them as thinly veiled fronts for Cần Lao domination. The American consul in Huế, John Heavner, paid a visit to both sites in 1959, as they had been built with US equipment and funds. At Hòa Mỹ he noted that Cẩn's party followers directed the aid money into a Cần Lao business growing kenaf for paper manufacturing. American food aid and equipment supported the settler-workers while profits directly benefited Cần Lao loyalists. At Nam Đông, he noted a similar mix of military and civic aid. Bulldozers cleared debris for new military posts while settlers depended on food aid arriving on trucks.[35]

At Nam Đông in particular, this new wave of development was a radical departure from earlier Việt Minh settlements in both ecological and social terms. Ecologically, the new settlement emphasized intensive agriculture in what had always been a swidden system. Further, the construction of an all-weather road from Huế opened up the valley's forested slopes to clearcutting, triggering mudslides. While in the past Vietnamese had ventured to Nam Đông by foot trails, the new road brought in half-ton GMC trucks, bulldozers, and armored vehicles. With materials arriving on flatbed trailers, a roadside town emerged with military post, school, dispensary, post office, and government office (figure 4.5). However, once the refugees arrived at their rows of hastily built homes on a new grid of gravel roads, they struggled to build an agricultural economy from the razor-thin topsoil. They remained dependent on aid. An RVN summary of the settlement at Nam Đông enumerated various schemes to expand rice paddies and plant industrial crops.

FIGURE 4.5. Nam Đông settlement. Source: Mission J7321, ON#94794, Record Group 373, US National Archives and Records Administration, College Park. Annotations by author.

None of the plans worked, and the instant community of resettled northern-ers remained dependent on aid shipments and the protection of the ARVN outpost across the river.[36]

This new development model at Nam Đông, a suburb-like village with gridded streets and a nearby base surrounded with guard towers and fencing, was also a radical social departure from the Việt Minh community that pre-dated it. The RVN government, especially President Diệm, insisted on estab-lishing *sedentary* agricultural communities in the highlands, a move that alienated the Katu people who had farmed swidden plots there for centuries.[37] Many RVN officials still viewed the Katu as "savages" (*mọi*) and fostered a divide between lowland settlers and the Katu. The settlement featured ethnic Vietnamese army posts and was developed exclusively for ethnic Vietnamese, cementing Katu support for the communists. The Việt Minh by contrast continued to encourage swidden cultivation partly as a means to survive and partly to retain vital Katu support. Lacking roads and foreign aid, they relied on Katu crops such as cassava. When party leader Lê Duẩn visited in 1953, he urged Katu comrades to "turn the hilly wilderness into swidden gardens."[38]

The relationships that Việt Minh leaders forged with the Katu during the interzone years proved resilient even during these RVN intrusions. American anthropologist Gerald Hickey noted this with Katu people and spoke publicly about the RVN's deep alienation of highland groups, drawing attacks from the Diệm government. Hickey encountered this tension firsthand when he visited a settlement a few mountain ridges south of Nam Đông in 1957. He traveled upriver from Đà Nẵng with a Katu-Việt merchant and an American missionary. Upon reaching the Katu village, he met men wearing loincloths, their long hair decorated with boar tusks. At the village, the group met with a village chief in a room decorated with the spears used in the group's "blood hunting" raids. When the American group attempted to present the chief with a donation of American medical supplies and rice, the chief surprised them by declining, explaining "the 'Viet Minh' would not like it." His son had "gone north" in 1954, "and the Viet Minh would be angry if we took food from [Westerners]."[39] Relationships between the Việt Minh and the Katu were key to sustaining highland trails.

REMILITARIZING THE HIGHLANDS

The refugee settlement at Nam Đông marked the beginning of a new American-backed military struggle in the highlands. The base-like settlement with its fenced-in grid and triangular footprint of an ARVN military post became a center for launching new raids in surrounding hills. The Ngô family and the Cần Lao Party ramped up police sweeps (càn quét) across South Vietnam in 1958–59 while stories of corruption and torture from the Nine Bunkers spread on the streets of Huế. This settlement at the end of the road was precariously perched on a political and ecological boundary where government-controlled land gave way to steep slopes and forests returning to Việt Cộng influence.

The combination of military sweeps and development campaigns insisting on the sedentarization of the highlanders triggered a new communist-led military response. Organized by communist and Katu leaders who had fled into the mountains, local self-defense units began to fight back.[40] Party cadres established a new headquarters four kilometers from Nam Đông and started their own campaign to "suppress traitors" (*trừ gian*) via harassment and assassination of RVN officials who participated in the sweeps. A party history of Nam Đông district notes that in 1957 party cadres assembled a self-defense force including lowlander cadres who had escaped sweeps in the lowlands, Katu youth, and some who had returned from the north. They rebuilt weapons stockpiles and trained the youth in guerilla warfare, forming the self-defense units into platoon-sized groups. They redoubled their efforts, too, to expand trails across the high ridges to Laos and North Vietnam.[41]

These local trail-clearing actions were born out of necessity, but they quickly demonstrated to such party leaders as Lê Duẩn in Hà Nội the value of trails should North Vietnam throw its support into a new war. Development of trails running through Laos, outside RVN borders, allowed delivery of new weapons and the return of experienced military officers who had gone north in 1954. Cẩn's police and paramilitary units had destroyed much of the underground network in the lowlands and hills during his reign of terror, but parts of the most remote trails in the highlands had survived. The Trị-Thiên Committee (a spinoff of the Interzone IV Committee) began work on a section of this new trail in Laos in 1956. As Cẩn's bulldozers expanded settlements, bases, and all-weather roads to Nam Đông and the more remote A Sầu Valley, the Laos trail became vital for maintaining communications from Hà Nội to parts of the south. By 1958 as Lê Duẩn promoted his "Road to the South" strategy with party leaders in Hà Nội, a few dozen travelers passed through its rest stations nightly. The trail outside Thừa Thiên–Huế Province had eight rest areas each a day's walk apart from the other. Each stop was managed by a Vietnamese cadre and nine youths from area highland groups. Katu, Pacoh, and other groups supplied the rest areas with tubers, manioc, and dry rice raised in swidden plots.[42]

The targeted assassinations of RVN officials and rumors of soldiers returning from the north caused even more repressive, violent responses from Sài Gòn. In May 1959 Diệm announced the draconian Decree 10/59 authorizing tribunals of ARVN officers to try suspected communist members, issue death sentences, and carry those sentences out immediately. These military tribunals became roving death courts; some even traveled with a portable guillotine. Local military commanders at the district level could detain anyone, determine whether he or she had committed treasonous crimes, and then determine a sentence without appeal.[43] Besides an immediate response from the party in the north to aid their southern brothers in arms, this suspension of any semblance of due process brought mass protests from students, Buddhist groups and, decisively, ARVN military leaders who had built extensive ties with the United States through officer training schools and frequent visits to other American-allied countries.

In Hà Nội that May, Lê Duẩn called for party comrades to reopen the trail system. He had already made trips to the Soviet Union to guarantee Soviet support and secret trips south of the DMZ to advance the plan with southern comrades. Party leaders were already assembled in Hà Nội for the fifteenth plenum, and Lê Duẩn used the opportunity to gain support for southern communists' military resistance. They passed Resolution 15 creating the 559 Transportation Group, a military division responsible for developing the trail system. After passage, China and the Soviet Union immediately pledged their support with the trucks, guns, and ammunition needed to rebuild a liberation army in South Vietnam.[44]

Farther away in Honolulu, the escalation of fighting in such places as Nam Đông and broader American concerns about Diệm's military tribunals caused a shift in US military advising too. On May 25 the US commander in chief, Pacific authorized American military personnel to accompany RVN military units on operational missions. Before 1959 the United States was prohibited by Diệm from sending US soldiers on operations with the ARVN; meanwhile, US Special Forces teams roamed much of Laos and reported on the trail building.[45] This decision did not commit ground forces, but it permitted MAAG advisers to visit RVN forts and outposts at Nam Đông and Hòa Mỹ. It also allowed US soldiers and spies opportunities to forge closer relations with ARVN commanders outside the watch of the Ngô family or their Cần Lao networks. These advisory visits contributed to rising fears in American intelligence communities that traffic on the trails through Laos might ignite a global conflict in the small country's rugged mountains.

At Nam Đông, the first battle in this new era took place in July 1960 during part of the party's General Uprising, timed to coincide with the sixth anniversary of the Geneva Accords. Party cadres and self-defense forces participated in a cluster of raids on RVN posts. They netted automatic weapons that the MAAG had delivered to RVN troops. Working with a mix of Việt and ethnic minority cadres, they expanded this local force from several dozen in 1960 to over a hundred by the year's end. They counted in their ranks key party officials of the Katu minority as well as several dozen Việt cadres who lived secretly among refugees in the settlement. Some Katu who had gone north in 1954 had now returned, too, now fluent in Vietnamese with military and political training.[46]

The July General Uprising worsened dissent between ARVN commanders and the Diệm government, causing a coup attempt that ended with ARVN military rule in the hills and mountains of Thừa Thiên–Huế. The November 11, 1960, coup attempt in Sài Gòn ended Cẩn's influence in the highlands and replaced it with military commanders. In Sài Gòn the commander of ARVN forces for Đà Nẵng and Huế, General Trần Văn Đôn, joined with other generals in the coup while his lieutenants advanced on RVN administrative posts in the hills. Diệm averted an overthrow by giving ARVN generals a greater say in regional and national governance, allowing them to take control over the border regions too. This lesser part of the conciliation, giving the generals and their officers control of such posts as Nam Đông, was a decisive turning point for the war in the highlands. It opened up these remote posts not only to more military units but to new levels of American military involvement as special forces and CIA counterinsurgency teams moved in.[47] Rather than redress local complaints or even attempt rapprochement with the highlanders or former Việt Minh supporters, the First Division initiated a wave of new offensives in 1960–61 to attack the trail networks. Down in Huế, the province chief (a Cần Lao loyalist) complained bitterly to South Vietnam's prime minister how this burst of new military operations was turning the entire district into a war zone.[48]

MAPPING INSURGENTS

The new military rulers in the uplands province introduced new political maps with light and dark pink shadings that conveyed their singular aim of counterinsurgency (figure 4.6). While such maps fed into national military planning for the RVN, they also informed American military allies who had for years been drawing up similar maps in neighboring Laos and Thailand.[49] The authors of this map used dark pink shading to indicate areas still largely under the communists' control. They used a lighter shade of pink to indicate lighter opposition in the hills west of Hòa Mỹ and southwest of another evacuated area, Khe Trái. As a cartographic projection of the ARVN's ambitions in 1960 for mopping up these bases of communist support, the map presented communist-controlled regions in symbolic terms very familiar to American counterinsurgency experts at the time. Small pie charts in each highlands commune showed, via colored

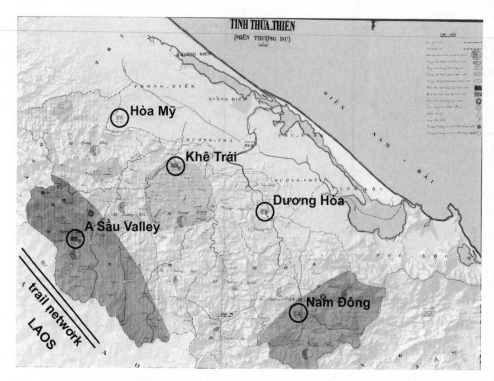

FIGURE 4.6. Map of upland district, 1960. Source: File 17331, Record Group ĐICH, Vietnam National Archives Center no. 2. Annotations by author.

sections, the approximate percentage of people who were "Việt Cộng in the region," still a majority across the hills. Lighter pink shading indicated areas with diminished support, and colored or empty circles indicated villages that supported a particular side or had been abandoned, respectively.

Excerpts of this map (plate 2) highlight the map's deep pink areas, the hills around Nam Đông and the A Sầu Valley. They bear closer inspection, for they show how ecological and political boundaries coincided, often separating ARVN posts from communist base areas by only a few kilometers. Reconstituted communist self-defense units and cells, pushed almost to annihilation during years of unrelenting police sweeps, extended their political and communications networks to the sources of streams on the highest slopes. ARVN troops could not easily penetrate the dense forests without support from Katus and highland groups while communist partisans retained the older practice of navigating by rivers and mountain ridges with help from native highlanders.

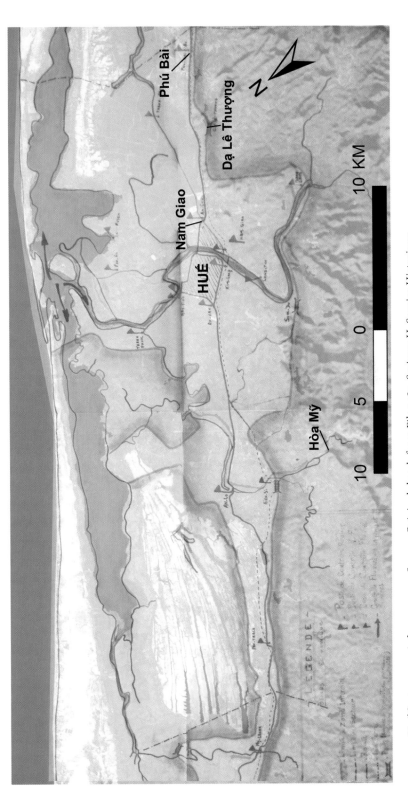

PLATE 1. Huế Sector occupied zones, 1952. Source: Original sketch from File 3482, Series 10H, Service Historique de la Défense, French Air Force Photo Archives, Fort de l'Est, Paris. Underlying imagery and shaded relief courtesy of ESRI Inc. Plate by author.

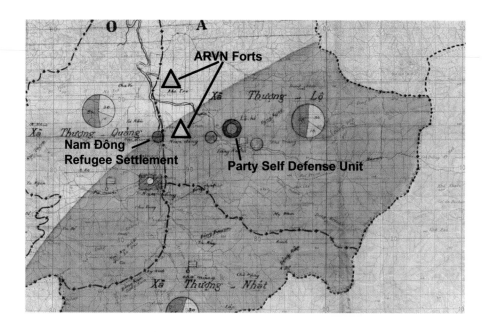

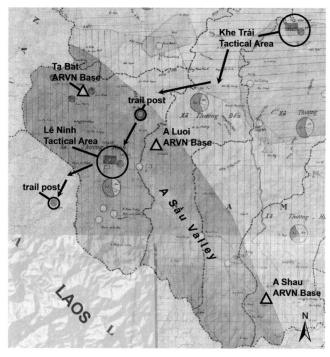

PLATE 2. (Top) Communist-held highlands near Nam Đông. Source: File 17331, Record Group ĐICH, Vietnam National Archives Center no. 2. Plate by author.

PLATE 3. (Bottom) A Sầu Valley with ARVN bases and communist tactical areas. Source: File 17331, Record Group ĐICH, Vietnam National Archives Center no. 2. Underlying shaded relief courtesy of ESRI Inc. Map georeferenced and annotated by author.

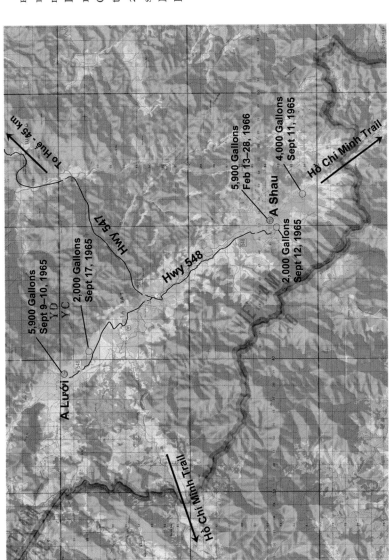

PLATE 4. Spray areas in A Shau Valley, 1965–66. Source: US Air Force Communications Service. HERBS Tape, Defoliation Missions in South Vietnam, 1965–71, Data by Province, 1985, Special Collections, USDA National Agricultural Library, accessed February 24, 2017, www.nal.usda.gov/exhibits/speccoll/items/show/1257. US Army Map Service Far East, Map Series L607. Plate by author.

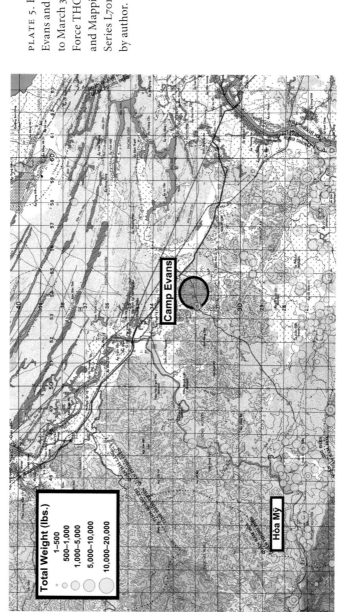

PLATE 5. Bombing in area of Camp Evans and Hòa Mỹ, December 1, 1966, to March 31, 1967. Source: US Air Force THOR GIS, National Imagery and Mapping Agency, Sheet 6442-II, Series L7014, 2nd edition, 1968. Plate by author.

Total Weight (lbs.)
1–500
500–1,000
1,000–5,000
5,000–10,000
10,000–20,000

Camp Evans

Hòa Mỹ

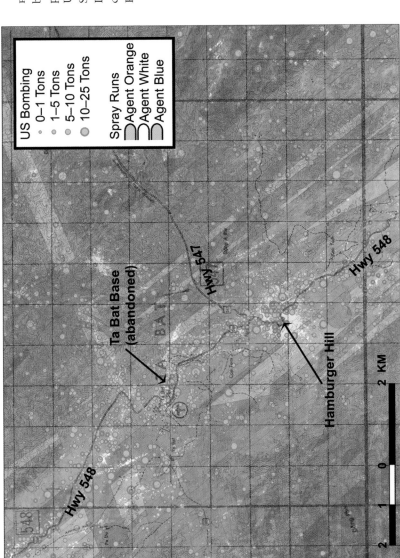

PLATE 6. Herbicide spraying and bombing in A Lưới. Source: Bombing point data, US Air Force THOR GIS; US Army Map Service Far East, Map Series L607; CORONA satellite image DS1045-1069DA081, January 29, 1968, courtesy of US Geological Service. Plate by author.

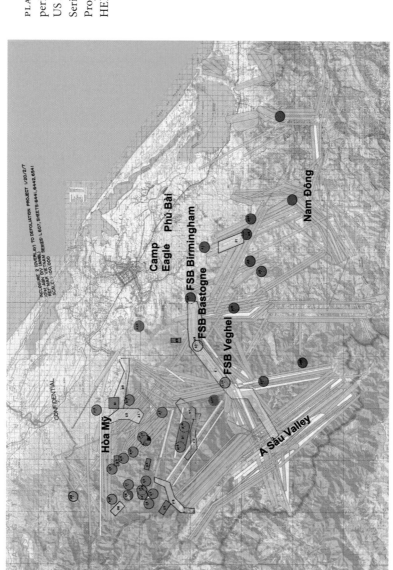

PLATE 7. Firebases targeted for perimeter defoliation, 1970. Source: US Army Map Service Far East, Map Series L607; Herbicide Operations Project 1/2/70; spray data from HERBS Tapes. Plate by author.

PLATE 8. View of former 160th Aviation Group Helipad. Photo by author, 2011.

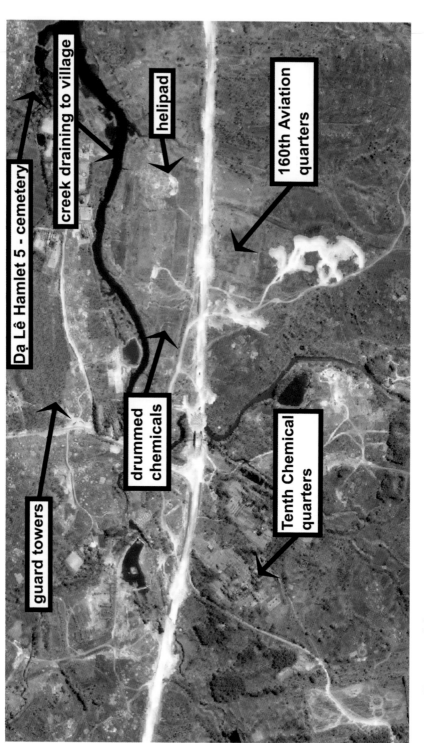

PLATE 9. Hotspot candidate sites in 2002. Source: IKONOS-2 satellite frame, courtesy of GeoEye Foundation. Plate by author.

Dạ Lê Hamlet 5 - cemetery

creek draining to village

helipad

160th Aviation quarters

guard towers

drummed chemicals

Tenth Chemical quarters

In this new era of increased military support to ARVN bases from South Vietnam and US counterinsurgency programs, the A Sầu Valley became a new focal point in a quickly globalizing conflict (plate 3). During the First Indochina War, this valley was largely outside the travels of French and Việt Minh forces alike. Việt Minh trails closer to the coast were sufficient for conveying troops and supplies north. However, as Cẩn's police units swept through Hòa Mỹ and Nam Đông in 1957, local party leaders retreated to this remote valley to forge new networks. From a tactical sense, however, the valley terrain was highly problematic. Two high ridges of mountains from one to two thousand meters high walled in a valley floor several kilometers wide that ran forty kilometers before exiting at both ends into Laos.

Only after development of trails in Laos became essential did communist groups focus on the A Sầu Valley. Controlling the valley required climbing its thickly forested rocky slopes. ARVN bases were located along the eastern side; the middle base at A Lưới included a small settlement zone, somewhat like Nam Đông, that was previously a Việt Minh area. One road connected A Lưới with Huế over thirty kilometers of rugged terrain, and a jeep track connected the three ARVN bases. Communist self-defense units reestablished control of an old Việt Minh tactical area, Khe Trái, and built a new one along a critical east-west gateway from the middle of the A Sầu Valley into Laos. A post across the border in Laos was a key communist rest area, a vital link in the new trail network.

This resurgent communist program of trail building supported larger attacks, culminating in December 1960 with the formation of a National Liberation Front to, once again, link up these local efforts into a coordinated national campaign. The NLF's declaration called for the creation of a national military, the Peoples Liberated Armed Forces (PLAF), in South Vietnam and a revolutionary government in areas liberated from the RVN. The pace of battles around outposts like Nam Đông and A Lưới picked up in 1961, as American officials grew more worried about the collapse of the RVN.

FORTIFYING THE LOWLANDS

After the 1960 coup, the city streets of Huế and villages along Highway 1 functioned as an increasingly important performance space both for supporting the NLF and fighting the Diệm government. The old villages of the

Inner Road in particular provided daily examples of the deep sectarian and ideological differences ripping traditional society apart. Cẩn's paramilitary approach with Cần Lao cronies and "brownshirt" youth triggered increasingly violent responses from pro-NLF residents in the early 1960s. After the formation of the NLF, communist groups retaliated against the most abusive of the Cần Lao officials and started nighttime attacks on military convoys on the highway. These triggered increasingly violent and sectarian responses from Cần Lao units. Residents of Dạ Lê Village described one retaliation, a sweep operation that took place on Wesak Day, a Buddhist holiday, in 1962. At approximately 5 A.M., several hundred army soldiers moved in a line from the highway through the village. Three PLAF commandos fled but ran into another group of waiting soldiers and were killed. The sweep resulted in about thirty other men being detained and interrogated while the Cần Lao paramilitaries looted chickens, ducks, a sewing machine, and cash. One peasant recalled that after every sweep, "they made more friends for the V.C."[50]

While villagers, Buddhist monks, and students at Huế University increased their protests about the Ngô family's abuses, Cẩn attempted to contain the widening array of protesters by turning one of the oldest villages on the Inner Road, Thanh Thủy Thượng, into a strategic hamlet (ấp chiến lược). The strategic hamlet program was a favored strategy of Cẩn's brother Nhu in Sài Gòn, but he assented to build one along Highway 1 as a showcase likely to appease Americans traveling into Huế from the airport. Cẩn had openly disagreed on the utility of strategic hamlets in central Vietnam's coastal villages. Instead he preferred to use paramilitaries who volunteered and trained in a military-style boot camp with indoctrination into the Cần Lao Party. The US consul in Huế in 1961, John Helble, noted that in central Vietnam strategic hamlets mostly began and ended with iconic bamboo fences. Helble and local American counterinsurgency specialists concurred that Cẩn's paramilitary strategy was more effective than Nhu's strategic hamlets because it recognized that insurgents were "more deeply rooted in the village than the Government has been willing to admit."[51]

Perhaps just to appease Americans or Sài Gòn bureaucrats, the provincial government built its "showcase" strategic hamlet at Thanh Thủy Thượng, conveniently located on Highway 1 between the airport and Huế. Thanh Thủy Thượng was one of the oldest Vietnamese villages on the central coast, and youth of the village had participated in revolutionary struggles since the August Revolution. The main village area had for centuries existed with little

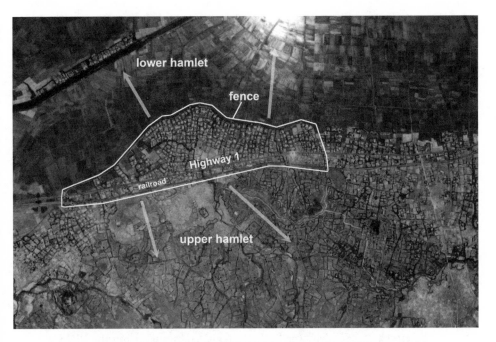

FIGURE 4.7. Aerial photo of Thanh Thủy Thượng, 1963, with USGS topographic overlay. Source: Mission F4634A, ON#69708, Record Group 373, US National Archives and Records Administration, College Park. Annotations by author.

changes in house plots or buildings in the narrow coastal strip lying between the highway and railroad and the rice fields. In this urban-like strip of land, family shrines and a Buddhist pagoda sat surrounded by houses and hedgerows of the village's founding families. Highway 1 and the national railroad bisected this strip, separating it from the hilly back slopes.

While Cẩn's sentiments toward the fortification project may have been minimal, locally, the construction of barricades and manning of checkpoints was deeply disruptive. By fencing in *just* the residential portion of the village, cutting people off from estuary fields in the lower hamlets and ancestral tombs in the upper section, the chief effect was not protection but a new form of militarized enclosure. Villagers were forced to build three rows of bamboo stockades separating the residential area from their fields and tombs (figure 4.7). Once complete, every resident had to produce papers upon entering and leaving this stockade, even if traveling to rice fields or the hills. Residents in Thanh Thủy Thượng had to face Popular Force soldiers at each checkpoint, and their children were required to serve in these units as well as Cần Lao patriotic organizations such as the Republican Youth. A commune history describes this strategic hamlet as a "prison camp," as the barricades deterred many people from leaving their homes for fear of abuse or shakedowns at checkpoints.[52]

While the strategic hamlet program was by most accounts deeply restrictive, the construction of barricades and increase in military checkpoints on Highway 1 reflected the Huế government's mounting concerns over the communists' gradual regaining of the upland territories. Since 1961 PLAF platoons had engaged in dozens of battles against ARVN patrols around the mountain bases. They extended their controlled areas across most of the A Sầu Valley and the mountains surrounding Nam Đông. At midnight on March 3, 1963, Company 105 of the PLAF attacked the ARVN camp at Hòa Mỹ, pushing the boundaries of the liberated zone almost to their original area in 1947. In a one-hour assault, they killed twenty-seven ARVN soldiers, took six Cần Lao officials hostage, destroyed two tractors, and took two tons of rice along with the post's radios, guns, and ammunition.[53]

The attack on Hòa Mỹ was both strategic—demonstrating the PLAF's capacity to strike in the hills—and symbolic. The first Việt Minh tactical zone established in 1946, after 1954 Hòa Mỹ had become one of Cẩn's pet development projects. Both sides understood the historical and tactical significance of Hòa Mỹ as a gateway into the highlands, and the PLAF's destruction of the camp, turning it to ruins again, sent an important message to the population. Cẩn had sent loyal Cần Lao operatives to manage the settlement and defended it with two platoons of paramilitaries. As a development site close to Huế, Hòa Mỹ attracted more official and foreign visitors than the mountain sites. Greater foreign attention resulted in richer stocks of rice, medicine, tractors, and especially guns.

This string of NLF victories in early 1963 was followed by waves of RVN political reprisals that produced a firestorm of media attention on Diệm's government and Kennedy's "special war" at home in the United States. In Huế on May 8, 1963, the army and police fired live ammunition into a crowd of Buddhist protesters, killing nine, including two children who were crushed under armored personnel carriers. The Buddhist Crisis escalated that summer when a monk from Huế, Thích Quảng Đức, immolated himself in protest in a Sài Gòn street intersection. From June until the army coup that eliminated the Ngô brothers on November 2, the American consul in Huế, John

Helble, provided Washington with regular updates on protests and police actions on the streets of Huế. The old imperial city on the narrow coast, just sixty kilometers south of the DMZ, became a focal point for global concerns about an escalating war.

Cẩn's final day in Huế on November 5, 1963, marked a surprising reversal to the homegrown authority he built in the shadows of an American- and Sài Gòn–driven buildup of military and civilian aid. After years of avoiding direct contact with Americans and other foreigners in Huế, Cẩn sought safe passage via American aircraft and the State Department. He showed up at the consulate in the back of an old Citroën, lying on the floor while a man dressed as a priest drove. Consul Helble cabled Washington for instructions and asked Cẩn where he would like to go for asylum. Cẩn replied, "Tokyo." A few hours later, Helble together with a CIA officer and American military advisers drove in a convoy to Phú Bài airport, where a CIA-owned C-46 landed and picked Cẩn up without incident. The plane whisked Cẩn off to Sài Gòn's Tân Sơn Nhất Airport, where the Vietnamese military intercepted the plane, dismissed Helble, and took Cẩn into custody.[54] The postcoup government tried him in April 1964 and executed him in Huế on May 9, one year and a day after the RVN troops in Huế had fired on Buddhist protesters.

A NEW WAR BEGINS

The deaths of Diệm and Nhu and the arrest of Cẩn marked an important turning point not only for RVN-US relations but also for the NLF and North Vietnam's position in the war. At the ninth meeting of the central committee in Hà Nội in December 1963, the party formally committed the material and personnel of the People's Army of Vietnam to support NLF operations south of the DMZ. By early 1964 PAVN soldiers openly participated in combat operations against RVN troops, threatening the ARVN posts at Nam Đông and A Lưới.

Although most American histories of the Vietnam War begin with an alleged North Vietnamese torpedo boat attack on US navy ships in the Tonkin Gulf in August, in Huế a real battle involving PAVN troops and the killing of US soldiers began one month earlier at Nam Đông. Soldiers in two PAVN divisions fought with PLAF units to wage a concerted series of attacks on the mountain bases and along Highway 1. Consul Helble in Huế was one of the few Americans who reported this act of war to Washington, and for unknown reasons senior American diplomats and military commanders buried the story. Helble was celebrating his farewell party at the consulate on July 2 after completing a long tour as Huế's American consul. During the party in his villa, a courier notified the ARVN's First Division general that PAVN and PLAF forces had blown over forty bridges on Highway 1 and were attacking the ARVN military post on the highway just seventeen kilometers north of Huế. Two captured soldiers wore PAVN unit insignia, and they confessed that their battalion-sized force (six hundred men) had camped and trained with PLAF units for ninety days in the A Sầu Valley before commencing the attacks. Helble cabled this news to Washington, as it constituted a direct attack by North Vietnamese soldiers across the DMZ on Americans. William Westmoreland, a new American commander at a rapidly expanding headquarters for the Military Assistance Command Vietnam (MACV) in Sài Gòn, discounted Helble's report and denied PAVN involvement.[55] The combined attacks that summer marked Hà Nội's decision to wage all-out war in the south, and this concerted uprising (đồng khởi) focused on demolishing the RVN's strategic hamlets and, if possible, overrunning the mountain bases supported by US Special Forces.[56]

Regardless of Westmoreland's political maneuvers with Washington, for the American soldiers camped at Nam Đông war began decisively on July 6, 1964, when the PLAF 802nd Battalion supported by PAVN troops attacked the American special forces A-team there. Approximately nine hundred communist troops attacked the special forces camp with artillery and human wave assaults just after midnight. Twelve Americans served in the A-team with a protection detail of sixty Nung ethnic minority soldiers, highlander mercenaries who fought with French troops near the mountainous Chinese border before 1954. Outside the American camp was a base with over three hundred ARVN troops. Anthropologist Gerald Hickey, one of the only Americans to have studied the Katu, happened to be at the camp the day before to interview local Katu residents. He describes the American group's defense in a chapter titled "Victory at Nam Dong" in his memoir, *Window on a War*. Roughly one hundred of the ARVN troops secretly supported the NLF and attacked sleeping comrades to reduce the defenses while opening a hole in the base perimeter for the attacking NLF battalion. The Americans, Nungs, and remaining ARVN soldiers emptied their arsenal on the attackers, holding the offensive off until morning when American planes arrived from Đà Nẵng. The grisly scene that morning included over one hundred ARVN soldiers dead, sixty PLAF dead, several American soldiers dead, and one Australian soldier dead. Marine helicopters transported scores of wounded combatants and civilians to hospitals in Đà Nẵng.[57]

RUINATION

In a period that most political histories of the Vietnam War describe as either a peaceful interlude or a time of competing nation building, the view from the ground in Thừa Thiên–Huế was more one of violently targeted ruination. Physical vestiges of the French–Việt Minh war, the Nine Bunkers and the former tactical zones, became focal spaces for new military activity. In the hands of Cẩn's secret police, the Nine Bunkers were reborn as a space for torture, and the former "cradles of the revolution" were reborn as model settlements ruled by Cần Lao party loyalists and military authorities.

In sites such as Hòa Mỹ and Nam Đông, the outward appearances of constructive activity—building refugee camps and roads—masked a targeted form of annihilation by replacement. Through paramilitaries and the Cần Lao, Cẩn worked hard to destroy traditional village relationships, dissolving forms of communal autonomy that had survived since colonial rule. Whether through police sweeps or by surrounding a village with barricades, these actions brought violence and corruption into village life, as the government encouraged children to report on parents and neighbors to act against each other. Finally, the combined PAVN-PLAF assaults on Hòa Mỹ and Nam Đông in 1964 marked a retaliatory form of ruination, largely destroying what ARVN troops and American funds had built.

Evacuated Việt Minh camps and evacuated French bases became signposts for what was, from 1954 to 1964, a most violent period. Cẩn drew globally from such groups as the brownshirts of Nazi Germany to give a logic to his program of destruction. His followers understood the deeper colonial and communist contours of the landscape. Into this deeply inscribed, militarized space littered with physical and political wreckage came American soldiers and an American military intent on socially and physically reengineering the landscape yet again.

FIVE

CREATIVE DESTRUCTION

AMERICAN MILITARY INTERVENTION AFTER 1964 WAS MARKED NOT
only by unprecedented destruction but also by extraordinary construction.
Lt. Gen. Carroll H. Dunn, in charge of US military base construction in 1972,
remarked:

> In February 1966, the Directorate of Construction was established in the Mil-
> itary Assistance Command, Vietnam, to provide centralized management of
> the U.S. program. . . . Embracing ports, airfields, storage areas, ammunition
> dumps, housing, bridges, roads and other conventional facilities, the con-
> struction program was probably the largest concentrated effort of its kind in
> history.[1]

Contrasted with the Americans' urban sprawl, too, were the persistent constructive efforts of NLF and People's Army supporters to maintain critical
bunkers and shelters despite unimaginable waves of bombing. Trần Mai
Nam, a North Vietnamese journalist traveling through the hills above Huế
in 1967, recalled:

> But soon my eyes are drawn to some precise points on this picture. Little
> houses scattered among the bomb craters. . . . For a quarter of a century, bombs
> and bullets have not stopped raining on this narrow strip of land. . . . Those
> mud and straw houses, so tiny, breathe an indomitable courage like those
> fighters who keep themselves going on wild plants, go barefoot. . . . On my

left lie the ruins of an enemy outpost destroyed by the P.L.A.F. On my right, a long trail of denuded nothing running up into the mountains, indicating the run of B-52s. . . . This was where the B-52s made their first raid on the Tri-Thien area. Before the bombing, the enemy dropped millions of leaflets over the area, carrying a photograph of these planes and information about their formidable cargoes of death.[2]

Working out of landscapes defined by earlier layers of military construction and destruction, American and Vietnamese combatants escalated their efforts after 1965. The American base-building effort to 1972 turned older bases and airstrips into base cities with round-the-clock air traffic and tens of thousands of American troops. Meanwhile in the hills thousands of NLF and North Vietnamese volunteers operated thick networks of trails crossing high mountains with trucks, diesel fuel pipelines, and ammunition bunkers. Matched with these duel constructive efforts were unprecedented acts of violence. The B-52 strikes noted by Trần Mai Nam brought a destructive capacity several orders of magnitude greater than bombing during the French war. Besides saturation bombing, Americans introduced new ecologically destructive technologies such as chemical defoliants and mass drops of napalm that had devastating effects on both natural and built environments.

While levels of construction and destruction were unprecedented, the logics behind these new landscape constructions followed older patterns. Communist forces returned to original strategic zones such as Hòa Mỹ despite repeated American and RVN attempts to clear the area. The former tactical zones reemerged as critical gateways. While the American constructive presence, especially its sprawling bases, transformed horizons on the coast with radio towers, jets, and row upon row of barracks, for communists the many small shacks dotting the bomb-cratered hills held an equally important symbolic value. B-52 strikes in the area in 1966 produced lines of craters visible from space, but the underlying logic of this space—the gateway function of the strategic zones and the concentration of foreign troops along Highway 1—had not changed much since 1947.

In some senses, the American struggle to escape this historical spatial logic, a contest between the coastal highway and the highland forests, led war advocates to propose ramping up the intensity of bombing and destruction. Harvard political theorist Samuel Huntington, in a famous essay supporting the American war effort, even revisited the old notion of "creative destruction" as articulated by Werner Sombart in *Krieg und Kapitalism* (1913) and Joseph Schumpeter in *Capitalism, Socialism and Democracy* (1942). Huntington noted, as did Sombart, that the intensive bombing was slowly turning South Vietnam into an urban nation. Refugees from the mountainous conflict areas flooded into cities such as Saigon and Danang while other new villes popped up around bases at Nha Trang, Pleiku, Buôn Ma Thuột, Kon Tum, Chu Lai, and Quy Nhơn.[3] After three years of base-building and strategic bombing, Huntington noted that South Vietnam had a greater precentage of its population living in urban areas than Sweden, Canada, and all of Southeast Asia except Singapore. Most of the surge, of course, was due to war refugees living in slums, but Huntington nevertheless seized on it and drew wide attention in the United States. Possibly this was a means of escaping Vietnam's history and its landscapes.

Huntington wrote: "The effective response [to national liberation movements] lies neither in the quest for conventional military victory nor in the esoteric doctrines and gimmicks of counter-insurgency warfare. It is instead forced-draft urbanization and modernization which rapidly brings the country in question out of the phase in which a rural revolutionary movement can hope to generate sufficient strength to come to power."[4] Aside from the moral problems inherent in this deadly means of encouraging urban development, Huntington's thesis also failed to appreciate a key feature of the NLF's revolutionary movement. It, too, was focused on an urban and industrial future. While communist networks lacked the concrete-hardened edges of airport runways, docks, and bunkers, their vision for Vietnam was an urban, socialist one built out of cities. While political cadres stressed smashing feudalism and imperialism in villages and the cities, they did not advocate physically smashing the villages and cities. Destroying physical landscapes, as NLF forces learned in their 1968 Tết Offensive in Huế, threatened to unravel popular support that was vital to sustaining their cause. Villages, cities, and even the mountain bases were not just temporary communities to be evacuated after the conflict. To carry out a socialist revolution, party leaders understood that historic landscapes were important as platforms for "cultivating" new followers and launching new construction out of the old.

This chapter follows the spatial tensions dividing American, ARVN, and communist logics of landscape as Americans brought new technology, especially aerial technology, to float above the layered surfaces below. It begins with the Americans' amphibious entry, on the coast, of US Marines in 1965 and then traces Vietnamese responses to the fighting, especially protests and fighting on the streets of Huế. Rather than following central political maneuvers and military decision making in Sài Gòn or Hà Nội, it focuses on the landscapes of the central coast and what engagements in those spaces meant for evolving, global debates over creative destruction in Vietnam.

AERIAL VISIBILITY

From the first days in 1943 when Army Air Force planes began their flights over Indochina, one of the biggest challenges facing Americans in Vietnam was literally seeing the land surface below. Especially in the higlands, dense forests and cloud cover obscured it. When American aid officials attempted to reach many towns in 1950, they found roads in disrepair and runways too short to land DC-3s. After 1954 much of the civilian aid given to the Republic of Vietnam went into the construction of runways and the installation of navigational equipment. After the ARVN's attempted coup in 1960 and the formation of the National Liberation Front, American aid for airbases went into overdrive. The airbase and depots at Phú Bài mushroomed into a web of roads and compounds, plus a runway long enough for jets. American aid paid for construction of an aerial platform allowing increased surveillance, faster troop transports, and a workaround for the friction of terrain. In the early days of the United States' expansion after 1960, new airstrips popped up like small islands carved into the hills beside ARVN outposts.

At Nam Đông and the A Sầu Valley, new airfields became a vital link for keeping the bases supplied in the event of attack. By late 1961 the dirt runways and helipads became the bases' primary link to Huế as PLAF forces cut the roads. American covert aid concentrated on a string of three bases in A Sầu as ARVN teams bulldozed an all-weather road along the valley floor (plate 3).[5] Seeing these bases from above with the sea in the background revealed their closeness to the coast. At eleven thousand feet, the A Sầu Valley was but a ten-minute flight from Phú Bài (figure 5.1). However, besides the friction of difficult terrain limiting movement on the ground, dense cloud cover for much of the year obscured aerial views and made landings treacherous (figure 5.2). Forests straddling the mountainous Vietnam-Laos border were almost always shrouded in low clouds.

FIGURE 5.1. Oblique view of A Shau airfield, November 1961. Source: Frame 08, Mission J5921, ON#69611, Record Group 373, US National Archives and Records Administration, College Park.

The American drive to see wider areas on both sides of the DMZ, in Laos and in neighboring China led to technological advances in several aspects of aerial surveillance, especially high-altitude aerial photography. Views from eleven thousand feet produced a sense of proximity between mountains and sea, while views from seventy thousand feet showed proximity to Chinese bases on Hainan Island as well as PAVN camps in the north. Just days before he left office in 1961, President Dwight D. Eisenhower established the National

FIGURE 5.2. Close-up of A Shau, 1961. Source: Frame 11, Mission J5921, ON#69611, Record Group 373, US National Archives and Records Administration, College Park.

Photographic Interpretation Center as a clearinghouse where several thousand photo interpreters, working for intelligence services and the military, pored over newly snapped images of central Vietnam to assess the military assets of communist forces. This new photographic effort was part of a broader American campaign to innovate high-altitude spy planes and satellite photography to monitor Cold War adversaries. Concerns over activity on the trails in Laos drew some of the first high-altitude spy missions using the new U-2 aircraft. Figure 5.3 shows the winding path of one U-2A plane at seventy thousand feet as it photographed the DMZ and Chinese military bases on southern Hainan Island.

From 1961 until the end of the war, this unending stream of high-altitude spy photography over Vietnam became a staple of presidential briefings on the "Vietnam situation." Year after year, the photography and interpretive reports of the National Photographic Interpretation Center improved, shaping US policy and reliance on this aerial perspective. The center produced a series of photographic intelligence reports focused on road building in the Laos panhandle with excerpted images from U-2s and other aircraft outlining

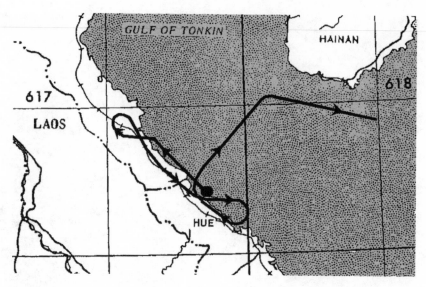

FIGURE 5.3. Path of U-2 Mission G 3018. Source: CIA Photographic Intelligence Center. "Mission G 3018 3 January 1961," Document CIA-RDP02T06408R0003000 10004-3, US National Archives and Records Administration, College Park.

PAVN rest areas and bivouacs. The American desire to view Vietnam from high altitude even figured into the space race programs as the United States launched a series of keyhole photographic satellites, codenamed CORONA, under the cover of its civilian Discovery program. By 1965 these satellites, carrying twin cameras, produced high-resolution black and white prints covering long segments (keyholes) of territory roughly thirty kilometers wide and 240 kilometers long.[6]

All of this photographic imagery, however, could not cut through the clouds, foliage, tunnels, and camouflage hiding much of the PLAF and PAVN infrastructure below. The Americans' need to see through dense layers of vegetation brought one of the most controversial aerial technologies, herbicide spraying, in an attempt to physically modify the landscape to suit the aerial perspective. From the first tests of herbicides in 1961, senior policymakers including John F. Kennedy and Ngô Đình Diệm themselves acknowledged the legal and ethical challenges of such a tactic.[7] Considering the growing network of villages and upland strategic areas under communist control as well as concern about communist gains around key cities such as Huế, the US Department of Defense along with its RVN counterpart viewed the use of herbicides for clearing rights of way as a top priority for securing roads and exposing communist base areas to aerial surveillance. A secret US history of the herbicide program noted President Kennedy's particular concerns about the international political optics of this program. At a September 25, 1962, meeting with the RVN's secretary of state, Kennedy replied to RVN requests for immediate crop destruction in the highlands with the following two concerns: "First that the GVN could differentiate between Viet Cong crops and Montagnard crops and secondly, that the usefulness of such an exercise would outweigh the propaganda effect of communist accusations that the US was indulging in food warfare."[8] Americans understood the propaganda downside to this tactic, but their aerial bias led them to downplay the spillover effects of destroying crops. The very notion that a reconnaissance officer in a spotter plane might be able to differentiate which crops went to Montagnards and which to communist soldiers ignored what was then common knowledge about the communist reliance on swidden crops.

The American decision in 1963 to start spraying highland crops signaled an abrupt shift from clearing lines of communication and base perimeters to a direct attack on the communist trail network. A joint US-RVN team targeted three hundred hectares of crops in the southern tip of the A Sầu Valley for crop destruction on February 16, 1963. After delays from bad weather and the observance of the Tết holiday, a chemical crew in an H-34 helicopter marked with the gold- and red-striped flag of the RVN took off from Đà Nẵng. This southern end of the valley marked a key junction where the Hồ Chí Minh Trail in Laos met paths running east toward Nam Đông and the coast. The first five flights carried an arsenical herbicide (later known as Agent Blue) used for killing rice. The last two flights carried Agent Purple, a precursor to Agent Orange with the same dioxin-tainted herbicide, 2,4,5-T. It attacked woody vegetation and broadleaf crops such as cassava. Flying the slow-moving helicopter near the ground exposed the crew to ground fire, and the crew aborted most of the runs. Helicopter pilots also contended with steep terrain, radarless navigation, and rapidly changing weather conditions. After one week they had sprayed just fifteen hectares.[9]

While these spray missions had little if any effect on the fighting in the A Sầu Valley, they added potent fodder for antiwar activists and galvanized the prowar camp in Hà Nội. Local NLF leaders in the valley decried the "poisonous sprays" dropped by the "US-puppet regime." General Võ Nguyễn Giáp, commander of the People's Army, drew on this new phase in the spray missions to accuse the United States of engaging in chemical warfare and violating the 1925 Geneva Protocol. He brought a formal complaint to the International Control Commission that the spray missions in A Sầu violated two articles of the 1954 Geneva Accords too. While the RVN government produced radio broadcasts and newspaper articles explaining that the herbicides were not poisonous to humans, DRV and NLF "Liberation Radio" programs amplified their charges. On June 6 the DRV ran a radio program likening the sprayings to the Nazi gas chambers used in the Holocaust.[10]

As communist forces expanded their networks in the A Sầu Valley in 1964–65, this new chemical approach held limited positive benefits while exposing new ecological challenges. MACV initiated a series of intensive spray operations in late 1965 and early 1966 in a last-ditch effort to secure the badly embattled special forces bases in the highland valley. PAVN and PLAF forces continued to expand their own posts on the slopes fringing the valley floor, and they cut off travel by road to Huế. MACV sent thousands of gallons of Agent Orange to the base perimeters via C-123 cargo planes outfitted with sprayers on the wings. This new spray aircraft delivered a two-hundred-meter-wide path of herbicides over a distance of six kilometers. The planes filled their tanks at Đà Nẵng, sprayed in circles around the airstrips, then returned for more runs (plate 4). Because Agent Orange was an herbicide that killed broadleaf vegetation but not grasses, it destroyed woody brush but then opened the valley to fast-growing grasses and reeds that thrived in the heavy rainfall and open sun. One of the most pernicious grasses was an invasive that hitchiked from American bases in Guam: elephant grass (*Pennisetum purpureum*). This grass, along with species of cane and the food crop sorghum, thrived in the defoliated perimeters of the bases, producing a two-meter-tall savannah. Communist troops adapted to the grass, forging new paths and adding new camouflage.[11]

In addition to advancing new forms of high-altitude photography and aerially sprayed herbicides, American forces also brought new radio technologies for communications and war. Built into the expanded base facilities at Phú Bài in 1962 was a state-of-the-art radio-listening post operated by the US Army Security Agency's Eighth Radio Research Unit (RRU). Managed by the National Security Agency and operating until the end of the US military's encampment, the Eighth RRU was one of the most heavily defended sites in the province. Surrounded by networks of trenches encircled by minefields, it enabled long-distance secret communications and supported a novel radio detection program designed to "peer through" mountain foliage to locate PLAF and PAVN radio transmissions.[12]

The Phú Bài station was part of a top-secret network of electronic listening stations that US intelligence agencies had operated across mainland Southeast Asia since 1961. Airborne radio direction finding (ARDF) had become an important feature in electronic warfare since World War II, and technological innovations accelerated rapidly during the Cold War. An ARDF hit, for example, led ARVN forces and their US advisers into the disastrous Battle of Ấp Bắc on January 2, 1963. As the war expanded in 1963, so did the RRU facilities. One NSA analyst at the Eighth RRU in Phú Bài later broke the NSA's code of secrecy and told journalists that he and hundreds of other NSA and military communications specialists worked at these stations, triangulating signals and calling in airstrikes.[13]

After the 1963 coup toppled Diệm and brought in a ruling junta of ARVN generals, the US MACV moved quickly to expand radio operations from the secret RRUs to more public broadcasting including one American staple of the Cold War, the Voice of America (VOA). The stretch of highway between Huế and the bases at Phú Bài turned into a frontier for American and South Vietnamese broadcasting. On May 12, 1964, US Ambassador Henry Cabot Lodge requested that the junta's leader at the time, General Nguyễn Khánh, locate a parcel near that stretch of highway for the United States to install radio antennas for VOA. With a US consulate in Huế and the RRU facility at Phú Bài, this was the ideal location for a forward transmitter to send American radio programs into communist-controlled areas. Because of this highly symbolic land use, implanting the "voices" of America in Vietnam's airwaves while taking valuable village fields, General Khánh personally signed the decree awarding the land just five days after the passage of the Tonkin Gulf Resolution.[14] Compared with the Diệm era, when Ngô Đình Cẩn would have stringently opposed such a move, the ARVN generals ensured a speedy transfer.[15]

While the expansion of these American radio transmitters and the research units reflected American concerns over airspace in Vietnam, the creation of radio broadcasting facilities opened up new opportunities for Vietnamese voices as well. Just south of the new VOA antennas on Highway 1, US engineers refurbished the transmitter and towers for Radio Huế (Đài Phát Thanh Huế). Radio Huế, like the VOA, broadcast a variety of Western and Vietnamese pop music as well as "Voice of Freedom" programs aimed at listeners in "controlled" and "liberated" areas.[16] Linked to Radio Huế's studio in the European quarter of Huế, the radio station would become an important protest tool when Buddhist and student demonstrators took over the studio in 1966.

AMPHIBIOUS LANDINGS

All of this aerial activity, however, could not alleviate the worsening situation for the RVN in mid-1964. While visual evidence confirmed the expanding construction of communist trail networks in the hills, photography could not halt them without commitments to large-scale bombing. The gains of PLAF and PAVN troops, especially in the A Sầu Valley in 1964, triggered rapid American responses to prevent what by July looked to be a dire situation. Nine months after Diệm's assassination, communist forces had regained control over most of former Interzone IV. American special forces units and ARVN soldiers struggled to retain the camps at Nam Đông and A Lưới and required constant helicopter support. After communist soldiers destroyed the US base at Nam Đông, the Tonkin Gulf Incident in August 1964 provided the US president with a pretext to order bombing in North Vietnam while escalating military actions in the south.

The subsequent American move to rapidly escalate the air war in February 1965 did, according to local sources, check the advances of northern troops via bombing north of the DMZ. However, it did little to prevent over ten thousand PAVN soldiers already south of the DMZ from operating. These men and women came primarily from two PAVN divisions, the 324th and 325th, comprised mostly of natives from the central coast. ARVN military commanders—most of them also native sons—wrote sobering reports that a "sea change" was continuing in the countryside despite the bombing. The bombing had little effect on the PAVN and NLF battalions active in the hills west of Quảng Trị, Huế, and Đà Nẵng.[17] They had built bunkers, new tunnels, and defensive positions around the A Sầu Valley and along the trails in Laos. After the assaults in July 1964, PLAF forces took back the agricultural development centers at Hòa Mỹ and Nam Đông. The next summer, in 1965, they moved downhill from one settlement to the next, taking over villages and even crossing Highway 1 in several coastal areas. One evening, several squads even returned to the strategic hamlet Thanh Thủy Chánh just outside Huế and razed the bamboo palisades.[18]

Recalling Huntington's comments about American bombing and "forced-draft urbanization," the South Vietnamese commander provided a sobering corrective. Cities alone would not save South Vietnam. Without the countryside, the new urbanites would starve. Furthermore, communist military operations suggested that after surrounding the cities they would not stop. These ground truths, the necessity of food and access to fields, brought RVN and US leaders to an understanding that US soldiers would be needed to protect the air bases and reclaim the urban fringes to prevent an impending invasion.

The American ground war in Vietnam began on the central coast on March 8, 1965, when two battalions of the US Ninth Marine Expeditionary Brigade landed on the beach near Đà Nẵng. Their first mission was to secure the perimeters of the American base complex there. A month later two more battalions arrived and were airlifted by helicopter to Huế–Phú Bài. Given concerns about local responses to foreign troops, the military government in Sài Gòn limited the American troops to small tactical areas of responsibility (TAORs) around each base. The TAOR in Đà Nẵng consisted of two hills west of the airbase and at Phú Bài the bare land across the highway from the airport. The marines moved a larger force from Okinawa to Vietnam in late April 1965 to expand a third base for fighter jets at Chu Lai, then described as an "uncultivated waste" on the beach seventy-five kilometers south of Đà Nẵng.[19]

Even with these first landings, American military commanders were highly aware of the symbolic significance of a mission that they envisioned as different from the "expeditionary" missions of French soldiers. They even changed their name to reflect this aim. A marine history of the landings noted: "on 7 May 1965, III Marine Expeditionary Force was redesignated III Marine Amphibious Force (III MAF) for political reasons. The word, expeditionary, smacked too much of the gunboat imperialism of a bygone era and had been used by the French forces which entered Vietnam at the end of the Second World War."[20] This relatively small detail points to a deeper problem for US ground forces in Vietnam, embedding in a landscape long defined by foreign military occupations.

The marines' mission was amphibious not just in the traditional sea-to-land sense but also in terms of their mixed military-civil presence in old villages such as Phù Bài. Their tactical area overlapped with the outer hamlets of Phù Bài Village (figure 5.4). As a protective force for the airbase, the marines also engaged in civilian duties termed "civic action." Civic action, military

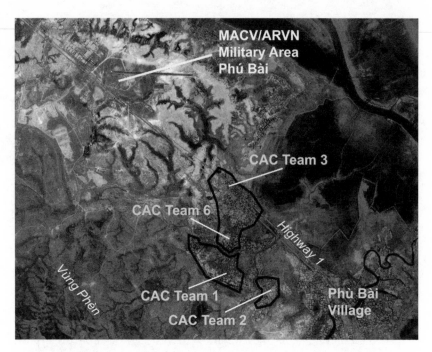

FIGURE 5.4. TAOR for combined action companies at Phú Bài, 1965. Source: Russel H. Stolfi, *U.S. Marine Corps Civic Action Efforts in Vietnam, March 1965– March 1966* (Washington, DC: Headquarters US Marine Corps, 1968), 2b. Base image derived from a composite of a 1963 aerial photograph showing the base area and a 1968 CORONA satellite image showing the larger surroundings including Phù Bài Village and the hills. 1963 image: Mission F4634A, ON#69708, Record Group 373, US National Archives and Records Administration, College Park; 1968 image: CORONA Frame DS1050-1006DF129, courtesy of US Geological Survey Earth Resources Observation and Science Center. Composite image by author.

leaders proposed, would distinguish the American military occupation from earlier armies as the "amphibious" name change suggested. Communist propaganda already labeled the Americans as invaders (*kẻ xâm lược*), linking them with earlier French, Japanese, Chinese, and Mongol invaders. In contrast, revolutionary campaigns were described as the "resistance" (*kháng chiến*) or the "national resistance against foreign invaders" (*toàn quốc kháng chiến chống ngoại xâm*).

The marine mission was also amphibious in the sense that American soldiers integrated their operations with South Vietnamese troops. This was a conscious effort to break with the Japanese and French forces that segregated themselves in the 1940s. From mid-1965 this image of American and Vietnamese soldiers working side by side in local civic and military affairs circulated widely in American media. The marines called this integrated fighting unit a combined action company, later a combined action platoon (CAP). Four of these integrated teams assembled as a company in Phú Bài in mid-1965, and a former US Special Forces adviser, First Lieutenant Paul Ek, headed them. Following the model of special forces advisers in the highlands, Ek sought to "blend" his teams in everyday life. He took an intensive course in Vietnamese at Okinawa and gave his teams a two-week course on Vietnamese customs and the unique nature of their combined mission before they arrived at Phú Bài.[21] In an interview he stressed the importance of this strategy of embedding in the village landscape: "We tried to get the people to accept us as members of the community. The Marines' training was geared to teach them as much as we could about Vietnam and the Vietnamese people so that they could actually live with them in a close relationship, not as an occupational force but as members of that village . . . at the same time carrying out their primary mission of a military capability."

Becoming "members of the community," however, was both difficult to imagine and dangerous to carry out. The marines spent much of their energy bouncing back and forth between military and nonmilitary activities: policing checkpoints, providing free medical care, setting up ambushes, repairing roads, interrogating prisoners, and teaching English. Some in the US military championed this blended approach to counterinsurgency, but many others criticized it for forcing soldiers trained in military boot camps to place themselves in situations for which they'd received little training.[22] The Americans also had little sense of the history of their Vietnamese allies in the village. Many of the Popular Force paramilitaries came from families who had affiliated with the Cần Lao just a few years earlier. Their bid to win over Việt Cộng sympathizers was often undermined by allies who had a reputation for past violence.

While the Americans in the CAPs lacked a deep knowledge of the village's history or the personal histories of their local allies, from time to time their detective work revealed glimpses of the underground networks moving food, supplies, and people from village markets into the hills. For instance, they observed that older women tended to smuggle rice. An extreme drought in summer 1965 forced the NLF to seek additional rice in lowland village markets, providing cash for women to buy it at the markets. These older women acted as mules, buying rice in quantities slightly larger than permitted and delivering the surplus to underground caches. Since the French war, the RVN had placed strict limits on amounts of rice that villagers could store in their homes or buy at the market. The CAPs and the Popular Forces recorded patterns of activity that appeared unusual, identifying individuals where possible. When Lieutenant Ek and his Vietnamese counterpart detained several women, they admitted right away to working as food carriers for the NLF. The CAP interrogators then attempted to recruit them as double agents, but only one woman turned, revealing the location of several rice caches. The other women endured the detentions and weeks later were caught buying rice again.[23]

A story that played well with American audiences at home, American policymakers repeatedly highlighted these CAP success stories to boost support for their rapidly expanding, conventional buildup. Civic action success offset the bad news coming in via secret channels from the highlands. The CAPs, especially the teams at Phù Bài Village, reinforced the arguments of MACV commander General Westmoreland asking Congress for more combined activity together with funds to carry out strategic bombing on PAVN troops in the highlands. Marine commanders advertised CAP operations as "little victories" in press reports that were republished in the 1966 US Senate spending bill for the war. The US$4.7 billion appropriations bill supported an increase in ground troops to over four hundred thousand persons and included funds for building new ports, roads, and base facilities. In the middle of floor debate about troop numbers and the enormous costs, military experts mentioned a report titled "Phu Bai: Model of Counterinsurgency" that emphasized the blended approach.[24] The article downplayed the military aspects of CAP work and instead emphasized their socially constructive aims:

> Civic action is conducted at all levels, from an individual marine teaching
> a child to read, all the way up the scale to the use of large units on projects
> which are national in scope. An example of a really large project would be the
> development of the Ohio River Valley by U.S. Army Corps of Engineers. The
> extensive road net built by the Roman legions in the time of the Caesars is
> another . . . civic action is taken at every level and, in a campaign of the sort
> we're conducting in Vietnam, it's often those individual or group local proj-
> ects which pay the biggest dividends.[25]

The strange reference to Roman legions hints at the imperial scale of this building project for what was to be an occupation army. Roman roads may have been durable, the ancient world's autobahns, but first and foremost they conveyed Roman armies. Juxtaposed against the obvious windfall that the bill brought to American construction and engineering firms, the "success stories" from villages like Phù Bài were targeted at winning support from skeptical senators who were more interested in President Lyndon Johnson's domestic War on Poverty. The Senate nonetheless passed the spending bill, voting 93–2 in favor.

What the civic action reports did not emphasize, however, was the intensely dangerous nature of this work for foreign soldiers attempting to embed in the ancient landscape. Village inhabitants, by contrast, had been forced to adapt to several decades of police sweeps, detentions, and military actions. In many cases, persons who appeared least likely to carry out violent attacks—seniors and young women—became the most dangerous. Women often had an easier time crossing checkpoints and patrols, and some volunteered to carry out suicide attacks. While military-age men in the villages often left to avoid detention or conscription into the ARVN, women stayed behind, procuring supplies and providing the NLF with intelligence. While American reports highlighted the CAPs' successful ambushes and detective work, party histories emphasize NLF successes. On one occasion, an NLF commando force attacked a CAP team in its residence on Highway 1 at Dạ Lê Village. A month later two women from Dạ Lê Village smuggled antipersonnel mines inside their bags and detonated them in an infirmary where Americans were receiving treatment, killing several US soldiers and an American nurse.[26]

WAR IN THE HIGHLANDS

While Americans attempted to eliminate the NLF's political infrastructure in coastal villages, combined PAVN-PLAF units focused a series of attacks on US-ARVN bases in the highlands, including a successful defeat of the A Shau Special Forces Base on March 9 and 10, 1966.[27] In their spatial and environmental logics, the communist attacks on American bases in the hills were mirrors of the American operations in the lowland villages. Where Americans struggled to move from an aerial perspective to one grounded in the daily movements of people in village markets and on the roads, the communist forces attempted to use force on the ground to destroy the Americans' aerial platform.

Compared with the Americans' "success story" in Phù Bài Village, communist forces pointed to their "success story" in the devastating assault on A Shau. A vicious battle that left several hundred dead and wounded, it demonstrated how after years of trail construction and with material support from China and the Soviet Union, communist ground networks could severely limit the Americans' aerial platform.

At A Shau in the winter of 1966, communist forces used a thick layer of low clouds hanging over the valley to conceal their early preparations for the assault. They opened the attack with 80-mm guns planted on the mountain slopes with views of the base below the cloud line and views of incoming aircraft above the clouds. Among the first targets of their assault was the radio communications hut on the base. The first strikes commenced at 3:50 A.M., instantly cutting radio links to Phú Bài and Đà Nẵng. Only after four hours of artillery barrages did US soldiers reestablish a radio contact and call for air support. However, when the bombers and gunships arrived, they could not see PAVN troops through the clouds, and batteries of anti-aircraft guns in the hills began shooting *down* at American planes from the ridgeline. An AC-47 Spooky, a DC-3 plane with heavy guns mounted on one side, circled over the camp to provide covering fire, but 80-mm guns destroyed it. American cargo planes attempted to drop ammunition and rations inside the embattled camp, but they dropped many supplies in areas already overrun. ARVN and US Marine transport helicopters attempted to land and effect a rescue, but several were attacked with heavy fire and destroyed. At sundown, PAVN-PLAF forces launched a new attack on the base with 75-mm recoilless rifles, reducing many buildings to rubble.

The following day, PAVN-PLAF infantry commenced a ground assault, moving through dense thickets of elephant grass that concealed their movements. Because the grass had rapidly spread around the defoliated perimeter, covering a belt of landmines, ARVN troops would not move out into the grass to engage the communist troops. On the evening of the second day, communist forces overran the base. Of 434 persons in the camp—US special forces, Nung guards, ARVN soldiers, interpreters, and civilians—248 went missing while 172 were confirmed killed. What the after-action report described as "the disaster at A Shau" was not an isolated incident either. Across the highlands, mixed PAVN-PLAF forces engaged in similar large-unit offensives. The surviving Americans fled the base and their dead comrades on March 10. Only two months later on a dry, cloudless day in May did a detachment of soldiers from Đà Nẵng bring nine helicopters to the grisly scene at A Shau to bury the dead. They found twenty-four Vietnamese bodies and only one American. They collected information on the Vietnamese bodies and buried them on-site; then they lifted the lone American body in a body bag and flew it to Đà Nẵng for the journey home. Investigators suspected more bodies were concealed in the thick elephant grass covering the destroyed perimeter of the cratered airstrip, but they feared attack from communist snipers or inadvertently setting off landmines.[28]

While there are no communist after-action reports available, one captured document from Nguyễn Đức Bống, a platoon leader in the PAVN 325A Regiment suggests that these offensives took a devastating toll on communist troops too. Bống's notebook detailed a blacklist of individuals who criticized the wisdom of the attack on A Shau after a large percentage of men died, especially in the second wave of assaults through the grass. The notebook recorded personal details of the troops killed, destined to inform families at home. The platoon commander recommended measures to "purify the unit politically," too, sending soldiers who were too shell-shocked to fight to perform support duties.[29] However, neither the notebook nor the soldiers reached their destinations. An American infantry unit destroyed the platoon when they assaulted another mountain base later that summer.

BOMBING THE HILLS, MOVING SOLDIERS BY AIR

Such bitter encounters with PAVN-PLAF forces in the highlands in 1965–66 produced a sobering realization among American policymakers at home. They could not win the war in the mountains with air support alone; instead, they approved an increase of several hundred thousand American ground troops along with assault helicopters and high-altitude bombers. General Westmoreland drastically expanded aerial attack capabilities, advancing what would become a signature feature of the war, helicopter-borne "air cavalry" offensives. Considering the three elevational zones of the central coast, this air cavalry approach signaled a new effort not just to dominate the air above fighting zones in the hills but to quickly ferry hundreds of soldiers by helicopter to the fighting. Additional marine and army units arrived on the coast in mid-1966 to fill out these operations, expanding camps along Highway 1 and outside the air bases. They mounted helicopter-borne search-and-destroy missions into the coastal hills, often clearing lone huts and attacking lone individuals caught in these areas. To seal off the hills, MACV ordered heavy bombing in the highlands too. Around South Vietnam's borders, they dropped electronic sensors and increased air surveillance. PAVN units, however, countered with "mop up" operations, overrunning isolated camps and rebuilding new tactical areas around these ruined camps.[30]

As American troops continued to pour into Vietnam's ports and communist forces expanded areas of control in the highlands, the deforested, bare hills in between once again became a volatile battlefront. US Marines encountered especially strong resistance near Hòa Mỹ in December 1966 when they launched sweeps in the hills while establishing new camps along Highway 1. The PAVN 324th Division had been expanding its offensives eastward from trails in Laos along Highway 9, the region's main highway connecting Laos with Quảng Trị Province and the coast. One of the 324th's battalions, the Sixth, operated with the PLAF 802nd Battalion further south in Thừa Thiên–Huế Province with the aim of reopening the east-west trail system to Hòa Mỹ. As the marines pushed west into the same hills, both forces met in a series of scattered attacks near this former "cradle of the revolution." Over one thousand PAVN-PLAF soldiers opened attacks on the American camps, assaulting base perimeters along Highway 1 with small weapons and lobbing artillery and rockets inside. The marines had not expected communist attacks deep in the lowlands on the highway, and MACV added three more battalions (over 1,500 men) to counterattack while bomber aircraft razed the hills with napalm and B-52s engaged in saturation bombing around Hòa Mỹ. On Christmas Day 1966, the marines opened Camp Evans, named for the first American killed in the communist offensive.[31] The battles continued for four more months with no substantial gains in territory.

This particular location, the marine camp on Highway 1, and the communist movements through Hòa Mỹ, represented in the starkest of environmental terms the difficult position of American and ARVN forces along the highway. Communist forces repeatedly attacked not only from the mountains but also from the marshes and dunes. The Americans responded by calling in intensive bombing strikes on both sides. American bombing over a four-month period leveled Hòa Mỹ and ten surrounding hamlets in the hills. When communist soldiers attacked the camp from the coastal dunes, an AC-47 Spooky gunship emptied three thousand pounds of bullets on them. A map of recorded American bombing missions derived from a US Department of Defense database shows the intensity of bombing in just this four-month period (plate 5).[32]

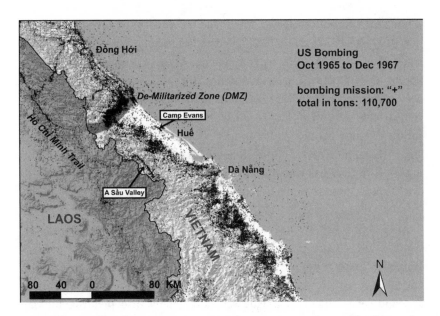

FIGURE 5.5. US bombing missions on central coast, 1965–67. Source: Bombing point data, US Air Force THOR GIS. Background layers courtesy of ESRI Inc. Map and annotations by author.

This sudden escalation of troops and bombing in 1967 produced an unprecedented phase of base construction along the coast while pounding the hillsides with thousands of tons of munitions. Here the idea of creative destruction was being tested in the extreme. The cratering of the hills produced the "forced-draft urbanization" that Samuel Huntington described, sending refugees from bombed areas fleeing for their lives to refugee camps near American bases on the highway. The bare hills and "waste lands" that had borne the brunt of fighting in many past wars now received most of the American bombs dropped in the course of these expanded operations. This search-and-destroy campaign with bombing and helicopter assaults was no longer isolated to a few remote bases in the mountains or civic action around the air bases.

The fighting around Hòa Mỹ and Camp Evans in 1967 was one small part of a much wider string of operations in the belt of low hills fringing the central coast. Figure 5.5, derived from the same bombing database as in plate 5, shows the clustering of bombing operations in central Vietnam in 1966 and 1967. South of the DMZ, the densest areas of bombing occurred in the foothills. North of the DMZ, American bombing concentrated on the coast, where PAVN forces traveled by rail or road before turning inland to the trails in Laos. A tally of all the bombs dropped in the missions captured in this frame counted 110,000 tons. Eighty-one percent of these were general-purpose bombs while 8 percent were incendiaries (napalm, white phosphorus) and 4 percent were cluster bombs. For comparison, the area in figure 5.7 is roughly equivalent to the area of West Virginia or Norway (62,000 square kilometers). In just this one part of Vietnam, the tonnage dropped in these two years amounted to more than half of all bombs dropped over Western Europe in 1943.[33] With the exception of some battlefields in World War I, nowhere on earth had received so many bombs in such a concentrated space.

WAR AND THE CITY

While the greatly expanded areas of US bombing and military operations may have, à la Huntington's theory, produced a bifurcation of populations and landscapes, cities such as Huế were never wholly insulated from the war. Military and political conflict in Huế did not begin with the 1968 Tết Offensive but instead grew out of earlier student and Buddhist protests against the Sài Gòn government, the military, and especially the US troop buildup. The rapid escalation in American military operations in 1966, especially the increased bombing in the hills, triggered a new current of popular resistance on the streets among a spectrum of people, including ARVN military leaders, Buddhist leaders, and even officials in Huế.

After protests by students and Buddhist monks against the Diệm government, a new Struggle Movement led by a Unified Buddhist Church emerged on the streets of Huế and Đà Nẵng in 1966. Protests erupted in March 1966 when the head of the military junta in Sài Gòn, Nguyễn Cao Kỳ, removed a charismatic ARVN commander of I Corps, General Nguyễn Chánh Thi. Thi had a long career in the Vietnamese military, was active in past coup attempts against Diệm, and was a Buddhist. Like many military leaders in central Vietnam, he was alarmed by the Kỳ government's antidemocratic policies and by Kỳ's ready acquiescence to American requests to expand military operations. Thi, together with other military, civilian, and Buddhist leaders in central Vietnam, refused orders from Sài Gòn to break up student protests, leading Kỳ to order his removal.[34]

Considering the mostly urban and coastal spaces where US military and civilian agencies pursued civic action, the Struggle Movement in Huế was a direct challenge to the notion that Vietnam's urban areas were firmly allied with the Americans. After General Thi's ouster, student protesters descended on Radio Huế, where they commenced broadcasting anti-American programs. Huế's civilian and military leaders offered no resistance. Radio station staff in Huế and Đà Nẵng allowed the students to broadcast for several hours each day. Neither Huế's police nor ARVN troops followed orders from Sài Gòn to remove the students for several months. Given the "radio corridor" established by the United States from 1963 to 1964 with antenna farms and the RRU at Phú Bài airfield, this move struck at the heart of US ambitions to win Vietnamese hearts and minds over the airwaves. In Huế and Đà Nẵng, city officials and staffers encouraged what Kỳ and others argued was an open rebellion against Sài Gòn and a public condemnation of the expanding American military presence, especially its bombing missions.[35]

While protesters aimed their anger at the military junta too, they eventually clashed with US soldiers in Huế. On March 26 a US enlisted man pulled down an anti-US banner. The move triggered an immediate response on Radio Huế where protesters and their ARVN supporters demanded that the enlisted man publicly apologize and replace the banner. General Westmoreland ultimately intervened, offering an apology to prevent a spectacle.[36] Protests continued that spring as more American troops arrived. In May an American soldier shot an ARVN soldier who accompanied the protesters, triggering another wave of anti-US protests with strong support from ARVN soldiers. After the man's funeral on May 26, protesters burned down the US Information Service library in Huế. Kỳ then ordered the ARVN's First Division, the Huế military unit whose leaders had refused to put down the protests, to relocate to Quảng Trị. In protest of this move, protesters sacked the US consulate.

As American-made tanks driven by pro–Sài Gòn military units approached the city to restore order, the protesters adopted a new tactic of resistance, placing family ancestral altars wrapped in Buddhist flags in the middle of city streets. This symbolic act, placing one's ancestral altar in the path of approaching tanks, was a highly unusual but deeply effective form of protest. The tanks avoided the altars and waited outside the city limits of Huế and Đà Nẵng.[37] This small-scale act of family-centered defiance highlighted a deep conflict for many Vietnamese whose family ties reached beyond the urban periphery into the same stretches of countryside subjected to carpet bombing and search-and-destroy missions. Many of Huế's families were but one generation removed from ancestral villages, and many thousands of youths had left families in the countryside for schools in the city. Because of family ties linking students (and ARVN soldiers) to ancestral homelands in the war zones, American military actions in these hilly border zones often had indirect impacts on young people living in Huế. Base construction also exacerbated tensions as the RVN seized village lands, especially areas with tombs. During the escalated fall 1966 operations, marines operating at Phú Bài took one hill in a hamlet of Dạ Lê and renamed it LZ Tombstone for the many graves around the makeshift landing zone.[38]

• • •

The communist Tết Offensive that began on January 30, 1968, marked a pivotal turning point in the spatial and landscape terms of the conflict. The Battle of Huế began in the early morning hours on the Lunar New Year, January 31, 1968, and lasted over a month as over four thousand PAVN-PLAF forces took control of the city, flying the NLF's red and blue flag with its central gold star above the citadel. This takeover was a surprise, and it punched a hole through Huntington's urbanization theory, proving that the cities were not impregnable strongholds of American sympathizers.

For many communist troops and their families, it was also a return of sorts. The 1968 battle was not the first Tết offensive in recent memory but the second. Several thousand Việt Minh youth fled the city when French troops invaded Huế in February 1947. That year the Việt Minh Trần Cao Vân Regiment together with irregulars fought unsuccessfully at blown bridges and trenches to thwart the invasion. They retreated to the safety of the tactical zone at Hòa Mỹ and redoubts in the highlands. This regiment, later named the 101st, became a part of the People's Army 325th Division in 1951. After 1954 soldiers in the regiment relocated north while extended families stayed behind, many of them suffering reprisals for being "VC in the region." Twenty years later in 1967, the Trần Cao Vân Regiment fought in the Trị-Thiên front along Highway 9 in Quảng Trị. In May 1967 its political leaders reorganized with cadres from PLAF divisions and local district committees to form a Tactical Region IV Party Committee to coordinate the attacks from January 20 to 31.[39] The Trần Cao Vân prepared for a large-scale assault on the US Marine camp at Khe Sanh in the hills on Highway

9 just south of the DMZ.[40] In May 1967 artillery units from the regiment probed American and ARVN defenses along the highway with rocket attacks. On May 27 a PLAF artillery unit sent rockets into Huế to test the city's defenses, hitting the American MACV office, the ARVN First Division headquarters, and the broadcasting office of Radio Huế. During the fall these units stockpiled over sixty-one thousand tons of supplies at caches in the hills along trails and at recovered tactical zones at A Lưới and Nam Đông.[41]

In social terms the communist assault on the city was also significant because Vietnamese troops had not led a major military assault against other Vietnamese troops defending the city since the Nguyễn fleet's invasion in 1801. Despite communist propaganda that repeatedly characterized the war as a resistance struggle against American "invaders" and Vietnamese "lackeys," this violent shift resulted in widespread destruction in the city and inadvertent killing of many civilians; it blurred the boundaries between liberators and invaders. As American and ARVN units eventually cut off PAVN-PLAF troops inside the old walled city, the communist units fought a violent, devastating retreat to the hills, leaving entire companies for dead along with hundreds of civilians caught in the crossfire.

Communist preparations for the attack, secretly hiding weapons and soldiers at homes inside the city, also illustrated the intense ideological differences dividing neighbors and families. Under the noses of ARVN soldiers and secret police, the PLAF smuggled into the city caches of weapons needed to supply several thousand soldiers. By December 1967 soldiers from the PLAF's Phú Xuân Sixth Regiment (1,800 soldiers), four infantry battalions (1,300 soldiers), one rocket company (100 soldiers), and another 1,000 local soldiers had managed to move into the city without detection.[42] Just outside the city in the hills, soldiers from the PLAF Ninth and Fifth Divisions and various special units added another 4,000 soldiers, who secretly took up positions outside the city to block movements of American and ARVN soldiers from such bases as Phú Bài.[43]

This secretive and successful preparation for the offensive highlights the vital role that families played in supporting, hiding, and feeding the troops. Many people who had in past eras suffered as "Việt Cộng in the area" supported the troops. North Vietnamese veterans of the battle recounted hiding with families for several weeks, taking care not to let neighbors hear their distinctive northern dialect.[44] Communist forces transported weapons that arrived in trucks carrying flowers and fruit to the holiday markets. Fake funeral processions delivered coffins filled with weapons and ammunition, and supporters buried them at pagodas and churches. Baskets of rice and vegetables concealed explosives. Communist soldiers arrived dressed in civilian clothes and some even in ARVN uniforms; they mixed into crowds gathered for Tết celebrations and holiday markets.[45]

The offensive began under heavy cloud cover that prevented American helicopters from safely reaching the city and helped communist units reach their targets. On January 31, 1968, at 2:30 A.M., PLAF forces poured shells and rockets at several dozen preselected targets in the city. Then, PAVN-PLAF infantry forces met at designated points and took over the citadel region north of the river, the old imperial city. By morning light, a giant NLF flag with a gold star in the middle was visible on the flagpole atop the old imperial fort in front of the royal palace. Over the next few days, PLAF forces on the other side of the river in the European quarter attacked government offices and almost overran the American MACV office before US Marines from Phú Bài reinforced the post. The ARVN First Division, quartered inside a walled fort in the citadel, barely held off repeat waves of attacks.[46] Over the next several days, PAVN and PLAF soldiers walked freely inside the old imperial city while troops across the river in the "new town" fought American units and inflicted heavy casualties.

As the clouds lifted days later, descriptions of the fighting blanketed radio and television airwaves, conveying scenes of NLF flags and street fighting to stunned global audiences. On February 6, CBS News aired a segment following two companies of US Marines who had broken out from the MACV headquarters and were fighting to take two city blocks around Huế University and the provincial headquarters. The news cameras followed as the marines blasted giant holes through homes and university buildings, coming up against communist forces crewing machine guns. At the end of the segment, the marines reached their objective and hoisted a US (not RVN) flag at the province headquarters, tearing up the captured NLF flag.[47] Such television accounts showed millions of viewers worldwide a degree of carnage that belied the confident reports of social scientists such as Huntington. CBS News anchor Walter Cronkite traveled to Vietnam two weeks after the Tết Offensive ended, reporting from Sài Gòn, Huế, and other cities. When he returned, he delivered a historic condemnation of the American war effort that galvanized public opinion against the war.[48]

The physical destruction brought by a month of fighting, conveyed in photographs and statistics, underscored the heavy costs to the city's mostly civilian population. Heavy shelling and use of tanks had destroyed over ten thousand homes and left 40 percent of the city's population homeless. More than five thousand civilians were listed as dead or missing.[49] In July 1969 the chief of the ARVN's military history division released a 490-page account of the Tết Offensive, devoting over forty pages with graphic images to the battles in Huế. This account highlighted the mass arrests of RVN officials and their subsequent killings by communist forces as they fled the city with the prisoners under fire. Drawing from captured NLF documents, it detailed plans for targeted arrests as well as assessments of the offensive after the retreat on February 23.[50] The official PAVN history of the war naturally avoids a discussion of the killing of over 1,300 "traitors" and "puppets" and the disposal of their bodies in a mass grave; however, it does in somewhat circuitous terms acknowledge breakdowns of discipline as communist forces fled under heavy fire from ARVN and US troops. The history states: "Our soldiers' morale had been very high when they set off for battle, but because we had made only one-sided preparations, only looking at the possibilities of victory and failing to prepare for adversity, when the battle did not progress favorably for our side and when we suffered casualties, rightist thoughts, pessimism, and hesitancy appeared among our forces."[51]

The urban experience of such devastating violence in Huế also catalyzed artists who produced some of the era's most famous songs and stories about the war. They noted scenes of dead bodies, wrecked homes, and people everywhere wearing white headbands in the weeks after the fighting, mourning deceased relatives and friends. The urban battles, because of their immediacy, highlighted the violence of fighting that had been raging in the hills for years; perhaps better than news stories, artistic responses pointed to the war's complex scarring of personal relationships and family histories. One of South Vietnam's most popular singers, Trịnh Công Sơn, wrote such songs as "Ballad for the Dead," recounting grisly scenes from his hometown:

> Xác người nằm trôi sông, phơi trên ruộng đồng
> Trên nóc nhà thành phố, trên những đường quanh co

Xác người nằm bơ vơ, dưới mái hiên chùa
Trong giáo đường thành phố, trên thềm nhà hoang vu

Corpses float on the river current, dry on the fields
On the roofs in the city, on the encircling roads
Corpses lying helplessly, under the eaves of the temple
In the city church, on the edge of the wastelands[52]

Author Nhã Ca's *Mourning Headband for Huế* relates in more personal details how the communist siege and American bombing shattered family and neighborly relations. She'd traveled to Huế before Tết to attend her father's funeral. She then spent several weeks hunkered in a bomb shelter, carefully rationing out stores of food and moving during pauses in the fighting. After surviving the fighting, she returned to Sài Gòn and published stories about the siege in a pro-peace newspaper, *Hòa Bình*.[53] Her stories detailed a non-aligned view on the terrors faced by civilians as families desperately sought to protect teenage boys and vulnerable loved ones from one side or the other.[54]

MILITARY CITY-BUILDING

While the American political response at home to the Tết Offensive developed in surges of protests and debates through the summer's Republican and Democratic party conventions to the November election, the military response was rapid and unprecedented. Within months new bases mushroomed along the central coast. MACV moved out from Sài Gòn's airport to a sprawling air base facility thirty kilometers north. It created a new Forward Command at Phú Bài and turned the hills of Vùng Phèn and the lands above Dạ Lê into a military city, lights blazing all night around helipads and a busy runway. Just weeks after the fighting in Huế had subsided, US Navy construction battalions (Seabees) arrived to repair damaged infrastructure and quickly erect scores of prefab barracks, hangars, and roads for some forty-five thousand troops slated to follow.

The communist offensive had caused severe disruptions to the existing infrastructure, especially the marine bases along Highway 1, disrupting flows of all materials from bullets to c-rations to oil. Sapper battalions had blown most of the major bridges from Huế to the DMZ, and infantry units had taken the mountain pass separating Huế from Đà Nẵng. They blew pipelines and damaged the tanks supplying aviation fuel to Phú Bài. During the fighting in February, US forces required resupply by air when the winter clouds parted. US troops consumed more than 2,600 tons of supplies each day that month. An additional 45,000 US Army troops were due to arrive by the summer, so the demand for housing and logistics facilities was particularly acute.[55] As MACV moved its offices, General Westmoreland ordered the US Army's 101st Airborne Division to relocate to the hills above Dạ Lê. Following President Johnson's emergency request to Congress for increased troops and spending, he added to the division a brigade (3,000 men) of the Eighty-Second Airborne Division and a US Marines Regimental Landing Team (approximately 1,000 men) from Southern California. The forward command included army and marine generals who negotiated with the navy and air force for coordinated campaigns involving units from all branches.[56]

The Seabees destined for Huế set off from Port Hueneme, California, in January 1968 with a fleet of transport ships carrying prefab buildings, bulldozers, cranes, and tools to repair broken infrastructure around Huế and construct the new army base. The annual yearbook of MCB Team 8 provides a vivid pictorial account of activities in the area. As the Battle of Huế wound down, MCB 8 repaired the fifteen-kilometer road connecting Thuận An with Huế, including vital bridges and the petroleum-oil-lubricant pipeline running from a tank farm near the coast to Phú Bài (figure 5.6).

As had the marines before them, the Seabees devoted part of their efforts to rebuilding civilian infrastructure; however, the team was not prepared for the extent of broken buildings, rubble, and trash they encountered that spring. Photographs in the yearbook detail the skeletal hulls of buildings in Huế—the shot-up Huế University building, blown bridges, and piles of rubble inside the citadel. When the Seabees arrived at the site for the army base, the marine staging area LZ Tombstone, they found the hill covered in a thick layer of garbage. The fighting in February covered the hill in empty tins, shell casings, boots, and boxes (figure 5.7). Two snapshots in the yearbook, one of a boy lacing up a pair of combat boots and the other of him and other boys inspecting materials in the rubbish heap, point to the high level of material consumption during the fighting. When MCB 8 arrived, accompanying ARVN troops permitted Dạ Lê's villagers to visit the rubbish piles to collect anything they wanted before bulldozers razed the site.

As the American military supply chain expanded on the central coast in 1968, nearby villages became mired in this new construction and its material

FIGURE 5.6. Reconstructed petroleum-oil-lubricant tank farms near Thuận An.
Source: US Navy Mobile Construction Battalion Eight, *MCB 8: Hue, Phu Bai, 1968*
(Minneapolis: American Yearbook Company, Military Division, 1968), 9.

flows, especially wastes. MCB 8's bulldozers shaved the hilltop and carved
out roads linking the army base with Phú Bài. The bulldozers plowed through
several dozen tombs before ARVN and village protests forced them to reroute
roads and buildings around them. By summer, army engineers and a private
firm, Pacific Architects and Engineers, arrived to complete construction of
cantonments for the 101st Airborne Division's Camp Eagle. By September
army units were in place and the base was operational. Residents of Dạ Lê
no longer dared to venture to their old hamlet, Dạ Lê Thượng, now laying
partially inside a perimeter of minefields and exploding incendiary *fougasse*
devices. A network of watchtowers, perimeter lights, and machine gun

FIGURE 5.7. Children gleaning materials from military waste at Hamlet 5. Source: US Navy Mobile Construction Battalion Eight, *MCB 8: Hue, Phu Bai, 1968* (Minneapolis: American Yearbook Company, Military Division, 1968), 108.

emplacements guarded the outside fringes too, as soldiers looked for any movement as a sign of an attack.[57]

Inside the fence, Camp Eagle was in material and cultural terms a small city. The skies buzzed with activity as helicopters took off and landed around the clock, ferrying troops and supporting a new network of hilltop firebases in the mountains. Each unit at Camp Eagle had its own club, and the base featured an ampitheater, the Eagle Entertainment Bowl, to host performers such as comedian Bob Hope and shows of dancing girls and rock and roll bands playing to crowds of ten thousand or more.[58] Some villagers sought day-labor work inside, lining up by entrance gates; several dozen worked blue collar jobs. The base produced great volumes of trash, and villagers helped haul it to makeshift dumps while others picked through it. In anthropologist James Trullinger's 1975 interviews with residents of Dạ Lê, villagers repeatedly recalled the dangerous trips to visit family tombs on the hilltops. One recounted being shot at by troops while attempting to clean a tomb with his son.[59]

By 1969 this constellation of military camps had grown as large as Huế. The camps, the roads, and even some of the hilltop firebases formed a new infrastructure visible from space. The following photograph, a declassified image taken from a top-secret American spy satellite on March 20, 1969,

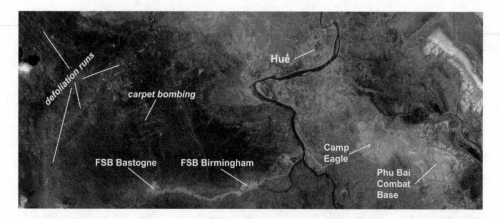

FIGURE 5.8. Base areas, March 20, 1969. Annotations by author. Source: CORONA Frame DS1050-1006DF129, courtesy of US Geological Survey Earth Resources Observation and Science Center.

shows the extent of this buildup after one year (figure 5.8). In the top center of this image, the squarish outline of the Huế Citadel gives a spatial reference. Each side measured two and a half kilometers in length. The 101st Airborne Division was headquartered at Camp Eagle while the MACV Forward Command and US Marine units were located at Phú Bài Combat Base. This section of what Washington's photo interpreters called a keyhole image was about one-third of the long, rectangular frame. A close-up detail from the image shows the city-like nature of these new base areas with buildings and roads forming dense grids (figure 5.9). The hedgerows of fields and households are visible on the fringes of the base.

In a violent reprise of the ancient founding village and upland satellite model, the US military established fire support bases (firebases) on the hilltops to direct artillery fire into the highlands. Like their ancient analogues, each firebase was like a hamlet, connected for supplies and direction to its parent base. Camp Eagle was a political and material center near Highway 1, sending people and materials via helicopter to these mountaintops. In figure 5.8, the white filament of a gravel road, provincial Route 547, snakes west from the base across the Perfume River into the hills. This road, like the root of a plant edging further into the soil, provided a vital conduit for truck convoys carrying artillery shells, troops, armaments, c-rations, beer, fuel, spare parts, and napalm to satellites such as Firebases Birmingham and Bastogne.

FIGURE 5.9. Phu Bai Combat Base, March 20, 1969. Source: CORONA Frame DS1050-1006DF129, courtesy of US Geological Survey Earth Resources Observation and Science Center.

From the moment of their violent creations to their evacuation several years later, the firebases were the most concentrated destructive sites of the war. The US military, the world's largest logistics organization in 1968, produced manuals with step-by-step instructions to guide commanders in rapidly constructing these hilltop fortresses. The following quote from a First Cavalry guide gives a sense of the destructive powers available:

> If the proposed site is one of dense jungle where it would take ground crews considerable time to clear even the smallest opening, it would be to the commander's advantage to use more efficient means, such as large Air Force bombs that would completely demolish all vegetation in the drop area. The 750-pound bomb called the "Daisy Cutter" detonates approximately ten feet above the ground, completely destroying all vegetation within a ten-foot radius and knocking down trees in a considerably larger area. The 10,000-pound bomb (instant LZ) performs the same devastation but over a much larger area . . . it is important that preparatory fire play a large part in clearing fire bases.[60]

FIGURE 5.10. Firebase Spear, April 2, 1971. Caption on the original photo reads: "Alpha Battery, 1st Battalion, 321st Artillery, 101st Airborne Division (Airmobile) is inserted." Source: Box 8, Information Officer Photographic File, 101st Airborne Division, Record Group 472, US National Archives and Records Administration, College Park.

In the hills west of Camp Eagle, military commanders ordered the "instant LZ." After the initial bombing, they followed additional guidelines. Cargo helicopters dropped drummed napalm in "flame drops" that incinerated the downed trees and burned away brush along the perimeter. An even larger helicopter, the CH-54 Skycrane, airlifted bulldozers and then howitzers as troops and engineers built bunkers, gun emplacements, and set up camp. Within days construction was complete. Helicopters from base camps ferried howitzers, shells, provisions, and people daily. Helicopters with spray rigs visited periodically to douse the base perimeter with herbicides and DDT to kill mosquitoes.

FIGURE 5.11. Firebase Spear, completed, April 22, 1971. Source: Box 8, Information Officer Photographic File, 101st Airborne Division, Record Group 472, US National Archives and Records Administration, College Park.

This airborne network of bases and firebases tested the limits of the American aerial platform to the extreme. However, even with the new base cities and a force of over five hundred thousand American soldiers on the ground, this system could not regain control over the highlands. In addition to communist attacks, the dense vegetation, steep slopes, and ever-present clouds challenged this hilltop approach. Figures 5.10 and 5.11 illustrate these challenges of this terrain as US forces with the 101st Airborne attempted to clear one hilltop and then airlift materials. In the center of each image, a CH-47 helicopter hovers over the site, giving a sense of scale. Despite the proximity of helicopters, big guns, and radio contact, firebases often lacked visibility of the lands below and remained shrouded in clouds from the skies above. In the fall and winter months, heavy rains added to soldiers' troubles, turning denuded hilltops into thick slopes of sticky mud.

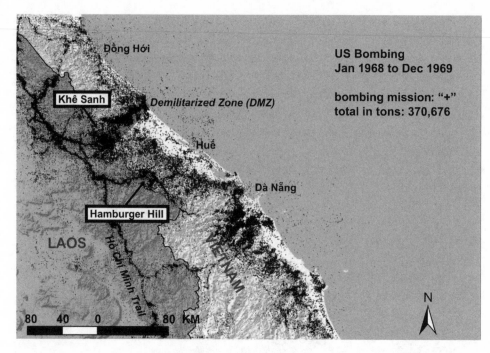

FIGURE 5.12. US bombing missions on central coast, January 1, 1968, to December 31, 1969. Source: Bombing point data, US Air Force THOR GIS. Background layers courtesy of ESRI Inc. Map produced by author.

From the opening days of the Tết Offensive through 1968 and 1969, this escalation in US troops and expansion of firebases was accompanied by a threefold increase in bombing compared with the 1966–67 period. Figure 5.12, depicting the same stretch of central Vietnam as in figure 5.5, shows US aerial bombing missions from January 1968 through December 1969. Using the comparison to World War II bombing in Europe, bombing in these two years was equal to almost double the volume of all Allied bombs dropped over Western Europe in 1943. Bombing intensified greatly over the Hồ Chí Minh Trail in Laos, and it extended westward from the cratered hills into the forested peaks, especially around the A Sầu Valley.

COMMUNIST RIGHT OF WAY

While Americans extended their airborne networks from base cities to firebases on the hilltops, communist forces ramped up their own infrastructure

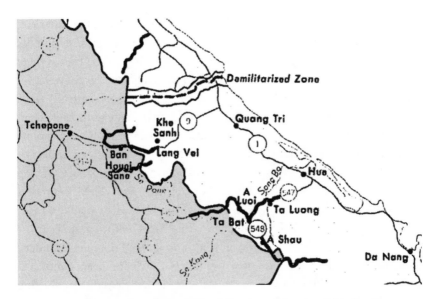

FIGURE 5.13. Excerpt from figure 1, "Road Construction 1967–68," in Intelligence Memorandum 68–48. Source: CIA CREST Declassified Documents, Report Number CIA-RDP85T00875R001500220048-6.

development along the trail networks and around base areas. CIA intelligence memorandums developed from U-2 and CORONA photographs reported that in the A Sầu Valley, PAVN-PLAF forces had, since their victories in mid-1966, expanded their own network of all-weather roads, improved wired communications (to avoid detection of radio transmissions), and even cleared the old runways on abandoned special forces bases, perhaps in anticipation of their own air cargo drops. After fending off the Tết Offensive, US bombers pounded these abandoned bases and any site that suggested evidence of communist camps. The CIA report highlighted suspect depots and camps in Laos, and it provided a map showing over two hundred miles of gravel roads that PAVN-PLAF engineers had completed linking the trails in Laos with battle-fronts along Highway 9 in Quảng Trị and in the A Sầu Valley (figure 5.13). Along these roads, still serviced by the 559th Transportation Group, construction units expanded vehicle depots, added anti-aircraft guns, reinforced barracks, and ran an eight-inch pipeline supplying diesel and kerosene.[61]

These top-secret discoveries in 1968 and 1969 pointed to a corresponding communist urbanization scheme that, contrary to the American construction along the coast, was establishing altogether new Vietnamese urban corridors in lands that before 1945 were hardly mapped. While the American bombing campaigns and military assaults after Tết were undoubtedly destructive for thousands of men and women working on the trail system, the systematic wasting of hilltops, communist roads, and large swaths of forests was a double-edged sword. In the short term, it forced trails to be rerouted, wires and pipelines to be reconnected. In the long term, the violent clearing of old growth rainforest and indigenous claims by B-52 Stratofortresses and napalm drops opened the slopes to communist state-builders.

With respect to the urbanization of networks in the region, the CIA map also pointed to another troubling spatial fact. As PAVN-PLAF engineers pushed their roads east, they would eventually reach the new roads and corridors that Americans had extended west from bases on the coast. Near the DMZ, the embattled marine camp at Khe Sanh marked the 1968 boundary while near Huế after the Tết Offensive, PAVN-PLAF engineers controlled Route 547 east to the 101st's Firebase Bastogne. If one viewed these dueling construction campaigns from space, one might even imagine they were two sides attempting to connect.

HAMBURGER HILL

While American pilots and firebase gun crews may have cursed the low clouds and heavy rain, the same torrential rain turned communist roads to muck and stalled this construction effort every fall and winter. Communist fighting was intensely seasonal. PAVN-PLAF forces planned a 1969 winter-spring offensive after the rains eased while they built up caches and troops over the rainy winter. This seasonality played into the timing of the 1968 Tết Offensive, and a year later it guided the first follow-up battle with reinforced American troops where the highways met.

This battle, later known by Americans as the Battle of Hamburger Hill, took place on the hills overlooking the embattled highway junction where the communist "highway" from Laos ran into the A Sầu Valley and the start of Highway 547. As the clouds and rains lifted in March 1969, both sides concentrated on this road junction as essential for advancing and protecting their efforts. The communists' Trị Thiên Region Committee ordered several thousand troops to the valley to protect road-building efforts and push east to the American firebases. With Camp Eagle fully operational, US Army planners were eager to draw upon their networks of firebases and helicopter groups to break the communist forces. The Trị Thiên Committee moved a regiment (approximately three thousand soldiers) of the PAVN 324th Division into the western hills above the junction of Highway 547 and 548 (figure 5.12). Soldiers dug trenches around hilltop bunkers and moved heavy guns including anti-aircraft weapons to the peak of A Bia Mountain. The PLAF Sixth Regiment, one of the main forces at the Battle of Huế, supported the effort, even cutting rice rations over the fall and winter to stockpile food for the battle.[62]

Comparing US military histories of the battle with People's Army histories, it may come as no surprise that both sides suffered high casualties but nevertheless claimed victory in what was by all accounts a meat-grinder engagement. One American report published by the air force in October 1969 paid close attention to coordinated ground and air-based attacks on communist troops on the hill. US-ARVN forces fought for ten days to take the peaks on A Bia. The fighting left over a thousand soldiers wounded and several hundred dead. As aerial bombing and artillery reduced the mountain to a moonscape, after the battle there was little of anything to claim. US-ARVN troops did not dare to build a firebase so deep in communist territory. Meanwhile, the PAVN-PLAF forces retreated to safe havens in Laos. Both sides waged smaller battles in the valley throughout the summer. Perhaps most important from an environmental standpoint was the decision by the US command after May 31 to designate the entire valley a Specified Strike Zone, meaning that airstrikes could be ordered without observing on the ground local allied units. A radio listener at Phú Bài or a photo interpreter could present evidence of communist troop movements to a commander, who could then order bombing at designated coordinates. This strike zone opened the valley to saturation bombing and increasing use of defoliants.[63]

As with the Tết Offensive, news of Hamburger Hill at this remote highway junction jolted US debates at home. Newspaper reporters in Sài Gòn wrote of the fierce resistance posed by PAVN troops and the cost of these battles in American lives. Two *Los Angeles Times* stories on May 28 and June 18 epitomized popular responses against these dangerous insertions into the mountains. The first headline read, "US Troops Abandon Viet Hill, Center of Congressional Storm," and the second read, "Reds Back on Viet Hill; US General Ready to Fight."[64] Heavy casualties and the seeming pointlessness of these battles deep in the mountains energized antiwar protests in the United States.

In addition to widespread public protests in the United States about these deadly stalemate battles, by 1969 scientists, environmental activists, and some military leaders began to express concerns about the environmental effects of US activity. In particular, the Department of Defense and the Department of State were concerned about 1968 reports that the herbicide 2,4,5-T in Agent Orange contained high concentrations of the contaminant, 2,3,7,8-TCDD (dioxin). While communist propaganda had since 1963 likened the chemical spraying to poison gas attacks, the troubling findings in 1968 suggested that if the operations were exposing people to dioxin, there might be a shred of truth to the claim. In January 1968 the American ambassador contracted senior scientists from the American Association for the Advancement of Science to commence investigations of the herbicide's alleged toxicity. The full report appeared in the association's flagship journal *Science* in January 1969. The report was inconclusive, but it galvanized scientists and the public at large to investigate a bevy of alleged health impacts from exposure to dioxin. The *Science* article triggered a public debate at American universities and around the world, even leading to the coining of a new word, ecocide, to describe the intentional destruction of South Vietnamese forests. US agencies, including the Department of Defense, and the president had since 1963 expressed concerns that targeted destruction of forests and fields might result in such charges of war crimes; antiwar activists seized on the reports and published their own accounts of ecocide.[65]

At the heart of this debate were the many chemicals that American troops used in Vietnam to open paths through forests or attack enemy camps. Besides Agent Orange and tactical herbicides, the US military introduced a broad suite of other chemicals to combat adversaries in jungle environments as well as to protect American bases from human and insect assaults. Chemical platoons assigned to individual bases managed supplies of tactical materials such as napalm and Agent Orange. They also managed use of pesticides inside the bases and defoliation using diesel fuel. The US Army introduced airborne drops of tear gas (CS and CS2) to push soldiers from underground bunkers above ground. American combat activities in war zones such as the A Sâu Valley involved a mix of tactics with soldiers, helicopter assaults, aerial bombing, electronic surveillance, and chemical spraying.

Teasing out military and scientific debates over the toxicity of Agent Orange from broader concerns about the war and chemical pollution in the 1960s remains difficult even fifty years later. While press reports in 1969 and 1970 focused on Agent Orange, they largely ignored the broader role of chemical units in both US-ARVN and PAVN-PLAF forces. Most large units had chemical companies or platoons for managing tactical chemicals such as explosives as well as nontactical disinfecants, insecticides, solvents, and other chemicals. While American antiwar activists in 1969–70 focused on Agent Orange, few paid much attention to the fact that the same dioxin-containing herbicide had been used at home in gardens and along rights of way since the late 1940s.[66]

Also lost in the Agent Orange–centered history is a more nuanced understanding of the wide array of other chemicals (many also later banned) used by American forces. For the 101st Airborne at Camp Eagle, the Tenth Chemical Platoon of the Army Chemical Corps managed the delivery of tactical chemicals like Agent Orange to war zones as well as spraying the base with DDT for mosquitoes. The chemical corps was formed in 1918 during World War I when US Army troops encountered gas attacks in Europe. After 1945 the chemical corps expanded its responsibility to biological, radioactive, and nuclear weapons, and during the 1950s it supervised the development of herbicides like Agent Orange for use in the challenging highland forests of Indochina. It also managed supplies of napalm and the tear gas CS. When the 101st Airborne set up at Camp Eagle, the Tenth Chemical's unit of officers, soldiers, and assault support helicopter pilots managed this chemical stockpile.

A one-day snapshot of the Tenth Chemical's operations at Camp Eagle suggests the scope of chemical activities. On the morning of January 21, 1970, helicopter pilots with the Tenth Chemical Platoon commenced aerial spraying around Firebase Bastogne with a 2:1 mix of Agent Orange (350 gallons) and diesel (200 gallons). Using a UH-1 Huey helicopter with a spray rig, they made five trips from Camp Eagle to the firebase. In the afternoon, Tenth Chemical soldiers at the helipad loaded a CH-47 Chinook helicopter with drums of napalm for a "bulk flame drop" (figure 5.14). Crew on board strapped a dozen drums together (660 gallons), and once over the target they pushed it out the rear hatch. As the drums fell to the ground, a fighter jet swooped in and strafed it with bullets to create a giant fireball that singed the ground and suffocated anyone hiding below. The Tenth Chemical ran eleven bulk

Members of 184th Chemical Platoon load 55 gallon drums of CS into CH-47 Helicopter

FIGURE 5.14. Loading CS tear gas drums into a CH-47. Source: Box 17, General Records, Command Historian, Headquarters US Army Vietnam, Record Group 472, US National Archives and Records Administration, College Park.

flame drops that afternoon, targeting a coastal area of marshes and dunes where the 101st Airborne's Third Brigade was fighting. After these missions concluded at 3:30 P.M., the Tenth Chemical ran one final operation reserved for dusk, a "sniffer mission." The "sniffer" crew piloted a "Huey" fitted with a high-tech, ammonia-sniffing device. They flew low and slow, just above the treetops, to record minute traces of ammonia in the air. For each ammonia trace detected, they recorded map coordinates, setting targets for air attacks that night or the following morning.[67] Figure 5.14, which pictures a different chemical platoon loading a CH-47, details a "bulk CS drop," in which crews dropped barrels of CS instead of napalm to produce giant clouds of tear gas over suspected communist tunnels.

Even though US military planners worked closely with RVN counterparts to select target zones for the herbicide spraying months in advance of missions, problems of spray drift and accidental destruction of noncombatant or "friendly" crops highlighted the volatile ecological and political effects of the chemicals. A US military review of the herbicide program noted that thousands of farmers petitioned the South Vietnamese military for damage to crops. The highly volatile form of 2,4,5-T used in Agent Orange tended to drift several kilometers with the wind. Another American study noted that failures to compensate farmers posed deep political and tactical problems. Some disgruntled farmers joined the insurgents, and American attempts to reimburse farmers presented opportunities for widespread corruption as the South Vietnamese government lacked sufficient oversight to verify crop damage claims.[68]

In both strategic and economic ways, Agent Orange's physical drift into friendly fields or onto allied soldiers pointed to deeper, underlying problems with the logic of using an herbicide to fight a war. Pilots of the sprayer planes, flying missions on predetermined coordinates, did not attempt to distinguish friends from enemies on the ground. After the Tết Offensive, many students and antiwar activists in South Vietnam began to protest the overall destructiveness of American operations; chemical damage only added to their claims. More scientific reports published in 1969 pointed to dioxin's potential hazards to fetal development, so US military leaders attempted to justify the noncivilian impacts of defoliation, even in such fought-over places as the A Sầu Valley. The following excerpt from a 1970 planning document illustrates how far the military's logic of mitigating damage to civilians had been stretched. It explained: "Intelligence estimates indicate approximately five regiments or a total of 10,000 NVA/VC troops are located within the target area. No friendly or pro GVN inhabitants are known to be living in the area and the Montagnard population is estimated to be approximately 9600. The resultant native population density of the entire area is less than four individuals per square kilometer."[69] This strange math, averaging the indigenous population across the area of the entire spray run, reflected a grim attempt to distract from the likelihood that concentrated villages of highlanders were squarely in the spray paths and would be exposed to a potentially teratogenic chemical while also losing their crops. This diminished valuing of highlander lives drew increasingly severe responses from South Vietnamese allies who faced criticism from senior leaders and protesters.[70]

In heavily bombed areas of the A Sầu Valley, much of the herbicide washed into circular, muddy ponds left by thousands of bomb craters. Residues of the oily herbicides broke down over several weeks in sunlight and washed into the A Sáp River, where people fished and turned the water to irrigate rice paddies. While the herbicide degraded, the heavier dioxin molecules settled in the sediment of the crater ponds. The former special forces bases, overrun by communist troops in 1966, were especially targeted for spraying and bombing in 1969 and 1970. A 1968 CORONA image (plate 6) shows white dots of bomb craters running in lines, the results of saturation bombing runs visible from space. Additional circles indicate bombing runs that took place after the 1969 battles. The spray missions visible in plate 6 reflect the plant-centered logic of herbicide spraying. The A Sáp River through the A Sầu Valley was a rice-growing area, so a different herbicide, Agent Blue, was used as it targeted grasses. Runs of Agent Orange and Agent White covered the mountain slopes on both sides of the valley. These selective herbicides killed trees and broadleaf crops.[71] When the fall and winter rains hit, these defoliated (and napalmed) forests tumbled down the slopes in mudslides, clogging and flooding the valley.

Besides the international and local political fallout from this chemical war, defoliating broadleaf plants also brought new ecological challenges. By selectively killing broadleaf plants, Agent Orange in effect created grass-lands, and communist troops adapted, forging new paths and adding new camouflage.[72] PAVN-PLAF veterans also adapted to the napalm attacks, chang-ing camouflage from light green (grasses) to gray (defoliated trees) to black (napalmed hillsides) as they traveled. Veterans interviewed by the author near Huế repeatedly touched on the challenges that spraying posed for camou-flage. One veteran of a PLAF unit described how American helicopters dropped "gasoline bombs" (bulk flame drops) that singed hills black while suffocating people hiding underground. After these runs hit his area, he cov-ered himself in blackened char to avoid being spotted by American planes.[73]

In North Vietnamese stories, these chemically devastated landscapes formed a popular backdrop in many war stories and later war movies. Travel-ing through post-spray hillsides in 1967 near Huế, North Vietnamese journal-ist Trần Mai Nam wrote: "We march in the desolate gray of the forest. Around us, giant trees, their foliage stripped by poison chemicals, thrust their stark branches into the sky. Their ghostly silhouettes march across a low and cloudy sky, heavy like a soaked quilt. . . . here, on these mountains once green with heavy growth, such a rage against nature seems insane. One finds himself asking: 'But what do they want?' Is it possible that the superforts [B-52s] fly all the way from Guam, so far through the air, just to change the color of this forest?"[74] By 1969 photographs of the dead trees and gray hillsides began appearing in American antiwar newspapers and pamphlets. In 1970 one antiwar activist, Barry Weisberg, published the first journalistic book on the subject, *Ecocide in Indochina: The Ecology of War*. Weisberg popularized the North Vietnamese argument that the military herbicide program amounted to a war crime and backed it up with pictures.[75] Agent Orange spraying ceased in April 1970 after President Richard Nixon ordered a partial ban on the 2,4,5-T herbicide, and spraying of all tactical herbicides ceased in 1971.

While audiences in Hà Nội, Washington, and Sài Gòn seeing pictures of blackened hillsides or color photographs of grayscale lands may have imagined total annihilation of South Vietnam's forests, the spray missions were usually very targeted. For the most part, they followed both communist and American roadways. In the 1960s, few Americans questioned the spraying because the same herbicides were used commercially at home for almost identical purposes, clearing rights of way along roads, powerlines, and airport runways. Power companies in the United States and Canada even employed helicopters with sprayers to deliver 2,4,5-T over rugged terrain in rural areas. Plate 7, a compilation of all recorded spray runs in the province, shows the spraying concentrated along the mountain highways (547 and 548) and around the communist tactical zones at Hòa Mỹ, Nam Đông, and the A Sầu Valley. In addition to the communist tactical zones and routes, sprayer planes also doused American firebases guarding the highways running to the coast. Three firebases on Highway 547, Birmingham, Bastogne, and Veghel, were exposed to both fixed wing spraying and perimeter spraying by army helicopters.

Of all the firebases in Vietnam in 1969–70, Firebase Bastogne was one of the most sprayed and attacked. The last stop on the gravel road running west from Camp Eagle, it was a mirror in some respects to communist gateway camps such as Hòa Mỹ. However, while communist tactical areas quickly moved people and supplies through, the firebases were troublingly static and confined spaces. Soldiers and materials arrived by truck or helicopter, but those stationed there did not venture far on foot from the heavily defended, defoliated perimeters. Besides problems of terrain and these air-supported networks, the name of this firebase in particular, Bastogne, provides some clues to the American military's view of this terrain and the struggle. The name derived from a Belgian town in the hilly Ardennes forest, the site of the 101st Airborne's successful defense against a Nazi German offensive in the December 1944 Battle of the Bulge.[76] Army leaders viewed the firebase's location in communist-controlled hills as one liable to large-unit sieges, as

Bastogne had been in World War II. The 101st Airborne's victory in 1944 also rested on critical reinforcements arriving by air including paratroopers and food. At that point, however, all similarities ended.

As this escalation of the war after 1968 delivered few tactical victories for MACV-ARVN forces, President Nixon and other US leaders opted to remove American grounds troops and "Vietnamize" their war effort. In central Vietnam this resulted in substituting ARVN soldiers in the American aerial platform as MACV-ARVN planners attempted an unprecedented push west on highways 9 and 547 across the border deep into Laos. Operation Lam Sơn 719 began in the Huế–Quảng Trị area in February 1971, and it was in some respects a last-ditch effort not unlike the 1953 French Operation Atlante described by Bernard Fall in Street without Joy. US and RVN military leaders attempted to destroy the main corridors of the communist trails in Laos by sending more than twenty thousand ARVN soldiers by tank, helicopter, and plane to communist base areas in Laos. More than ten thousand American troops, including units from Camp Eagle and Phú Bài, played a supporting role, flying aircraft and coordinating bombing strikes. Soldiers from Huế's ARVN First Division and other regional units traveled by helicopter above the bombed-out pavement of Highway 9 in Quảng Trị into Laos.

The operation, while bold in conception, was a disaster for the ARVN. In Laos ARVN soldiers attempted an airborne landing in the middle of what, by 1971, were trail cities, heavily fortified mountain bases supporting several thousand soldiers. PAVN-PLAF units here were reinforced with anti-aircraft batteries and tanks, and they shot down over one hundred aircraft and seized many ARVN artillery guns. Several years of Soviet and Chinese aid produced heavily armored, formidable defenses there. Roughly two thousand South Vietnamese soldiers were killed with another six thousand wounded. An ARVN general concluded that the essential weakness for ARVN troops was "lack of ground mobility," but the ARVN units struggled with the aerial platform as well as the terrain.[77] During five years of American operations, ARVN troops had fought mainly as infantry units while Americans operated most of the helicopters and operational control over high-altitude air strikes and aerial surveillance. While American units such as the 101st Airborne may have excelled in using these aerial technologies, ARVN troops had not.

The PAVN-PLAF victory derived from strong ground defenses in their base areas and increased sophistication on the airwaves. Communist radio operators took advantage of weak radio discipline by ARVN soldiers who routinely gave away positions by not speaking in code. Twenty-five years after Việt Minh forces established the first nationwide radio network, PAVN-PLAF units had in 1971 a plentiful supply of Chinese-made radio sets along with captured American Motorola backpack units. Communist radio operators by 1971 used radio-jamming technologies to cut off South Vietnamese units and interfere with the airborne radio-finding missions too. In his history of the operation, the ARVN general commended the communists on their radio discipline, taking special notice of a female voice he'd heard on the communist radio nets issuing combat orders. The presence of this female voice signaled both the total participatory effort involving women on the communist side as well as superior radio discipline.[78] This operational disaster combined with widespread public outrage in the United States over President Nixon's ordering saturation bombing deep inside Laos and Cambodia pressured the rapid removal of US troops. Troop levels were decreased from more than five hundred thousand in 1969 to fewer than fifty thousand in 1972.

LEAVING THE BASES

The American base closures in 1972 created a new "ruins" problem just as chaotic as the evacuations in 1954. The reduction in troops hollowed out an urban infrastructure of airstrips, radio towers, camps, and roads that primarily American funds and advisers had built since the early 1950s. On the plateaus of the central highlands, American bases at Kon Tum and Pleiku dwarfed the villages after which they were named. On the central coast, especially after 1966, such American bases as Camp Evans and Camp Eagle supported encircling towns of refugees and ARVN veterans. Like American bases elsewhere, these towns depended on the base for much of their income. The rapid American departure stunned local authorities and ARVN commanders. At Camp Eagle more than ten thousand men with tons of equipment disappeared in the first two weeks of January 1972. Compared with the process of building these spaces, the removals were frenzied. They left behind ghost towns to ARVN allies who would have to face new assaults from the mountains.

The turnover of Camp Eagle became a flashpoint for local protests in Huế, too, not about American troops leaving so much as over the ruins they left behind. Further angering ARVN generals was the news that American forces were not simply giving back these properties but selling them via long-term international loans. Per the terms of base agreements, the United States charged the RVN for all improvements on these lands.[79] Officially, MACV maintained that the bases would continue to support Vietnamese units in fighting communist adversaries. However, in practical terms, when American troops evacuated they took most essential elements of the base. This was not only due to the US military's need to conserve resources, redeploying them elsewhere, but also because the US military did not legally own much of the equipment. Given the rapid timeframe for base construction, the United States had paid construction companies such as Pacific Architects and Engineers to build and operate key parts of base infrastructure.[80] When the American military mission ended, property transfers between the US and South Vietnamese militaries did not include the contractors. The US military had also repositioned usable equipment such as fire trucks and radio equipment to smaller enclaves. Camps such as Camp Eagle were left without defenses and littered with industrial wreckage, garbage landfills, and pits of discarded chemicals. Essential systems—high voltage generators, perimeter lighting, air conditioners, water pumps, water treatment plants, telephone switchboards, radios, and signal equipment—disappeared.[81]

On January 21, 1972, NBC Nightly News aired a short segment showing the official transfer ceremony at Camp Eagle. The segment started with the lowering of the American flag while a bugler played "Taps"; then it cut to images of gutted buildings with empty holes left from removed air conditioning units. It finished by following American soldiers loading one of the wall-mounted units into a jeep.[82]

FILLING THE VOID

Just two months after the Americans cleared out of Camp Eagle, PAVN-PLAF forces launched one of the largest conventional mass offensives, the Easter Offensive, to take the central coast. An estimated forty thousand soldiers in infantry and artillery units marched with several hundred tanks across the DMZ down Highway 1 to Quảng Trị, taking the town's nineteenth-century citadel and surrounding areas. On Highway 9, the main east-west road linking the coast with Laos, PAVN-PLAF units marched east past Khe Sanh with

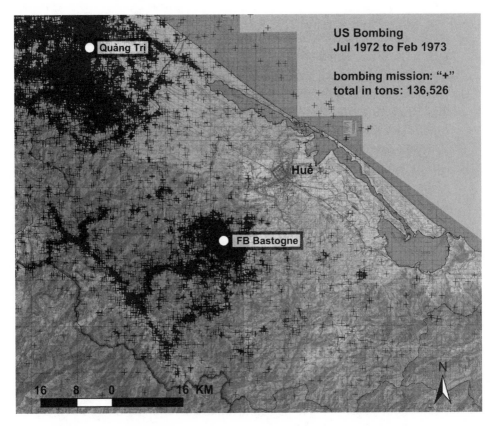

ease. They overpowered ARVN units stationed in former American bases, connecting with the groups that had marched south to Quảng Trị. In the A Sầu Valley, just as the winter cloud cover was starting to thin, communist forces marched to A Lưới past A Bia Mountain (Hamburger Hill) and started down Highway 547 toward Firebase Bastogne (figure 5.15). ARVN troops on the hilltop base took heavy fire all summer while US bombers pulverized the surrounding area. The PAVN 324th and PLAF Sixth Regiments seized Bastogne in July and then turned its guns toward Camp Eagle.[83] The speed of these communist advances surprised US and RVN leaders alike as they realized that American efforts to open paths with herbicides and bombs now aided PAVN units driving Soviet tanks over widened roads.

While military leaders and foreign journalists saw the 1972 communist offensive as a show of force during peace negotiations in Paris, locally in Huế journalists focused on the fight at Firebase Bastogne and fears of a total collapse. Malcolm Browne, famous for his iconic photograph of Buddhist monk Thích Quảng Đức's self-immolation in 1963, reported on the fall of Bastogne for the *New York Times*. As American B-52s pounded communist forces with round-the-clock bombing north of Quảng Trị, communist units in A Sầu Valley hit Bastogne and neighboring firebases with "several thousand shells a day."[84] Browne described a tidal wave of the communists' heavily armored military onslaught along Highway 547 followed by the equally catastrophic American air bombing campaign that stalled it. A map of US bombing missions from July 1972 to the final day of bombing, February 22, 1973, shows the extent of this targeted, intense bombing. Concentrated on the large PAVN-PLAF troop movements north of Quảng Trị and west of Bastogne, American bombers dropped more tons of bombs on these two areas in six months than they had over three years of fighting from 1965 to 1967.

CEASE-FIRE AND RUINS

Except for one important point, the Paris Accords signed on January 27, 1973, reprised the Geneva Accords of 1954. It produced a cease-fire, called for the creation of an international control commission, and permitted foreign nations to continue supporting their Vietnamese allies with existing levels of weapons and equipment. However, in one critical geographical aspect it differed: US negotiators dropped their demand that communist forces evacuate their tactical areas in the mountains of South Vietnam. An ARVN general in a history of the conflict's final years noted that communist forces had made uncontested claims to these territories that they again governed as they had before 1954. However, with the advances on Quảng Trị and Huế, they demonstrated the capacity to take these cities by force against a well-armed adversary.

Unlike Geneva, the Paris Accords signed on January 23, 1973, legalized communist government in highland areas, recognizing provisional revolutionary government (PRG) councils. There would be no political voids or troop relocations. After the cease-fire began on February 22, the PRG took every opportunity to challenge stipulated boundaries of the liberated zones in South Vietnam. They planted NLF flags at every key crossing point on roads and rivers, asking international observers to map each flag.[85] Their resolve to hold highland areas and endure American bombing stemmed from experiences in 1954 and 1968. PAVN-PLAF networks in the mountains had never been stronger than in 1973, while ARVN forces struggled to defend the emptied American bases.

After several failed general offensives, party leader Lê Duẩn paused. He emphasized building more political and material infrastructure in the hills. Mountain valleys such as A Sầu were no longer just corridors; they would become future towns. During the cease-fire, PRG troops played what one ARVN general called a "game of flags" where at night they moved boundary markers into RVN territory. By day, ARVN troops moved the flags back. International observers were like umpires officiating the contest.[86]

In material and landscape terms, what was most different in 1973 from 1954 was the quick retreat of American support for South Vietnam's coastal networks of bases, highways, depots, electric grids, ports, ammunition supplies, heavy weapons, and especially airplanes. The military and industrial infrastructure that two decades of US congressional appropriations had funded could not continue without new imports of heavy equipment, ammunition, and especially oil. The OPEC oil embargo in 1973–74 created severe shortages and price hikes for petroleum supplies in the United States too. This interruption in the global supply of oil meant delays in the supply chain to bases in Vietnam. (Ironically, oil explorers in 1974 identified offshore oil fields off the southern coast of Vietnam.)[87]

This final phase of the war before the communists launched their spring 1975 offensive highlighted a key weakness in the American militarization-urbanization strategy. The petroleum, chemical, electronic, and mechanical supply lines that enabled the world's most modern military to develop landscape-altering campaigns of airborne assaults and surveillance could, in their sudden absence, render these landscapes a liability. Even worse, the clearing of forests and hilltops to insert advance forces opened up ideal spaces for communist forces to position their own units. Communist histories about the 1973–74 period detail a steady expansion of military campaigns aimed to further hobble South Vietnam's military infrastructure. Party political leaders organized wave after wave of political protests in southern cities while military sapper units attacked ARVN infrastructure, blowing pipelines and crippling equipment. In June 1974 commandos detonated explosives destroying petroleum tanks and ammunition bunkers near Phú Bài. A tally of the damage inflicted from February to September 1974 included destruction of more than forty-seven thousand tons of bombs and bullets and fourteen petroleum tanks and seizure of the highest mountaintop observations posts within sight of the coast.[88] In these six months of small-scale battles, the communist forces around Huế had for the first time gained an *aerial* advantage over their adversaries.

In contrast with previous communist offensives that took advantage of lingering cloud cover, a newly combined People's Army II Corps (comprising the PAVN 324th and PLAF Sixth Regiments) planned the spring 1975 offensive in Huế to occur *after* the cloud cover had lifted. This was a first. With South Vietnam's military forces running out of vital supplies and no signs of American high-altitude bombers, they used the bright, clear skies to their advantage. With forces positioned north and south of Huế, they started their siege of the coast at 5:45 A.M. on March 8. Over the next two weeks, these units fought their way into Huế, taking control of the airstrip at Phú Bài and rushing past the abandoned barracks at Camp Eagle. The final Huế-area battles with ARVN troops concluded on March 24 and 25 at the beaches along Thuận An. The symbolism of the location—the point where French marines had started their invasion in 1884 and again in 1947—was not lost on communist military historians.[89] The following morning at 6:30 A.M., members of the PLAF Sixth Regiment climbed the historic citadel in front of the Noon Gate and raised the blue-and-red NLF flag above the city. The war, at least in Huế, was over.

SIX

POSTWAR

AFTER THE WAR ENDED IN 1975 THE PAVN MOVED IN TO THE OLD BASES while the Socialist Republic of Vietnam (SRV) commenced a new era of postwar governance. As in previous postwar moments, especially 1945 and 1954, this one in 1975–76 included its fair share of social and environmental ruins. Faced with international isolation, food shortages, and an economic depression in 1976, the unified socialist state had few resources to redevelop militarized areas. Nor was there a large-scale demobilization of military forces after 1975. The People's Army sent troops to occupy Cambodia in 1978, and in 1979 it fought a border war with China. As a socialist planned economy, the SRV was not inclined to follow Western countries that had redeveloped old bases into industrial parks. Instead, the SRV embarked on new campaigns for agricultural collectivization and small-scale industrialization while local gleaners picked apart scrap metal and any usable materials from the hills.

Given the scale of construction around Huế, especially after 1968, processes of deconstruction, salvage, and recovery were extremely slow at first. In 1980–81, a documentary film team from WGBH in Boston visited Huế collecting footage for *Vietnam: A Television History.* Footage shot along Highway 1 from the airport into Huế shows the hills running up to the former Camp Eagle. In figure 6.1, a tank and armored vehicle stand frozen in time from 1975, yet to be rendered into scrap metal. In the distance, two squares of utility poles form the outline of a helicopter hangar now stripped of its siding. This graveyard-like image of abandoned war machines, standing in

FIGURE 6.1. Screenshot from a 1981 WGBH film clip, "Destroyed US Army Base." Source: WGBH Media Library and Archives, *Vietnam: A Television History*, March 1, 1981, Phú Bài, Vietnam, http://openvault.wgbh.org/catalog/vietnam-713cae-destroyed-u-s-army-base.

place for over six years, suggests that removal of this equipment was not slowed just by the physical challenges of cutting armor plating with hand tools but by social and political indecision about what vestiges of the war to keep.

Especially for many PAVN and PLAF veterans, these dead tanks did not just signify victories but also served to remind people of the scale of destruction in the war, something easier to forget now that most of the war's remains have disappeared. While not discussed in official histories, these local debates over the preservation of war remains were common. I learned about them firsthand in 2001 while driving by motorbike on a stretch of highway north of Sài Gòn. I found a tank parked beside the highway, its large gun poking out of some trees. I stopped the bike and, without thinking, crawled up on the tank, curious as to why this war object had been left on the side of the road with no signs, no historical markers, no explanation. Moments later, an older man on motorbike drove by and then circled back, no doubt surprised to see a foreigner standing on the tank. He parked his bike next to mine and waited for me to climb down. When I addressed him in Vietnamese and answered his questions about where I came from and what I was doing in Vietnam (working toward my PhD), the conversation turned more than a little bit uncomfortable. I was an American on the upper edge of military-serving age with a shaved head, speaking Vietnamese. We talked about the tank. He'd served in a PLAF unit that fought along this highway, what American GIs referred to as Thunder Road (Highway 13). He explained that after the war, he and other veterans organized to keep the tank on the roadside as a memorial to the people who died there. In 2015 I drove the same stretch of highway again, but the tank was gone.

This decision about what vestiges to keep or let go is a complex one with many parallels around the world. Landscapes are often at the center of debates involving veterans and national history. Walls pockmarked by shrapnel or metal skeletons of tanks and downed planes often serve as focal points for state-guided reflection. Proponents of memorialization seek such ruined monuments so that people will never forget, while others seek to erase these old war vestiges to move on. Communities are often divided, too, in trying to balance the desires of veterans and the younger generation. Mr. Phương, a resident of Dạ Lê Village who fought with the 324th Regiment, described to me his shock after 1975 when the one-time cityscape of Camp Eagle "looking like New York, bright lights like crazy" turned into the empty wasteland in figure 6.1. A native of the village and a political officer with the 324th, he returned to the village in 1975 and hoped to preserve parts of Camp Eagle while also salvaging some of the metal siding to build his house. He went north to Hà Nội for training courses in the early 1980s (when the shot in figure 6.1 was captured); when he returned home the tanks were gone.

> They cleared [the hills] so that several years later there was nothing left; before when I looked from Chín Hầm out here it was like New York City, bright lights like crazy. But then they cleared out after several years and left it empty; they managed it so nobody could take anything. . . . I returned here and just farmed. My house then was an iron siding house, just built. At that time, I resolved to preserve one military tank here as a reminder, but then I went to Hà Nội to study and the people here took it [for scrap], removing everything. . . . I had intended to preserve the [American] base in Hamlet 5; because I lived near it I knew to preserve the base intact so that later our

children and people could come and visit. But they'd taken and broken up everything already. The stuff the Americans had left was all destroyed. . . . I only took some iron siding, brought a motorcycle cart to carry them, but I didn't take anything else.[1]

Half a world away in the United States, veterans and journalists also sparred over similar debates about these landscapes in Vietnam. Paul Scipione served in the 101st Airborne at Camp Eagle during the war, and he wrote a letter to the editor of the *New York Times* after reading journalist Craig Whitney's account of a return visit to Phú Bài and Camp Eagle in 1983. Whitney worked in Huế in 1972 and 1973 as a reporter, writing for the *Times* on the communist offensive and the fallout after the American troop withdrawals. In his essay Whitney remarked on scenes of new construction along Highway 1 and the empty spaces where the American bases once stood. Scipione responded in a letter to the *Times*:

I found Craig R. Whitney's retrospective, "A Bitter Peace: Life in Vietnam" (Oct. 30, 1983) provocative. However, I must respectfully disagree with his observation "that only stones were left where American bases had stood— Camp Eagle, home of the 101st Airborne Division; military airfield at Phu Bai." . . . As a former NCO [noncommissioned officer] in the 101st who spent a short but incredibly intense part of my life at Phu Bai and Camp Eagle, I know with certainty that more is left there than a few stones—things like honor and comradeship, our former naïveté and the blood of ourselves and others, in the sand. For those of us who fought there, Phu Bai and Camp Eagle remain something indelible—a place in our minds and memories, not just places on a map.[2]

Both Scipione's and Phương's struggles concerned the meanings of past traumas inscribed not only in the physical landscape but also in their minds. That Camp Eagle and Dạ Lê Village were halfway around the world from Metuchen was irrelevant.

PROBLEMATIC RUINS AND FAMILY REUNIONS

Contrasted with postwar moments in 1945 and 1954, the postwar period followed one of the most concentrated, physically destructive wars in modern history. War's footprints on the landscape—abandoned bases and millions of bomb craters—remained vivid, but there were countless internal scars too. Residents in Dạ Lê Village, for example, described major demographic shifts. First, many of the men did not come back; in the first years after the war, it was a village of women. Then, in the late 1970s and early 1980s, many pro-RVN families began to disappear, secretly escaping in the dark of night to fishing boats on the coast. Finally, new settlers from the north central province of Quảng Bình, a mix of PAVN veterans and refugees from zones north of the DMZ arrived. They attempted to reclaim the bare hills of Hamlet 5 inside the former Camp Eagle. One man recalled that until the mid-1980s not even eucalyptus trees would grow in these compacted, chemically sprayed soils.[3]

Vietnam's embargo on media descriptions of postwar troubles eased a bit in the early 1990s after the historic Đổi Mới (Renovation) reforms of 1986. Vietnamese veterans began publishing short stories and novels that pointed to painful personal tragedies, shattered marriages, and crippling post-traumatic stress. First published as a newspaper serial in 1991 and translated into English in 1993, veteran Bảo Ninh's *The Sorrow of War* has become a classic of this genre for foreign audiences, providing readers a glimpse of these seldom documented but widely acknowledged, stressful engagements with former war sites as well as struggles simply going home. While the following passage takes place near Hà Nội, it could have easily taken place in the villages around Huế. It describes the protagonist, Kiên, a veteran suffering from intense post-traumatic stress disorder who returns to Hà Nội only to find a city hollowed out by bombing where the love of his youth has forgotten him. The sorrow that Bảo Ninh conjures in a story that jumps back and forth in time and dissolves into dreamlike encounters with ghosts seamlessly joins individual suffering with dystopic landscapes. In describing Kiên's visit to a fallen comrade's family to return his personal items, Bảo Ninh writes:

> The landscape was half marsh, half rubbish dump. The scrawny children wore rags. . . . The hamlet's inhabitants were semibeggars, gathering garbage for their meager living, and there were small dumps of obviously stolen goods lining the paths where thieves had set up tiny stalls. Someone pointed Vinh's family house to Kiên. It was like all the others, a shanty of tin and old timber, surrounded by garbage. Vinh's little sister was barely fifteen then. Her eyes had swollen and sent tears down her cheeks as she recognized her brother's knapsack and his personal belongings. There was no need to ask why Kiên

had come to visit them. The sad news was there for them to touch. Vinh's blind mother sat with the girl, feeling the items as she handed them over. A cloth hat. A folded knife. An iron bowl. A broken flute. A notebook. When Kiên rose to leave, the old lady had reached up and touched his cheek. "At least you came back," she said quietly.[4]

Repeatedly in the novel, Bảo Ninh emphasizes the intense struggles that surround this soldier's return home in landscape terms—coming back to ruined spaces. The novel captures in such personal exchanges what has remained for decades after 1975 one of the most difficult processes of postwar recovery for millions of Vietnamese.

Especially in the former border provinces of Thừa Thiên–Huế and Quảng Trị, of the first landscapes to attract private attention were the lands dotted with tombs and family shrines. With the economic reforms of the 1990s, the SRV permitted remittances from overseas Vietnamese to relatives who stayed. These remittances quickly ran into billions of dollars. Much of the money went to ancestral homelands (*quê hương*), not only money for personal needs, medicine, and so on, but also to rebuild the village and especially family tombs.[5]

As a frequently traveling in-law (*rể*) in an extended Vietnamese family, with ties to a paternal homeland in Trung Đơn, a tiny village in Quảng Trị Province, and maternal relatives in Huế, I had frequent opportunities to attend village and family ceremonies while negotiating my own roles as a son-in-law to a founding family. Through my father-in-law, Lý Tô, I was privy to one man's experience of working with a cousin in Huế, Uncle Nghiên, to get money back to the village. Like many central Vietnamese families, the Lý family was split in its wartime affiliations mostly along gender lines. Tô's father encouraged him and his elder brother to get advanced educations; they matriculated through Huế's best schools and traveled to the United States on engineering scholarships. The same father, following traditional village custom, discouraged his four daughters from studying beyond the third grade. In the 1960s three of them joined the NLF, where they received a revolutionary education. They met their future husbands working with the PLAF and the party. At one family reunion in Huế, one of these "rebel aunties" half-joked with me saying she was in her youth just like the women in the black pajamas with the AK-47, "bang bang." This split family situation, some siblings moving to the United States and others staying in Vietnam, was not uncommon during the war, especially on the central coast.

As Vietnam expanded its diplomatic and trade relations with the United States in the mid-1990s, these split families began to reconnect. Tô and his brother Đãi joined an association of overseas Trung Đơn villagers and focused on supporting family reunions and village projects with other family clans, the Hoàng, Ngô, Hồ, and Nguyễn. As did other family- and village-based networks, they raised tens of thousands of dollars over twenty years to bring electricity to the village, rebuild roads, build bridges, and carry out other constructive works. The Trung Đơn Network raised funds for college scholarships at Huế University. Mostly Buddhists, they also raised funds to build a new Buddhist pagoda and restore family tombs. Uncle Nghiên acted as a go-between with overseas relatives, making sure the funds reached their destination.

As an in-law and a Vietnamese-speaking foreigner on trips to Trung Đơn, I enjoyed lavish feasts and a front-seat view on one family's effort to reconnect. We met the uncles who as war heroes helped manage government paperwork required to turn overseas remittances into roads and scholarships. A member of the village people's committee joined one death anniversary (*ngày đám giỗ*) feast for my wife's grandfather. After the meal several men from the family led me to the recently reconstructed Lý family shrine honoring the founding ancestor who had settled in the village in the mid-1500s.

In addition to overseas relatives, increasingly wealthy urban family descendants in Vietnam have joined in this family-centered form of history-making. Family members whose parents served in PAVN-PLAF forces and some whose parents served in the ARVN have joined these village networks, contributing to construction efforts, and have tapped in to family and village networks when they travel abroad. Provincial and communal public works departments have grown wealthier, too, and they have replaced remittance-funded projects with wider roads, more electric power, bridges, and other public services. Now more than forty years since the war's end, the increasing number of village festivals and family reunions and the ever-more-opulent tomb and shrine constructions suggest hopeful signs for rebuilding village landscapes and healing the tangible and intangible wounds of war.

CHEMICAL GHOSTS

Like the ghosts that haunt Kiên in Bảo Ninh's novel, the chemical remains of war on the central coast present a different political and environmental challenge. One of the most troubling remains from the war are the many toxic chemicals left not only from the herbicide program but also from industrial chemicals disposed at landfills around former bases. Lacking expensive, high-tech methods for genetic testing or mass spectroscopy in soils, many people living in former spray zones or near former bases are left to wonder whether clusters of birth defects or cancers are associated with invisible toxins. One resident of Dạ Lê Village born in 1925, Mr. Minh, described a familiar pattern of ailments that he believed were associated to his exposure to Agent Orange. He explained how he regrouped to the north in 1954 and then returned south along the Hồ Chí Minh Trail in Laos, where he worked during the war in the 1960s managing a fifty-person transport team in charge of five boats at a ferry crossing called Tà Khống. He and his team were repeatedly sprayed with herbicides. He suspected that his son's severely deformed legs may have been related to his exposure to these "poisons" but he had no way to prove it.[6] Minh's story is common in Vietnam, and over the decades newspapers, books, and films have popularized these fears with calls for justice and reparations from the United States.

My initial interest in using historical records to track these chemical footprints pushed my interest in the larger historical project, and it also raised my awareness of the more general problem posed by so many different chemical traces in the land. My research in Huế began around the research of historical maps and records identifying possible chemical hotspots near former US bases. I conveyed scans of the Tenth Chemical Platoon's daily records at Camp Eagle to the Director of Thừa Thiên–Huế Province's Department of Science and Technology, and we discussed using historical records to more accurately pinpoint suspected chemical dumps.[7] While Agent Orange remains a highly restricted topic for foreign research in Vietnam, this more general problem of toxic waste cleanups at former US base sites is of equal if not greater importance to local economic and development policies.

Using military text records and imagery, I worked with a handful of geographers and a remote sensing specialist in Huế to generate land cover maps of both Camp Eagle and the Phú Bài Combat Base. We digitized historic air photos of the base areas in 1972 as a starting point and then digitized land cover areas using the UN Food and Agriculture Organization's standard land cover categories. We digitized land cover layers from satellite imagery produced in 2001 and 2009, and we analyzed the 1972 air photos using text records and visual inference to locate suspected storage depots. In 2012 we presented the maps with suspect chemical hotspot candidate sites to officials from the province and the district. As is common with foreigners involved in such matters, the group politely accepted my data then said goodbye. I readily understood that local debates and follow-up strategies would not be open for the comment of historians, especially foreigners. Nevertheless, I believe that this method of researching public American and South Vietnamese records may support continuing environmental research, and this book is in some small ways tied to that more activist interest.

Of all the places we visited, one hotspot candidate in particular has remained a touchstone for me as I wrote this book. The helipad for the 160th Helicopter Group at Camp Eagle is still partially visible as a large asphalt rectangle on a hilltop separated by a ravine from the tomb-covered hills of Hamlet 5 in Dạ Lê (plate 8). This site, unlike most, is easily accessed by a new highway running through the center of the former Camp Eagle. Since 2012 I have returned to this spot on every visit to Huế as it gives me a link to the site's wartime past and an opportunity to study new constructions, from the tombs in the background to new construction across the road and, since 2016, a grid of acacia saplings planted in evenly spaced holes dug into the old, cracking pavement.

Comparing satellite photographs and air photos taken in 1972 with a map of base cantonments from the 101st Airborne Museum allowed me to reconstruct this site's association with this aviation group (figure 6.2). A composite image of these layered sources shows the helipad's location in the past compared with more recent satellite imagery of the site. This helped pinpoint the approximate locations of the Tenth Chemical Platoon, too, as its headquarters and depot for drummed chemicals was close to the helipad. This helipad was of interest to the province as it supported the sniffer missions, flame drops, and defoliation runs of the 101st Airborne. A closer view of this hotspot candidate site shows the asphalt helicopter pad as well as stacks of containerized materials. At the time these aerial photographs were taken, the US Army had already moved most of its troops and aircraft from the facility. The aviation depot area with a storage pad for drummed chemicals was one of the hotspot candidates (figure 6.3). Air photos from 1972 show the hangars used for aircraft repairs as well as the rows of metal clad buildings that served as quarters for the crews. They also show the perimeter with guard towers and a creek that drained runoff from the helipad area to Dạ Lê's fields below.

Even though scavengers had cleared off most of the buildings here by the late 1990s, the footprints of the old buildings and helipad were still visible in

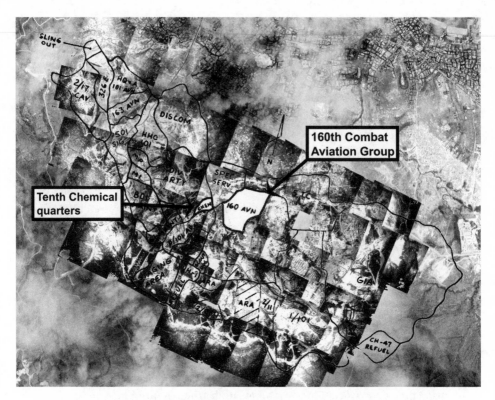

FIGURE 6.2. Map showing unit cantonments inside Camp Eagle, circa 1969. Source: "Camp Eagle Counterattack Plan," 101st Airborne Division Pratt Museum; Box 3, Military Assistance Command Vietnam Construction Directorate, Real Property Disposal Files, Record Group 472, US National Archives and Records Administration, College Park; CORONA Frame DS1117-2038DF144, courtesy of US Geological Survey Earth Resources Observation and Science Center. Annotations by author.

satellite images with little vegetation evident. Using an infrared layer from a 2001 satellite frame, we located the outlines of the old helipad by lines of weeds growing around its old rectangular form (plate 9).

While as a historian I appreciate the accessibility of this site and its relatively open state, which permit easy mental reconstructions, the lack of remediation here points to troubling problems of economic, local, and even international politics. A modern environmental cleanup of such a site in an industrialized country might run in the tens of millions of dollars for testing, soil remediation, and disposal. Limited resources and tight profit margins in Vietnam means that local governments must do what they can to

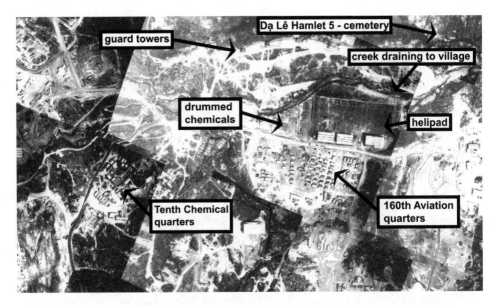

FIGURE 6.3. Hotspot candidate sites, 1972. Source: "Camp Eagle Counterattack Plan," 101st Airborne Division Pratt Museum; Box 3, Military Assistance Command Vietnam Construction Directorate, Real Property Disposal Files, Record Group 472, US National Archives and Records Administration, College Park; CORONA Frame DS1117-2038DF144, courtesy of US Geological Survey Earth Resources Observation and Science Center. Annotations by author.

generate new uses from these lands without incurring these costs and simultaneously without exposing people to hazardous materials. They do the best they can; they keep most of these sites reserved for industrial uses, capping them in asphalt or covering them in trees. Like militaries globally, the PAVN has also opted to retain many polluted properties as another way of mitigating liability. The helipad has been left alone, but the property just south of it across the highway, the former headquarters for the helicopter squadron, has become Ministry of Defense Vocational College 23 (figure 6.4). The PAVN has repurposed it for a relatively safe new use to minimize exposures, an asphalt driving course. A sign shows the largely paved, impermeable footprint of the new college destined to cover the hilltop. With so many potentially troublesome properties, states, communities, and militaries have opted to literally pave over past problems, capping damaged soils while they wait for new technologies or funds to do something about potential hazards in the ground.

FIGURE 6.4. Construction site for Vocational College 23 on top of the former 160th Aviation Group site. Photo by author, July 2015.

This local political debate over approaches to toxic sites also stems in part from difficult experiences in the 1990s with discoveries of Agent Orange/dioxin-contaminated sites and the negotiation of postwar relations with the United States. Foreign researchers and military teams identified major air bases of the American spray program as well as more remote hotspots where defoliants left concentrated plumes of dioxin in the ground. Publications about these sites have drawn extensive international attention, but locally these Agent Orange stories have brought problems too. Without tens of millions of dollars to clean soil, relatively poor rural governments in mountainous areas have few options but to mark off such sites as toxic and keep people out.

The former American A Shau Special Forces Base that was overrun in 1966 is one of the more famous of these upland sites with an unusually concentrated dioxin hotspot. A collaborative research venture between Canadian and Vietnamese researchers in the A Sầu Valley resulted in a comprehensive analysis of soils, animal tissue, human blood samples, and human breast-milk.[8] Soil tests conducted across the valley confirmed that dioxin sprayed from the airplanes had dissipated along the mountain slopes to "background levels" comparable with other sprayed lands such as golf courses in industrialized countries. They found levels from nondetectable to five parts per trillion. The only sites with highly elevated concentrations were the former American special forces bases in the valley where chemicals were likely stored in drums. At the former A Shau Special Forces Base, now known as Đông Sơn Commune, the team found that sediment in aquaculture ponds filling old bomb craters showed dioxin at a highly toxic concentration of 300–400 parts per trillion. The joint study recommended focusing attention to these "dioxin reservoirs" where the contaminant was moving through duck and fish fats into the bodies of people, especially babies in the womb.[9]

While the research helped to prevent new exposures at the site or via pathways of absorption via fish and ducks, this widely known history of A Shau as a hotspot has left a problematic legacy. I visited the former airfield and nearby Đông Sơn Commune with a group of American students and a Vietnamese ecologist in 2015. The visit, coordinated by an office in A Lưới District, featured stops at the former runway (figure 6.5), the hotspot site, and the commune's meeting hall.[10] Guides pointed our attention to a small infirmary funded by foreign and government contributions, and the chairman of the commune presented me with a gift of textiles made by the Ta Oi indigenous people who were the historic occupants in this part of the valley. He was a member of this group, as were roughly half of the people in the commune.

In the chairman's short welcome speech, he quickly got to the point about the Agent Orange and war legacy narrative and more specifically the hotspot story that had drawn our group there. Pointing to the infirmary, he said that what the commune did *not* need were more scientists and experts coming to draw people's blood and take it away to write their studies. They had a clear enough knowledge, he said, about hotspot locations and how dioxin moved through the food chain. The problem he identified as most vital to the commune's future development concerned affordable or free tests to confirm whether people's land, animals, or perhaps their DNA was now *clean*. He implored me, the ecologist, and the students to develop technologies to effectively map dioxin's presences and also its *absences* so that people could work, live, and build livelihoods in these areas. Farmers in the commune, he stated, despite general assurances from researchers, continued to encounter discrimination at urban markets when buyers asked their village of origin. The chairman's speech illustrated a particular struggle for those generally *not*

FIGURE 6.5. Former A Shau runway with bomb craters. Author photo.

affected by encounters with dioxin but nevertheless suffering under the weight of association with the war's chemical history.

REGREENING THE MILITARIZED LANDSCAPE

While comprehensive cleanups at bases and sites like A Shau remain limited, the economic reforms of the 1990s did set into motion new programs for land privatization in the hills that have, especially since 2000, resulted in a widespread return of vegetation in the form of plantation forests. State documents and newspapers long derided the problem of "đất trống, đồi trọc" (bare lands, eroded slopes), repeatedly using this term as a shorthand for damages blamed on US bombings, defoliation, and the war in general. Vietnam first recognized private leases in such lands in 1993 after land clearing during postwar decimated forests even further. Vietnam's total forest cover bottomed out at about 25 percent of total area and has since rebounded to over 44 percent, albeit almost wholly via plantations. Private investors have reforested an incredible area, over 5 million hectares of bare hills and other public lands.[11]

While this recent expansion in tree plantations is widely lauded in Vietnamese newspapers and television newscasts, it stems not just from recent approaches but also continues a legacy of colonial-era schemes to recolonize the hills with exotic species. Personalities such as Henri Guibier and Vietnamese foresters who followed him in the 1950s and 1960s continued to advance this type of green modernization. Huế's first postcolonial chief forester, Nguyễn Hữu Đính, continued Guibier's enthusiasm to reforest with exotics and worked with new foreign experts from the United States and Australia in the 1960s. Đính was responsible for developing new nurseries and plantations in secure areas. Later, he supported the National Liberation Front. He retired from government service in 1960, survived the Tết Offensive and post-Tết reprisals, and stayed in Huế after 1975 to develop a forestry school at Huế University. While the fighting in the hills west of Huế reached unprecedented levels of destruction by 1973, Đính and many forestry colleagues in both Vietnamese governments envisioned a postwar future with new regreening schemes. After the RVN and the communist PRG agreed to a cease-fire in January 1973, Đính sent a public report to RVN and PRG officials in Paris suggesting that they work quickly to develop a viable forest policy with fast-growing species that might support industries such as pulp and paper. He took advantage of his retirement status to offer advice to all sides, stating that the cease-fire presented an opportunity to "plant trees, *make flowers*" (make peace) and "*cease* forest destruction" (playing on the term "cease-fire").[12]

In some senses, regreening as an industrial enterprise is little different from the base-to-industrial-park conversions near Highway 1. Local governments may enthusiastically embrace development of plantation forests, but often when entrepreneurs attempt to stake off "cleared" or "waste" lands to regreen, debates arise. The PAVN victory resulted in postwar transfers of large parcels of land (the former American bases), producing what anthropologist James Scott calls an "abstract, theoretical kind of place."[13] However, military actors have remained active in this postwar enterprise too. Unlike in industrialized nations, where national militaries help support a domestic high-tech sector producing aircraft, surveillance technologies, and guns, armies such as the PAVN raise much of their funds through resource extraction and public businesses. For example, the largest telecommunications company in Vietnam, Viettel, is a military enterprise, building off of the military's radio and telecommunications networks. Like old military salary fields, many industrial forest plots, too, are managed by investments from military companies or provide jobs to military veterans.

Just as it's hard to erase such ghosts of old wars as tanks or trauma sites, leaving behind the military-social ties embedded in these landscapes is difficult. This is especially so around the former firebases. I learned this first-hand on a trip with forestry and conservation officials to the former Firebase Birmingham on old Highway 547 (now Highway 49). Responding to criticism from conservation organizations about monocropping in industrial forests, the local forest service office in collaboration with several nongovernmental organizations set aside this old military parcel as an experiment in natural forest regeneration. Even there, where government ownership is undisputed, foresters, villagers, and entrepreneurs appeared deadlocked on the economics and politics of natural reforestation and public ownership. Riding in a forest service jeep, we traveled from Huế on the same old road that once connected Camp Eagle with Bastogne. The driver turned the jeep off at a bend in the road, and we walked out onto a level bank about two hundred meters wide and five hundred meters long, the former runway of Firebase Birmingham. The old runway was barely recognizable except for some pieces of broken tarmac in the red dirt, buried for the most part under a dense thicket of tree saplings and scrub. We hiked down from the runway toward a creek crossing the plot. Saplings grew from seeds dropped by birds, they explained, and there was no regular plan to thin or selectively cut them. Despite the novelty of the "natural" plot and its historic location, the foresters held little hope that the plot would survive a coming round of budget cuts. Their bosses in Hà Nội saw the plot as a failure. It wasn't generating a profit, and located so close to a highway and a city, it wasn't ideally suited as a preserve. Area residents passed by carrying bundles of wood for fuel, and the NGO representative added that save for the honey harvested from the plot, the locals held a similar opinion of natural reforestation to that of the bosses in Hà Nội. Then they pointed my gaze to lush stands of acacia growing in industrial plots on nearby ridges and suggested that this green industrial fate awaited Firebase Birmingham. That model, they wryly noted, worked, while the experiment in natural regeneration lacked an easily defended economic or political logic.

DEMILITARIZING LANDSCAPE PASTS AND FUTURES

The arc of this history of the central coast's militarized layers, from the Ô Châu Terrible Lands to these postwar zones of industrial development and

FIGURE 6.6. Sign in Dạ Lê, Hamlet 5: "Military Area. PROHIBITED: Building Tombs, Burials, Graves." Photo by author, July 2015.

green capitalism, shows how legacies of militarization from one era often become entangled in the next. A core value for an environmental history in such a conflict zone rests in its power to challenge the stories that people, local or not, tell with respect to the ways land in the past was connected to national and international events as well as to the struggles of families, settlers, and farmers. Even in the present, these local and state histories of certain lands regularly conflict with one another. Individuals and families, for example, must often still negotiate with the state, especially the military, when they attempt to visit old tombs or create new ones nearby. As figure 6.6 suggests, this tension between military and nonmilitary uses shows few signs of abating, as locals simply ignore new claims to land that traditionally was part of the village commons. At the top of a hill overlooking the former 101st Airborne's headquarters at Camp Eagle, a broken sign next to a dirt road warns local inhabitants against the old practice of digging graves and burying ancestors. A thick screen of acacias screens off the old cemetery, barely visible behind the trees.

A quick ride down the road reveals a few dozen recently renovated tombs. Alone at this cemetery and mindful of my appearance as an American on a motorbike in a militaty zone, I am reminded of two things. First, the presence of broken concrete foundations from old Camp Eagle suggests how military claims often outlive the original militaries that established them. At this site, the American military lease of the hilltop was transferred in 1972 to the ARVN and in 1975 to the PAVN. Each army brought its own real estate agents to manage these transfers. Second, the site of new village tombs amid the young acacia trees and concrete ruins signals that despite these military claims, area residents continue to challenge them just as their ancestors had for centuries. They choose when and where to ignore the signs, and they build new graves, their own ancestral beachheads marking genealogical histories in this place. At least to me, this local choice of when to respect or violate state boundaries, carrying on an older and essential ancestral tradition, offers some hope. While graveyards are not normally the places people go for hope, the increasingly opulent shrines here signify one way that local communities and individual families continue to reclaim these lands from a violent past. Tree plantations and vocational colleges offer prominent signs of state-centered recovery, but these tombs reflect a more personal history. As commercial enterprises expand in the hills, highly contentious tomb-moving campaigns ensue as gravediggers attempt to clear certain hills. This visual push and pull in the hills between cemeteries and industrial spaces is, in my view, a sign of hope and also of complex challenges that face people in their attempts to reclaim these militarized landscapes from the layers of a troubled past.

NOTES

INTRODUCTION

1 "Eagle Turnover," January 16, 1972, Box 3, Real Property Management Division: Property Disposal Files, 1972, Military Assistance Command Vietnam (hereafter MACV) Headquarters: Construction Directorate, Record Group (hereafter RG) 472, US National Archives and Records Administration, College Park (hereafter NARA-CP).

2 Veterans' personal webpages and snapshots constitute an invaluable visual and historical resource. For one soldier's description of his 1969–70 tour at Camp Eagle and mention of the tombs, see Lee Hill, Photographs, 101st Airborne Division, HHC G2, last accessed September 21, 2017, http://mypage.siu.edu/leehill /Vietnam/VietnamPictures.htm.

3 Details of the cleanup can be found in Province People's Committee Decree 272, January 26, 2000, "Về việc phê duyệt thiết kế, dự toán công trình khắc phục hậu quả ô nhiễm môi trường do chất độc hóa học và bãi thải chiến tranh của Mỹ tại hồ Khe Lời, xã Thủy Phù, huyện Hương Thủy." More recently, the Vietnamese daily *Pháp Luật VN* returned to investigate alleged cancer clusters around the pollution site. See Thùy Nhung, "Nghi vấn thảm họa ung thư từ hầm chứa chất độc CS và kho trữ thuốc trừ sâu," in *Pháp Luật VN*, August 18, 2016, last accessed March 8, 2017, www.baomoi.com/nghi-van-tham-hoa-ung-thu-tu-ham-chua -chat-doc-cs-va-kho-tru-thuoc-tru-sau/c/20119429.epi.

4 These maps are described in more detail in chapter 6, and a collection of them can be referenced at the book's companion website, *Footprints of War*, at david biggs.net.

5 For a discussion of the mining see Bùi Thị Tân, *Về hai làng nghề truyền thống: Phù Bài và Hiền Lương* [Regarding two traditional craft villages: Phù Bài and Hiền Lương] (Huế: Thuận Hóa, 1999). Literally, đất phèn are acid sulfate soils in which dissolved iron produces red streaks and that can be toxic to plants. In local interviews area residents explained references to Vùng Phèn as a region of rust-red creeks cutting through the hills.

6 Within the growing subfield of military environmental history, the topic of post-military legacies and land uses is well covered. One exemplary collection focused on European and American sites is Chris Pearson, Peter Coates, and Tim Cole,

eds., *Military Landscapes: From Gettysburg to Salisbury Plain* (London: Bloomsbury, 2010).

7   Francis Sheppard, *London: A History* (Oxford: Oxford University Press, 1998), 8–12.

8   Keith Taylor, *The Birth of Vietnam* (Berkeley: University of California Press, 1983),
      63, 226.

9   Joseph Schumpeter, *Capitalism, Socialism and Democracy* (New York: Harper,
      1950), 83.

10   Sombart in particular noted the following passage from *Thus Spake Zarathustra*:
      "For earthquakes bury many wells and leave many languishing, but they also
      bring to light inner powers and secrets. Earthquakes reveal new wells. In earth-
      quakes that strike ancient peoples, new wells break open." See Friedrich Nietzsche,
      Thus Spake Zarathustra: A Book for All and None, trans. Walter Kaufmann (Lon-
      don: Penguin, 1968), 211. Historians of philosophy Hugo and Erik Reinert explain
      these compelling intellectual borrowings in "Creative Destruction in Economics:
      Nietzsche, Sombart, Schumpeter," in *Friedrich Nietzsche (1844–1900)*, ed. Jürgen
      Backhaus (New York: Springer, 2006): 55–86.

11   David Harvey, "Neoliberalism as Creative Destruction," *Annals of the American
      Academy of Political and Social Science* 610 (March 2007): 22–44; Naomi Klein,
      The Shock Doctrine: The Rise of Disaster Capitalism (New York: Picador, 2007).
      See also Naomi Klein, "Baghdad Year Zero: Pillaging Iraq in Pursuit of a Neocon
      Utopia," *Harpers*, September 2004: 45.

12   Two American historians who have helped launch these environmentalist and
      historical critiques of war are Edmund Russell and Richard P. Tucker in their
      book *Natural Enemy, Natural Ally: Toward an Environmental History of Warfare*
      (Corvallis: Oregon State University Press, 2004). In Asian Studies, Michael
      Szonyi's *Cold War Island: Quemoy on the Front Line* (Cambridge, UK: Cambridge
      University Press, 2008) examines long-term social and environmental effects of
      prolonged militarism at the local level. Another strain focuses on base closures
      and postconflict remediation. See Marianna Dudley, *An Environmental History
      of the UK Defence Estate, 1945 to the Present* (London: Continuum, 2012), and
      Chris Pearson, *Mobilizing Nature: The Environmental History of War and Mili-
      tarization in Modern France* (Manchester: Manchester University Press, 2012).
      Finally, comparative histories of militarization and war readiness open up oppor-
      tunities for examining different cultural responses to common problems such as
      radiation poisoning. See Kate Brown, *Plutopia: Nuclear Families, Atomic Cities,
      and the Great Soviet and American Plutonium Disasters* (New York: Oxford Uni-
      versity Press, 2013).

13   This global discourse on environmental cleanups and base closures has produced
      its own archives as well as a growing body of historical literature on such demili-
      tarization programs. In the United States, military agencies such as the Army
      Corps of Engineers have taken the lead in designing cleanup programs at for-
      mer sites. This work includes archive search reports and writing base histories.
      See, for example, Michael W. Harper, Thomas R. Reinhardt, and Barry R. Sude,

Environmental Cleanup at Former and Current Military Sites: A Guide to Research. (Alexandria, VA: Office of History and Environmental Division, US Army Corps of Engineers, 2001).

14 Political scientist Cynthia Enloe popularized the term in her studies on the impacts of military bases and militarized imagery on gender relations. A growing number of historians, geographers, and others have extended the term to study other processes, including environmental ones. See Cynthia H. Enloe, *Bananas, Beaches and Bases: Making Feminist Sense of International Politics* (Berkeley: University of California Press, 1990); Cynthia H. Enloe, *Maneuvers: The International Politics of Militarizing Women's Lives* (Berkeley: University of California Press, 2000); Szonyi, *Cold War Island*; Trevor Paglen, *Blank Spots on the Map: The Dark Geography of the Pentagon's Secret World* (New York: Dutton, 2009); and Mark L. Gillem, *America Town: Building the Outposts of Empire* (Minneapolis: University of Minnesota Press, 2007).

15 Geographer Denis Cosgrove in his 1984 classic, *Social Formation and Symbolic Landscape*, makes the provocative argument that the idea of landscape in art and politics was born out of the European turn to capitalist political economic models in the sixteenth and seventeenth centuries. Linking the rise of landscape art with the rise in capitalist modes of production, he writes: "Thus a landscape painted in accordance with pictorial rules, or nature observed by an eye trained to look at it as landscape, is in important respects far from being realistic. It is composed, regulated and offered as a static image for individual appreciation, or better, appropriation. For an important, if not always literal, sense the spectator owns the view because all of its components are structured and directed towards his eyes only." See Denis Cosgrove, *Social Formation and Symbolic Landscape* (Madison: University of Wisconsin, 1998), 26.

16 Jackson's vernacular landscape opens up an approach for interpreting competing military efforts to name and interpret subject landscapes as vital to larger political aims. With the foreign militaries of the United States and France, historic records and maps indicate a rapid-fire succession of place-names overlaid on top of older indigenous toponyms. The name "Camp Eagle," for example, was unique to the Screaming Eagles 101st Airborne Division and used in 1968 to designate a camp in the hills above the old village Dạ Lê. American military engineers first referred to the area by its Vietnamese name before shifting in 1968 to Camp Eagle. See John Brinckerhoff Jackson, *Discovering the Vernacular Landscape* (New Haven: Yale University Press, 1984).

17 This approach to landscapes in both their vernacular and topological significance is informed by urban and architectural theorists, especially philosopher Henri Lefebvre in *The Production of Space*. Space, he argues, consists of three components held in tension with each other: spatial practices, activities such as road building that alter a space's physical characteristics; representational space, symbolic spaces akin to J. B. Jackson's vernacular landscape; and representations of space, artifacts such as maps, bird's-eye photographs, and paintings that influence

how people "read" a space. Military organizations are powerful, state-backed organizations that can become deeply involved in this three-way spatial dialectic. See Henri Lefebvre, *The Production of Space* (Oxford: Blackwell, 1991), 38–39.

18   Ibid., 34. Lefebvre's final point, that space is generative, was his most controversial. It raises provocative questions about space and historical agency, especially in a highly contested, militarized area. Do spaces—imagined or real—shape human actions and thus influence the outcome of historic events? Do they shape military outcomes? Do postmilitary wastelands have agency, perhaps in fostering state-owned industrial parks? This is Lefebvre's point in arguing that space is generative; for him, it figured into the politics of his day in 1960s Paris as citizens clashed on the city streets. He was intimately concerned with the ways that majority political parties and state authorities used spaces to influence decisions of people to flee, conform or resist. Lefebvre's aim was not solely to develop a spatially inflected theory of political economy but more to detonate commonly held assumptions about the seemingly monolithic unity of space, especially modern, built spaces.

19   Heonik Kwon's *Ghosts of War in Vietnam* (Cambridge: Cambridge University Press, 2008) offers a fascinating anthropological analysis of the role that ghosts, especially wandering souls, play in everyday life. There are many Vietnamese books, films, and news stories about wandering souls, including some that are available in translation for global audiences. For example, see author Bảo Ninh's discussion of the "Jungle of Screaming Souls" in Bảo Ninh, *The Sorrow of War: A Novel of North Vietnam*, trans. Frank Palmos (New York: Pantheon, 1995). Ghosts also feature prominently in such films as Director Đặng Nhật Minh's *When the Tenth Month Comes* (Bao giờ cho tới tháng Mười) (1985).

20   Bernard Fall, *Street without Joy: Insurgency in Indochina, 1946–53* (London: Pall Mall Press, 1963).

21   Trần Mai Nam, *The Narrow Strip of Land (The Story of a Journey)* (Hanoi: Foreign Languages Publishing House, 1969).

22   Nhã Ca, *Mourning Headband for Hue: An Account of the Battle for Hue, Vietnam 1968*, trans. Olga Dror (Bloomington: Indiana University Press, 2014), xix–xx.

23   James Walker Trullinger Jr., *Village at War: An Account of Revolution in Vietnam* (New York: Longman, 1980).

24   For these online archives see CIA Electronic Reading Room, www.cia.gov/library /readingroom/document-type/crest; the Vietnam Center and Archives, www .vietnam.ttu.edu; and the National Security Archive, http://nsarchive.gwu.edu.

25   Historian of science Jeanne Haffner's *View from Above: The Science of Social Space* (Boston: MIT Press, 2013) tells a detailed story of such a transition from maps to air photos among French social scientists and geographers. See also David Biggs, "Aerial Photography and Colonial Discourse on the Agricultural Crisis in Late-Colonial Indochina, 1930–45," in *Cultivating the Colonies: Colonial States and Their Environmental Legacies*, ed. Christina Folke Ax et al., (Athens: Ohio University Press, 2011), 109–32.

26   The GIS-based work informs the book's larger arguments, while more detailed

discussions about the sources and particulars of georeferencing and analysis can be found on the book's companion website, *Footprints of War*, at davidbiggs.net.

27   Fernand Braudel, *The Mediterranean and the Mediterranean World in the Age of Philip II*, vol. 1 (Berkeley: University of California Press, 1995). For an account of Braudel's time in Algiers see Adam J. Goldwyn and Renée M. Silverman, "Introduction: Fernand Braudel and the Invention of a Modernist's Mediterranean" in *Mediterranean Modernism: Intercultural Exchange and Aesthetic Development*, ed. Adam J. Goldwyn and Renée M. Silverman (New York: Palgrave Macmillan, 2016), 1–26.

CHAPTER ONE: SUBTERRAINS

1   Heonik Kwon's *Ghosts of War in Vietnam*, 34, pays close attention to the many different ways that people relate to this past through the construction of ancestral shrines (*lăng họ*) and the worship of wandering ghosts at former military sites such as outposts or bomb shelters. Christina Schwenkel's *The American War in Contemporary Vietnam: Transnational Remembrance and Representation* (Bloomington: University of Indiana Press, 2009) focuses more on official practices of remembrance through war martyr monuments, exhibits, and photography.

2   See Nguyễn Thế Anh, "The Vietnamization of the Cham Deity Pô Nagar," in *Essays into Vietnamese Pasts*, ed. Keith W. Taylor and John K. Whitmore (Ithaca, NY: Cornell University Press, 1995), 42–50. "Tháp Mỹ Khánh: Dư địa chí Thừa Thiên Huế" [Mỹ Khánh Tower: Geography guide of Thừa Thiên Huế], last accessed March 24, 2014, www3.thuathienhue.gov.vn/GeographyBook/Default.aspx?sel=3&id=21.

3   Political anthropologist James Scott has become well known for his 2009 study of this highlands region that he terms *zomia* following the work of Willem van Schendel. Scott's work has attracted much debate for various claims, but one useful contribution of it concerns his notion that steep, forested slopes produced a "friction of appropriation" that challenged coastal peoples from gaining control. Like the seas, the highland forests also offered avenues of attack and thus acquired a reputation of danger. See James Scott, *The Art of Not Being Governed: An Anarchist History of Upland Southeast Asia* (New Haven, CT: Yale University Press, 2009), 198–99. Willem van Schendel by contrast does not argue for consideration of *zomia* as a discrete area in Southeast Asia but rather as a dynamic borderland that challenges what he calls the "statist" assumption implicit in area studies. See Willem van Schendel, "Geographies of Knowing, Geographies of Ignorance: Jumping Scale in Southeast Asia," *Environment and Planning D: Society and Space* 20 (2002): 655. This scholarly tension parallels that between the statists and marginal peoples even at the village level. Military groups from armies to outlaws to rebels typically occupied the spaces where state rule ended and "anarchy" began. Military forces, along with rebel groups, fought not only over land but also over many "non-state" peoples to expand territory and "cultivate" its inhabitants. For

much of its ancient history, the narrow strip of villages lining the central coast formed a constantly expanding and contracting state space hemmed in by the highlands and the sea.

4   Andrew Hardy, "Eaglewood and the Economic History of Champa and Central Vietnam," in *Champa and the Archaeology of Mỹ Sơn* (Vietnam), ed. Andrew Hardy, Mauro Cucarzi and Patrizia Zolese (Singapore: National University of Singapore Press, 2009), 107–26.

5   Nguyen Kim Dung, "The Sa Huynh Culture in Ancient Regional Trade Networks: A Comparative Study of Ornaments," in *New Perspectives in Southeast Asian and Pacific Prehistory*, ed. Philip J. Piper, Hirofumi Matsumura, and David Bulbeck (Canberra: Australia National University Press, 2017).

6   Nguyễn Hữu Thông, ed., *Katu: Kẻ sống đầu ngọn nước* (Huế: NXB Thuận Hóa, 2004), 24–25.

7   Vietnam was ruled by Chinese imperial governors for almost one thousand years (111 BCE–958 CE). The portion of the central coast north of Ngang Pass and bordering this contact zone was Cửu Chân District. After gaining independence, Việt rulers renamed the area Hà Tĩnh and Nghệ An Provinces. In Vietnam this area is seen popularly as a cradle of rebellion, as it fostered the anti-Ming uprising in 1420 and especially the communist-led uprising in 1930.

8   Like Vĩnh Linh, this pass also became famous during the Indochina Wars as a key gateway for North Vietnamese soldiers and supplies entering South Vietnam.

9   A recently published history of Thừa Thiên–Huế Province, a collective work including many of Huế's most prominent historians and archeologists, provides one of the most richly annotated histories of early history on the central coast. See Nguyễn Văn Hoa, ed., *Địa chí Thừa Thiên Huế: Phần lịch sử* (Hà Nội: NXB Khoa Học Xã Hội, 2005), 24–25.

10   Taylor, *Birth of Vietnam*.

11   Nguyễn Văn Hoa, *Địa chí Thừa Thiên Huế: Phần lịch sử*, 31–32.

12   Ibid., 38.

13   Georges Maspero, *The Champa Kingdom* (Bangkok: White Lotus Press, 2002), 87–88. See also Nguyễn Văn Hoa, *Địa chí Thừa Thiên Huế: Phần lịch sử*, 47.

14   Sun Laichen, "Military Technology Transfers from Ming China and the Emergence of Northern Mainland Southeast Asia (c. 1390–1527)," *Journal of Southeast Asian Studies* 34, no. 3 (October 2003): 510.

15   Scholars continue to revise earlier presentations of Champa as a single, unified kingdom; newer archaeological research, including maritime archeology, suggests that there were multiple Cham polities along the coast, tied together in a federation of sorts. Historian Michael Vickery provides two such revisionist or archipelagic histories of the central coast in recently published edited volumes. See Michael Vickery, "Champa Revised," in *The Cham of Vietnam*, ed. Trần Kỳ Phương and Bruce Lockhart (Singapore: National University of Singapore Press, 2011), 363–420. See also Michael Vickery, "A Short History of Champa," in *Champa and the Archaeology of Mỹ Sơn (Vietnam)*, ed. Andrew Hardy, Mauro

Cucarzi, and Patrizia Zolese (Singapore: National University of Singapore Press, 2009), 45–60. One of the first historians to make such a claim for Champa as well as Vietnam as an archipelagic space is historian Keith W. Taylor, "The Early Kingdoms," in *The Cambridge History of Southeast Asia: Volume 1, Part 1*, ed. Nicholas Tarling (Cambridge: Cambridge University Press, 1999), 153.

16   Li Tana, *Nguyễn Cochinchina: Southern Vietnam in the Seventeenth and Eighteenth Centuries* (Ithaca, NY: Cornell Southeast Asia Program, 1998), 41; Charles Wheeler, "Re-Thinking the Sea in Vietnamese History: Littoral Society and the Integration of Thuận-Quảng, Seventeenth-Eighteenth Centuries," *Journal of Southeast Asian Studies* 37, no. 1 (February 2006): 123–53.

17   Hồ Trung Tú, *Có 500 năm như thế: Bản Sắc Quảng Nam từ góc nhìn phân kỳ lịch sử* (Đà Nẵng: NXB Đà Nẵng, 2013), 87.

18   Ibid., 112.

19   Li Tana, *Nguyễn Cochinchina*, 37.

20   Nguyễn Văn Hoa, *Địa chí Thừa Thiên Huế: Phần lịch sử*, 75.

21   Ibid.

22   Thích Đại Sán (Thạch Liêm), *Hải ngoại kỷ sự* (Huế: Viện Đại học Huế—Ủy ban Phiên dịch Sử liệu Việt Nam, 1963), 107. Translation by Hoàng Thị Bình Minh: "Còn những nơi vì núi biển cách trở, thánh vương đánh dẹp chẳng đến, lễ giáo khó thông; dân cư tụ tập, tự làm quân trương với nhau, quen tập thói quê mùa hủ lậu; chẳng biết lễ nghĩa là gì. Chỉ biết lấy oai lực phục nhau, thì hay sinh ra chiến tranh, mà trong việc chiến tranh, cần phải biến ảo thần kỳ mới hơn người được. Vì thế trong nước hay bàn việc võ-bị, chẳng chuộng văn-đức."

23   Christoforo Borri, *An Account of Cochinchina: Containing Many Admirable Rarities and Singularities of That Country* (London: Robert Ashley, 1633), 28. For a thorough account of Borri and the *Account*, see Olga Dror and Keith Taylor, *Views of Seventeenth-Century Vietnam: Christoforo Borri on Cochinchina & Samuel Baron on Tonkin* (Ithaca, NY: Southeast Asia Program, 2006).

24   Village-based historians and genealogists have compiled and translated (from Chinese or Nôm scripts into modern Vietnamese) many fragments of village records that survived colonialism and modern wars.Vietnamese family associations have also recently published (online) family genealogies that point to founding ancestors who landed on the central coast. These sources cannot support fine-grained local studies, but they do at least point to some common contours in early modern Vietnamese village life.

25   "Dòng Họ Vũ-Võ Việt Nam," last accessed June 1, 2014, http://hovuvovietnam .com. The surnames Võ and Vũ are transliterations of the same Chinese character for the surname Wu (武).

26   The TV documentary presents a relatively novel juxtaposition of family history merging with state history, once taboo in the socialist era. The TV newscast depicts family descendants at the celebration exchanging courtesies with local officials, representatives of the state. This image of family-state relations may be new since the socialist era, but it points to a relationship between families, land,

27 "Họ Phạm Miền Trung—Tây Nguyên," family geneological website, last accessed
April 22, 2014, www.hophammientrung.com/tin-ve-coi-ngon/2/198/ho-pham
-ba-lang-thanh-thuy-thuong/cong-nghe-so.html. The authors of the *Địa chí Thừa
Thiên Huế* note that the surname Phạm generally applied to people of Cham
descent. See Nguyễn Văn Hoa, *Địa chí Thừa Thiên Huế: Phần lịch sử*, 34.

and the state that was a central feature of early modern politics, frequently tested
through negotiations of taxes and military service. "Lễ Thanh Minh của họ Võ
làng Thần Phù," last accessed June 1, 2014, http://hovuvovietnam.com/Ho-Vo
-lang-Than-Phu-phuong-Thuy-Chau-TX-Huong-Thuy-Thua-Thien-Hue_tc
_294_0_1110.html.

28 Lê Vũ Trường Giang, "Sự vận động của làng xã cổ truyền, bản Thuận ước và
những dấu ấn văn hóa ở làng Thần Phù," *Tạp Chí Sông Hương*, no. 302 (April
2014), accessed June 1, 2014, http://tapchisonghuong.com.vn/tin-tuc/p2/c15
/n15136/Su-van-dong-cua-lang-xa-co-truyen-ban-Thuan-uoc-va-nhung-dau-an
-van-hoa-o-lang-Than-Phu.html.

29 "Họ Phạm Miền Trung—Tây Nguyên."

30 Nola Cooke, "Nguyen Rule in Seventeenth-Century Dang Trong (Cochinchina),"
Journal of Southeast Asian Studies 29, no. 1 (March 1998): 137.

31 Lam Thi My Dung, "Sa Huynh Regional and Inter-Regional Interactions in the
Thu Bon Valley, Quang Nam Province, Central Vietnam," *Bulletin of the Indo-
Pacific Pre-History Association* 29 (2009): 68–75.

32 Nguyễn Đình Đầu, *Chế độ công điền công thổ trong lịch sử khẩn hoang lập ấp ở
Nam Kỳ Lục Tỉnh* (Hà Nội: Hội Sử Học Việt Nam, 1992), 18–20; Yumio Sakurai,
"Chế Độ Lương Điền Dưới Triều Nguyễn," in *Việt Nam Học: Kỷ yếu hội thảo quốc
tế lần thứ nhất*, by National Center for Social Sciences and Humanities (Hà Nội:
Thế Giới, 2002), 577–80.

33 Throughout the book, I use the traditional name of the village, Phù Bài, with ù,
to differentiate it from the area a few kilometers north that became the Phú Bài
base and airfield and, more recently, a ward of Hương Thủy Town. The spelling
with ú has become most common today, while the traditional name has mostly
disappeared from maps. Today the village is known administratively as Thủy Phù
Commune, a name that preserves the original ù. The meaning of the name
deserves mention too. A *bài* (*lá bài*, *lệnh bài*) meant a sacred card used by a village
god or magician to help locals avoid ghosts or misfortune. *Phù Bài* describes a
card that brings people support or patronage to avoid bad luck. *Phú Bài* means
a card that brings riches for the people. While the current administrative name
has changed, local elders in the village still use the traditional name, so I have
kept it here and I add the term *village* to further distinguish the residential area
from the industrial and base area. Thanks to Bùi Trúc Linh for help on this. See
also Bùi Kim Chi, Phù Bài làng xưa, *Tạp Chí Sông Hương*, no. 274 (December
2011), last accessed February 13, 2018, http://tapchisonghuong.com.vn/tap-chi
/c253/n9543/Phu-Bai-lang-xua.html.

34 Bùi Thị Tân, *Về hai làng nghề truyền thống*, 78.

35 Ibid., 60.

36 Nguyễn Đình Đầu, *Nghiên cứu địa bạ Triều Nguyễn: Thừa Thiên* [Research on Nguyễn dynasty land registers: Thừa Thiên] (Hồ Chí Minh City: Hồ Chí Minh, 1997), 165.

37 Lê Vũ Trường Giang, "Sự vận động của làng xã cổ truyền."

38 Nguyễn Khắc Thuần, ed., *Lê Qúy Đôn tuyển tập: Phủ Biên tạp lục (phần 1)* [Frontier Chronicles (part 1)] (Hà Nội: NXB Giáo Dục, 2007), 173.

39 Ibid.

40 Ibid., 174–75.

41 Trương Hữu Quýnh and Đỗ Bang, eds., *Tình hình ruộng đất nông nghiệp và đời sống nông dân dưới triều Nguyễn* [Situation of agricultural land and agricultural livelihood under the Nguyen dynasty] (Huế: Thuận Hóa, 1997), 69.

42 Nguyễn Khắc Thuần, *Lê Qúy Đôn tuyển tập*, 173.

43 Trương Hữu Quýnh and Đỗ Bang, *Tình hình ruộng đất nông nghiệp và đời sống nông dân dưới triều Nguyễn*, 70.

44 Historian George Dutton notes in his history of the Tây Sơn period that many of those who welcomed Trịnh army troops in 1774 soon grew outraged by their alleged abuses and in 1786 welcomed the Tây Sơn troops as their liberators. Fifteen years later, villagers living under Tây Sơn rule welcomed the Nguyễn army's return after enduring more famines, economic hardship, and relentless demands for conscripts and materials. See George Dutton, *The Tây Sơn Uprising: Society and Rebellion in Eighteenth-Century Vietnam* (Honolulu: University of Hawaii Press, 2006), 165–70.

45 Louis Cadière, "La Pagode Quoc-An: Les divers supérieurs," *Bulletin des amis de Vieux Huế* 2, no. 3 (July 1915): 306.

46 Barisy's letters and those of other Frenchmen in service to the emperor are compiled in Louis Cadière, "Documents relatifs à l'époque de Gia-Long," in *Bulletin de l'École Française d'Extrême-Orient* 12 (1912): 1–82.

47 Ibid., 42–43.

48 Ibid., 49–51.

49 Jean-Baptiste Chaigneau married a Vietnamese woman from a prominent family in Huế and raised several children before returning to France in 1825. His son Michel Đức Chaigneau published a popular account of his life growing up in the imperial capital. See Michel Đức Chaigneau, *Souvenirs de Hué* (Paris: Imprimerie Impériale, 1867).

50 For a comprehensive survey of rural life in the nineteenth century, including a detailed account of storms and famines, Trương Hữu Quýnh and Đỗ Bang, *Tình hình ruộng đất nông nghiệp và đời sống nông dân dưới triều Nguyễn*, 150–53.

51 Viện Sử Học, *Đại Nam Thực Lục* [Chronicles of Đại Nam], vol. 6 (Hà Nội: Giáo Dục, 2006), 622–23.

52 Viện Sử Học, *Đại Nam Thực Lục*, vol. 1, 717.

53   Nguyễn Đình Đầu, *Nghiên cứu địa bạ triều Nguyễn*, 165, 198.

54   Trương Hữu Quýnh and Đỗ Bang, *Tình hình ruộng đất nông nghiệp và đời sống nông dân dưới triều Nguyễn*, 155–57.

55   Two English-language histories that focus on the second Nguyễn emperor's turn to more Confucian and anticosmopolitan policies are Alexander Woodside, *Vietnam and the Chinese Model: A Comparative Study of Nguyen and Ch'ing Civil Government in the First Half of the Nineteenth Century* (Cambridge, MA: Harvard University Press, 1971), and Choi Byung Wook, *Southern Vietnam Under the Reign of Minh Mạng (1820–1841): Central Policies and Local Response* (Ithaca, NY: Southeast Asia Program, 2004). Both works draw deeply from royal edicts and histories to show the complex factors that weighed on this monarch as he broke decisively with the policies of his father and his ancestors the Nguyễn lords.

56   Historian Bradley Davis in particular explores this role in shaping not just state building but ethnography of non-Việt peoples. See Bradley Camp Davis, "The Production of Peoples: Imperial Ethnography and the Changing Conception of Uplands Space in Nineteenth-Century Vietnam," *Asia Pacific Journal of Anthropology* 16, no. 4 (2015): 323–42.

57   Choi Byung Wook, *Southern Vietnam*, 101.

58   Ibid.

59   For a survey of Q'ing cartographic enterprises, see Laura Hostetler, *Qing Colonial Enterprise: Ethnography and Cartography in Early Modern China* (Chicago: University of Chicago Press, 2001). I suggest that the Nguyễn court turned to this more common East Asian style of mapmaking only because the Gia Long government had experimented with planimetric and navigational maps developed through its correspondence with French and other European military surveyors. Historian John K. Whitmore's pioneering essay "Cartography in Vietnam" remains one of the most authoritative studies on Vietnamese cartography, even though he saw it as just a beginning. It provides an excellent synopsis of key cosmological elements guiding Vietnamese ideas of territory, especially the juxtaposition of mountain peaks and rivers. See John K. Whitmore, "Cartography in Vietnam," in *The History of Cartography: Volume 2, Book 2*, ed. J. B. Harley and David Woodward (Chicago: University of Chicago Press, 1994), 478–508.

60   This local usage of the term *động* is still current in central Vietnam today, especially in reference to certain upland valleys such as Động Chuối that supported Việt Minh resistance zones in the late 1940s. Older locals can still recite common sayings about *cốc* and *động*. The term *cốc* is of unknown etymological origin; Vietnamese around Huế today use it to describe the wildest, most remote mountains. The term *động* is also unusual in its use. It does not refer to the commonly associated term *cave* used today but rather to upland valleys settled by non-Kinh people. The usage may derive from a classical Chinese term *dong* that historians James Anderson and John Whitmore note was a Tang dynasty term for mountain valley settlements. See James A. Anderson and John K. Whitmore, eds., *China's*

Encounters in the South and Southwest: Reforging the Fiery Frontier over Two Millennia (Leiden: Brill, 2015), 3. Thanks also to Hoàng Thị Bình Minh.

61 These three books were condensed into one in the most common 1910 republication, which was translated from Chinese into Vietnamese and republished again in 1961. See Nguyễn Văn Tạo, *Đại Nam nhất thống chí: Thừa Thiên Phủ; Tập Thượng, Trung và Hạ* (Sài Gòn: Bộ Quốc gia Giáo dục, 1963).

62 Pierre Brocheux and Daniel Hémery, *Indochina: An Ambiguous Colonization, 1858–1954* (Berkeley: University of California Press, 2009).

63 Those treaties included two ceding Sài Gòn and the Mekong delta to France (1862, 1867), one granting a port concession in Đà Nẵng (1868), and two granting concessions in Huế (1873) and Hà Nội (1873).

64 Jules-Léon Dutreuil de Rhins, *Le royaume d'Annam et les Annamites* (Paris: E. Plon and Cie, 1879).

65 Ibid., 289.

66 Ibid., 282–83. Translation by author: "Plus de la moitié du sol cultivable de la province de Hué est encore inculte, ce qui tient aux différentes causes dont nous avons déjà parlé, principalement à la paresse des Annamites et à leur pitoyable gouvernement.... L'Annamite, à qui le commerce extérieur est interdit, n'a aucun intérêt à faire des cultures riches qui d'ailleurs lui coûteraient trop de fatigues, et il n'est pas encouragé à produire des céréales au delà des besoins de sa consommation, car les mandarins, aussi lâches et rampants avec leurs supérieures que durs et rapaces avec leurs inférieurs, le dépouilleraient bien vite de son superflu."

CHAPTER TWO: TERRAFORMING

1 For a detailed account of the naval assault on August 20 and succeeding negotiations for the Treaty of Hué on August 25, see Lucien Huard, *La guerre illustrée, Chine-Tonkin-Annam, Tome 1: La guerre du Tonkin* (Paris: L. Boulanger, 1886), 110–22 and 122–130, respectively.

2 Albert Billot, *L'affaire du Tonkin: Histoire diplomatique de l'établissement de notre protectorat sur l'Annam et de notre conflit avec la Chine, 1882–1885* (Paris: J. Hetzel, 1888), 171–84.

3 Brocheux and Hémery, *Indochina*, 52.

4 Ibid., 55.

5 Known generally as Quốc Học or Quốc Học–Huế, this public school remains one of the most prestigious high schools in Vietnam today. In 1932 it was renamed Khải Định Lycée after the deceased emperor; and it was renamed Quốc Học–Huế shortly after the creation of the Republic of Vietnam in 1955. Many of the central region's most famous leaders, including Hồ Chí Minh, Ngô Đình Diệm, and General Võ Nguyễn Giáp, attended the school.

6 This set up a legal gray zone as French administrators signed off on transactions and taxes went to the Résidence Supérieure d'Annam but all legal claims and torts

were to be settled by Vietnamese customary laws. R. Bienvenue, "Régime de la propriété foncière en Annam," doctoral thesis, University of Rennes, 1911.

7   Brocheux and Hémery, *Indochina*, 156.

8   Ibid., 128.

9   Paul Doumer, *Situation de l'Indo-Chine (1897–1901)* (Hanoi: Schneider, 1902), 92–93. Translation by author: "De plus, le Roi faisait abandon, au profit du Gouverneur Général de l' Indo-Chine, de sa prérogative de disposer des biens du domaine non affectés à des services publics, et, par conséquent, de concéder les terres vacantes et sans maitres. C'était la faculté pour les colons de s'établir en Annam, et l'on sait qu'ils en ont fait un heureux usage."

10 Henri Brenier, *Essai d'atlas statistique de l'Indochine Française* (Hanoi: Extrême-Orient, 1914), 12–13.

11 Land Concession Agreement, October 27, 1900, Folder 220, Resident Supérieure de l'Annam (hereafter RSA) Record Group, Vietnam National Archives Center no. 4 (hereafter VNA4).

12 Ibid. Translation by author: "Il est outre stipulé que S.E. le Vo-Hiên Hoàng Cao Khải aura la priorité sur qui que soit sur les terrains formant le polygone de l'artillerie ils étaient désaffectés."

13 Khải commanded a band of some four hundred mercenaries in the late 1880s, and his group led colonial military forces into major battles against Cần Vương leaders in the north. See Charles Fourniau, *Annam-Tonkin 1885–1896: Lettrés et paysans vietnamiens face à la conquête colonialie* (Paris: Harmattan, 1989), 169.

14 Ibid., 168.

15 The estimate is derived from the announcement of the fire school's personnel and schedule dated February 2, 1910. See "Le Capitaine LAZARE Commandant la 3ème Batterie au Chef de Bataillon Commandant le Subdivision Militaire Territoriale à HUE au sujet des écoles à feu de la 3ème Batterie," Folio 627, RSA Record Group, VNA4.

16 See my discussion of the East Forest in the previous chapter. See also Lê Vũ Trường Giang, "Sự vận động của làng xã cổ truyền."

17 January 14, 1911, Les membres du Conseil de Regence à Monsieur le Résident Supérieure en Annam, Folio 627, RSA Record Group, VNA4. Translation by author: "Cependant, déplacer l'autel pour recevoir les listes et abandonner le culte pour faire le service, ce sont des choses contraires aux sentiments des habitants et qui feraient maître des murmures de leur part."

18 April 8, 1910, Le Résident de France à Thua-Thiên à Monsieur le Résident Supérieure en Annam au sujet du séjour de l'artillerie à Huong-Thuy, Folio 627, RSA Record Group, VNA4.

19 August 24, 1911, Résident Supérieure en Annam à Monsieur le Chef de Bataillon, Commandant de la Subdivision Militaire Territoriale à Hue, Folio 627, RSA Record Group, VNA4.

20 December 5, 1911, Le Général de Division PENNEQUIN, Commandant Supérieur des Troupes du Groupe de l'Indochine à Messieurs le Général Commandant de

la 3ème Brigade et le Chef du Bataillon Commandant la Subdivision de Hué, Folio 627, RSA Record Group, VNA4.

21 December 27, 1911, Le Résident de France à Thua-Thiên à Monsieur le Résident Supérieure en Annam, Folio 627, RSA Record Group, VNA4. Translation by author: "Au moment précisément où les tendances du Gouvernement paraissent être de donner à la population indigène la tranquilité et le calme dont elle a besoin, l'obligation faite aux villages peu fortunés de la région de Huong-Thuy de loger encore, pendant plus d'un demi mois, un contingent de plus de 100 hommes, semblera certainement très pénible à la population de cette région."

22 Léopold M. Cadière "Sauvons Nos Pins!," *Bulletin des amis de vieux Hué* 3, no. 4 (1916): 437–43.

23 Ibid., 442. Translation by author: "Aujourd'hui, ce sont les gardiens eux-mêmes, qui abattent ces pins. Aujourd'hui, c'est le ravage sans frein, la dévastation sans mesure. Il nous faut agir."

24 Pamela D. McElwee, *Forests Are Gold: Trees, People, and Environmental Rule in Vietnam* (Seattle: University of Washington Press, 2016), 47–49.

25 Frédéric Thomas, "Protection des forêts et environnementalisme colonial: Indochine, 1860–1945," *Revue d'histoire moderne et contemporaine* 56, no. 4 (2009): 104–36, 122–23. Thomas challenges historian Richard Grove's assertion that European imperial science, especially in India, played a formative role in the development of environmentalist ethics. See Richard Grove, *Green Imperialism: Colonial Expansion, Tropical Island Edens and the Origins of Environmentalism, 1600–1860* (Cambridge: Cambridge University Press, 2003).

26 Henri Guibier, *Situation des forêts de l'Annam* (Saigon: Imprimerie Nouvelle Albert Portail, 1918), 31.

27 Ibid., 31. *Sartage* is an archaic form of forest burning once practiced in the Ardennes region of southern Belgium. Where villagers lacked sufficient field acreage, they burned sections of forest and then planted them in wheat or oats.

28 Ibid., 38. For more detailed information on the pine nursery, see M. H. Palisse, Garde Général des forêts à Monsieur le Résident Supérieure en Annam au sujet de l'achat d'un terrain pour l'installation d'une pépinière, Folio 682, RSA Record Group, VNA4.

29 Frédéric Thomas, *Histoire du régime et des services forestiers français en Indochine de 1862 à 1945: Sociologie des sciences et des pratiques scientifiques coloniales en forêts tropicales* (Hanoi: Thế Giới, 1999), 39.

30 Brett M. Bennett, "The El Dorado of Forestry: The Eucalyptus in India, South Africa, and Thailand, 1850–2000," *International Review of Social History* 56, no. 4 (2010): 27–50, 42.

31 Jared Farmer, *Trees in Paradise: A California History* (New York: W. W. Norton, 2013), 112.

32 Indochine Française, *Historique de l'aéronautique d'Indochine* (Hanoi: Imprimerie d'Extrême-Orient, 1931), 19.

33 Ibid., 45–46.

34   Ibid., 45–46, 57. For a deeper investigation into the highlander revolts and colonial pacification campaigns, see Oscar Salemink, *The Ethnography of Vietnam's Central Highlanders: A Historical Contextualization, 1850–1990* (Honolulu: University of Hawaii Press, 2003), 106. The landing field at An Khê also served from 1965 to 1972 as a major American military base and airfield, located approximately halfway from the port city of Quy Nhơn to the central highlands town Pleiku.

35   L. Gallin and Indochine Française, *Le service radiotélégraphique de l'Indochine* (Hanoi: Imprimerie d'Extrême-Orient, 1931), 7.

36   Gouvernement Général de l'Indochine, *Service géographique de l'Indochine: Son organisation, ses méthodes, ses travaux* (Hanoi: Imprimerie d'Extrême-Orient, 1931), 12.

37   "Terrain d'atterissage de Phú Bài, 1924–1926," Folio 1438, RSA Record Group, VNA4.

38   Gouvernement Général de l'Indochine, *L'aéronautique militaire de l'Indochine* (Hanoi: Imprimerie d'Extrême-Orient, 1931), 50.

39   Gouvernement Général de l'Indochine, *Service géographique de l'Indochine*, 32.

40   "Transfert de la station météorologique de Hue sur le terrain d'aviation de Phu Bai," Folio 3655, RSA Record Group, VNA4.

41   Christopher Goscha, *Vietnam or Indochina? Contesting Concepts of Space in Vietnamese Nationalism (1887–1954)* (Copenhagen: Nordic Institute of Asian Studies, 1995), 19.

42   Ibid., 20.

43   Harry A. Franck, *East of Siam: Ramblings in the Five Divisions of French Indo-China* (New York: Century Company, 1926), vii.

44   Ibid., 128–31.

45   "Inventaire du domaine militaire à Thừa Thiên, 1925–26," Folio 1769, RSA Record Group, VNA4.

46   Jean-Pierre Caillard, *Alexandre Varenne: Une passion républicaine* (Paris: Le cherche midi, 2007), 120–21.

47   Phan Châu Trinh, *Phan Châu Trinh and His Political Writings*, ed. and trans. Vĩnh Sính (Ithaca, NY: Cornell Southeast Asia Program, 2009), 36–38.

48   Phan Thi Minh Le, "A Vietnamese Scholar with a Different Path: Huỳnh Thúc Khang, Publisher of the First Vietnamese Newspaper in Quốc Ngữ in Central Vietnam, *Tieng Dan* (People's Voice)," in *Viêt-Nam Exposé: French Scholarship on Twentieth-Century Vietnamese Society*, ed. Gisele L. Bousquet and Pierre Brocheux (Ann Arbor: University of Michigan Press, 2002), 217.

49   Ibid., 224–31.

50   William J. Duiker, *Ho Chi Minh: A Life* (New York: Hyperion, 2000), 173–77.

51   Thường Vụ Huyện Ủy Hương Thủy, *Lịch sử đấu tranh cách mạng của đảng bộ và nhân dân huyện Hương Thủy (sơ thảo)* [A history of the revolutionary struggles of party cells and the people of Hương Thủy district] (Huế: Thuận Hóa, 1994), 43–45.

52   Ibid., 47.

53   For my discussion of this political turn to air photography and aerial surveillance, see Biggs, "Aerial Photography and Colonial Discourse," 110.

54   Pierre Gourou, *Les paysans du delta tonkinois; étude de géographie humaine* (Paris: Les éditions d'art et d'histoire, 1936). For a discussion of Gourou's approach to tropical geography in the 1930s, see Armand Colin, "L'évolution de la pensée géographique de Pierre Gourou sur les pays tropicaux (1935–1970)," *Annales de géographie* 498 (March–April 1981): 129–50. Finally, for a recent study highlighting Gourou's influence in subsequent use of aerial photography more globally, see Haffner, *View from Above*, 19–23.

55   Historian of science Jeanne Haffner's *View from Above* tells a compelling story of this transition among many of Vidal's disciples in Europe. For example, she tells the tale of Jean Brunhes and philanthropist Albert Kahn who embarked on a project titled Archives of the Planet with an aim to produce a photographic survey of the globe to present the diversity and harmony of all mankind. See *View from Above*, 24–25. In the United States, Carl O. Sauer's work in geography, notably his essay, "The Morphology of Landscape," *University of California Publications in Geography* 2, no. 2 (1925): 19–53, advanced a similar perspective.

56   M. H. Palisse, Garde Général des forêts à Monsieur le Résident Supérieur en Annam au sujet de l'achat d'un terrain pour l'installation d'une pépinière, Folio 682, RSA Record Group, VNA4.

57   "Tình Hình quân cộng sản ở Tầu," *Ánh Sáng*, April 13, 1935, 1, and April 15, 1935, 4.

58   Điền Dân, "Ước gì có cái 'làng' thích hợp với đời mới này," *Tiếng Dân*, serialized on the following dates in 1939: August 24, p. 1; August 31, p. 1; September 2, p. 1; September 6, p. 1; September 7, p. 1; September 9, p. 1; September 12, p. 1; September 16, p. 1; September 23, pp. 1–2; September 26, pp. 1–2. See also William Ravenscroft Hughes, *New Town: A Proposal in Agricultural, Industrial, Educational, Civic, and Social Reconstruction* (London: J. M. Dent, 1919). For a discussion of Hughes's work with garden cities and early twentieth-century utopian experiments in England, see Dennis Hardy, *Utopian England: Community Experiments, 1900–1945* (New York: Routledge, 2012), 84–97.

59   Điền Dân, "Ước gì có cái 'làng' thích hợp với đời mới này," *Tiếng Dân*, August 31, 1939, 1.

60   Nguyễn Tú and Triều Nguyên, eds., *Địa chí Hương Thủy* (Huế: Nhà xuất bản Thuận Hóa, 1998), 380. Thanh was later released and rose to the rank of general in the People's Army. He was a chief military commander for the National Liberation Front, and before his death in 1967 he was a principal architect of the 1968 Tết Offensive.

61   Vietnamese were well aware of the Japanese military's violent expansion for almost three years before it crossed the borders of Indochina. From the outbreak of the Second Sino-Japanese War in July 1937, Vietnamese-language newspapers featured front-page essays chronicling the latest events of the Trung Nhật Chiến Tranh. For example, the March 16, 1939, issue of *Tiếng Dân* described the Japanese military invasion of Hainan Island and its establishment of air force and naval

bases there. See "Nhật lo lập nơi căn cứ không quân và thủy quân ở Hải-Nam," *Tiếng Dân*, March 16, 1939, 1. These new bases brought Japanese forces less than four hundred kilometers from Hà Nội. On November 21, 1939, another Huế paper reported that Japanese forces had seized Beihai, a Chinese coastal port located approximately 120 kilometers north from Indochina on the Tonkin Gulf. See "Trung Nhật Chiến Tranh: Quân Nhật đã đổ bộ ở Bắc Hải rồi chăng?," *Tràng An Báo*, November 21, 1939, 2, 4.

62   For a detailed account of these military actions and diplomatic negotiations see Hata Ikuhiko, "The Army's Move into Northern Indochina," in *The Fateful Choice: Japan's Advance into Southeast Asia, 1939–1941*, ed. James William Morley (New York: Columbia University Press, 1980), 155–280.

63   Nagaoka Shinjiro, "The Drive into Southern Indochina and Thailand," in *The Fateful Choice: Japan's Advance into Southeast Asia, 1939–1941*, ed. James William Morley (New York: Columbia University Press, 1980), 237. See also Kiyoko Kurusu Nitz, "Japanese Military Policy towards French Indochina During the Second World War: The Road to the 'Meigo Sakusen' (March 9, 1945)," *Journal of Southeast Asian Studies* 14, no. 2 (1983): 329.

64   Nguyễn Tú and Nguyên Triều, *Địa Chí Hương Thủy*, 380.

65   Nitz, "Japanese Military Policy," 329.

66   Ralph B. Smith, "The Japanese Period in Indochina and the Coup of 9 March 1945," *Journal of Southeast Asian Studies* 9, no. 2: 269.

67   For in-depth treatment of the March 9 coup and reactions among Vietnamese nationalists, especially the royal court, see David G. Marr, *Vietnam 1945: The Quest for Power* (Berkeley: University of California Press, 1995); and Pierre Brocheux, *Histoire du Vietnam contemporain: La nation résiliente* (Paris: Fayard, 2011).

68   For an in-depth military history of photographic and signals intelligence, see John F. Kreis, *Piercing the Fog: Intelligence and Army Air Forces Operations in World War II* (Washington, DC: Air Force History and Museums Program, 1996). For a discussion on American campaigns to decipher Japanese naval codes from the mid-1930s, see 99–102. For in-depth discussion of the Fourteenth Air Force's photo intelligence and bombing programs, see 312–20.

69   For a detailed discussion of the K-18 cameras and others used in World War II photoreconnaissance, see Roy M. Stanley, *World War II Photo Intelligence* (New York: Scribners, 1981), 149–53. Veteran websites for the Twenty-First Photo Recon Squadron list the Lockheed P-38 (F-5) as the principle aircraft for these missions, with planes taking off from Guilin, China, when figure 3.4 was taken in October 1943. For details on the squadron see Maurer Maurer, *Combat Squadrons of the Air Force; World War II* (Washington, DC: USAF Historical Division, 1969), 111–12. For details on the specific photo mission and interpretation of figure 3.4, see "Military Intelligence Photographic Report No. 373," File Number 20487, Box 222, MIPI Series, Record Group 341, Records of Headquarters US Air Force (Air Staff), 1934–2004, NARA-CP.

70   Ronald Spector's history of the relationship forged between the OSS and the Việt Minh in 1945 is one of the most thoroughly researched essays on the topic. See Ronald Spector, "Allied Intelligence and Indochina, 1943–1945," *Pacific Historical Review* 51, no. 1 (February 1982): 23–50, 36–39.

71   Historian William Duiker provides a thorough account of interactions between Hồ and Zhang at Liuchow in Duiker, *Ho Chi Minh*, 267–76.

72   Spector, "Allied Intelligence," 40.

73   David G. Marr, *Vietnam 1945: The Quest for Power* (Berkeley: University of California Press, 1995), 429.

74   Nguyễn Tú and Nguyên Triều, *Địa chí Hương Thủy*, 382.

75   Ibid.

76   This officer, Phùng Đông, not only stood down, but he soon joined the Việt Minh army and by 1946 had risen to the position of chief of staff for the Trần Cao Vân Regiment. He was caught by the French in April 1947 and executed. See Thường Vụ Huyện Ủy Hương Thủy, *Lịch sử đấu tranh cách mạng*, 58–59.

77   Ibid., 59.

78   Voice of Vietnam, "A special radio broadcast on September 2, 1945," last accessed October 6, 2014, http://english.vov.vn/Society/A-special-radio-broadcast-on-September-2-1945/264418.vov.

79   In English see Marr, *Vietnam 1945*, 364–65.

80   Duiker, *Ho Chi Minh*, 324.

CHAPTER THREE: RESISTANCE

1   Đảng Bộ Huyện Hương Thủy, *Lịch sử lực lượng vũ trang Huyện Hương Thủy (1945–2005)* [History of the armed forces of Hương Thủy District (1945–2005)] (Huế: NXB Thuận Hóa, 2008), 38. Translation by author: "Bám vào nhân dân, chỉ có tổ chức được nhân dân mới đánh được địch. Rừng rú, chiến khu cần phải có nhưng nhân tố quyết định là tổ chức nhân dân đánh địch trong làng xã mình."

2   Hùng Sơn and Lê Khai, eds., *Đường Hồ Chí Minh qua Bình Trị Thiên* (Hà Nội: Quân Đội Nhân Dân, 1992), 28–29.

3   Ibid.

4   Fredrik Logevall, *Embers of War: The Fall of an Empire and the Making of America's Vietnam* (New York: Random House, 2012), 199.

5   Ibid. See also Marr, *Vietnam 1945*; and Marr,*Vietnam.*

6   Nguyễn Tú and Nguyên Triều, *Địa chí Hương Thủy*, 384.

7   Nguyễn Tú and Nguyên Triều, *Địa chí Hương Thủy*, 389.

8   Historian Christopher Goscha has written several major works on Việt Minh and communist networks extending beyond Vietnam throughout Southeast Asia and into China. For reference to the regional trading around Huế, see Christopher E. Goscha, "The Borders of Vietnam's Early Wartime Trade with Southern China: A Contemporary Perspective," *Asian Survey* 40, no. 6 (November 2000): 1004. For his work on networks extending across Southeast Asia, see Christopher E. Goscha,

Thailand and the Southeast Asian Networks of the Vietnamese Revolution, 1885–1954 (Richmond, UK: Curzon, 1999).

9   For an in-depth discussion of the modus vivendi agreement see Stein Tonneson, *Vietnam 1946: How the War Began* (Berkeley: University of California Press, 2000), 65–70.

10   Nguyễn Văn Hoa, *Địa chí Thừa Thiên Huế: Phần lịch sử*, 330.

11   Vietnamese sources differ on numbers in Thừa Thiên–Huế from 1,300 to over 2,400 by summer 1946. A district-level party history of Hương Thủy notes that the 850 soldiers sent to the French quarter of Huế came from the Franco-Laotian guerilla forces in Laos. They marched from Savannakhet, Laos, through the mountains to Quảng Trị via Highway 9 and then headed south to Huế. See Thường Vụ Huyện Ủy Hương Thủy, *Lịch sử đấu tranh cách mạng*, 81–82.

12   The Trần Cao Vân Regiment was formed in autumn 1945 shortly after the August Revolution in Huế. Trần Cao Vân was a patriotic member of the royal court who was executed by colonial authorities in 1916. The regiment included many French- and Japanese-trained Vietnamese officers and soldiers who had served the pre-revolution Vietnamese government supported by the Japanese military. One such officer, Hà Văn Lâu, took command of Việt Minh forces openly fighting French units around the southern port city of Nha Trang. He returned to his native Huế to command the Trần Cao Vân regiment in December 1946 following the outbreak of hostilities with France in the north. For an in-depth interview with Hà Văn Lâu see Voice of Vietnam Online, "Giao lưu trực tuyến với Đại Tá Hà Văn Lâu và ông Lê Danh" [Online exchanges with Colonel Ha Van Lau and Mr. Le Danh], September 11, 2006, last accessed November 21, 2014, https://archive.today /20120716145957/vov.vn/Home/Giao-luu-truc-tuyen-voi-Dai-ta-Ha-Van-Lau-va -ong-Le-Danh/20069/42212.vov#selection-705.0-705.56. See also Marr, *Vietnam*, 168.

13   Thường Vụ Huyện Ủy Hương Thủy, *Lịch sử đấu tranh cách mạng*, 82.

14   Christopher Goscha, *Vietnam: Un état né de la guerre 1945–1954* (Paris: Armand Colin, 2011), 63.

15   Binh Chủng Thông Tin Liên Lạc, Quân Đội Nhân Dân Việt Nam, *Lịch sử bộ đội thông tin liên lạc, 1945–1995* [History of military communications, 1945–1995] (Hà Nội: NXB Quân Đội Nhân Dân, 1996), 28–29. One of many famous quotes attributed to Hồ Chí Minh concerns his words about the need for modern communication technologies: "Communications is one of the most important in the work of revolution, because it determines a unified command and the distribution of forces thus ensuring victory." Translation by author: "Việc liên lạc là một việc quan trọng bậc nhất trong công tác cách mệnh, vì chính nó quyết định sự thống nhất chỉ huy, sự phân phối lực lượng và do đó bảo đảm thắng lợi." For a discussion of the quote see Đỗ Trung Tá, "Sáng mãi lời dạy của Chủ tịch Hồ Chí Minh đối với công tác đảm bảo thông tin liên lạc" [Eternal lessons of President Hồ Chí Minh related to the work of preserving communications networks], *Việt Báo*, August 14, 2006, last accessed on November 10, 2014, http://vietbao.vn/Chinh-Tri

/Sang-mai-loi-day-cua-Chu-tich-Ho-Chi-Minh-doi-voi-cong-tac-dam-bao
-thong-tin-lien-lac/65063156/96/.

16 Marr, *Vietnam*, 168.

17 Nguyễn Văn Hoa, *Địa chí Thừa Thiên Huế: Phần Lịch sử*, 339; Nguyễn Tú and
    Nguyên Triều, *Địa chí Hương Thủy*, 340.

18 Thường Vụ Huyện Ủy Hương Thủy, *Lịch sử đấu tranh cách mạng*, 89.

19 Nguyễn Văn Hoa, *Địa chí Thừa Thiên Huế: Phần Lịch sử*, 339–42.

20 Thường Vụ Huyện Ủy Hương Thủy, *Lịch sử đấu tranh cách mạng*, 92.

21 Nguyễn Văn Hoa, *Địa chí Thừa Thiên Huế: Phần lịch sử*, 348–49.

22 On D'Argenlieu's politics with Bảo Đại, see Oscar Chapuis, *The Last Emperors of
    Vietnam: From Tu Duc to Bao Dai* (Westport, CT: Greenwood, 2000), 146. For
    a discussion of the decision's impact in Hương Thủy see Thường Vụ Huyện Ủy
    Hương Thủy, *Lịch sử đấu tranh cách mạng*, 94–97.

23 Thường Vụ Huyện Ủy Hương Thủy, *Lịch sử đấu tranh cách mạng*, 115.

24 Ibid., 116. Translation by author: "Chiến khu là nơi của nhiều thương nhớ, niềm
    phấn khởi, nơi đoàn tụ và lòng nhân ái, ở đây là sự sống cơ sở quí giá của con
    người . . . Những chiều hôm, nhân dân Phú Vang và Hương Thủy tại quê mình
    nhìn lên chiến khu, những dãy núi xa, lại nhớ khi đi dân công, tải thương, tiếp
    tế, vận chuyển, lần đầu tiên đi vào chiến khu."

25 Hùng Sơn and Lê Khai, *Đường Hồ Chí Minh qua Bình Trị Thiên*, 67.

26 For a general overview of the Vietnamese gazetteer tradition see the introductory
    comments by historian Đào Duy Anh, ed., *Đại Nam nhất thống chí: Tập 1*, trans.
    Phạm Trọng Điềm (Huế: Thuận Hóa, 1992), 5–12.

27 Nguyễn Văn Hoa, *Địa chí Thừa Thiên Huế: Phần lịch sử*, 349. Translated from
    Vietnamese by the author: "bằng nằm giữa sông Ô Lâu—Rào Quao va dải núi
    rừng sát chân động Chuối."

28 Nguyễn Văn Hoa, *Địa chí Thừa Thiên Huế: Phần Lịch sử*, 356.

29 Gerald C. Hickey, *Window on a War: An Anthropologist in the Vietnam Conflict*
    (Lubbock: Texas Tech University Press, 2002), 71–75.

30 Ngô Kha, ed., *Lịch sử đảng bộ huyện Nam Đông (1945–2000)* [History of the Party
    in Nam Dong District (1945–2000)] (Hà Nội: NXB Chính Trị Quốc Gia, 2003),
    48, 54.

31 Thường Vụ Huyện Ủy Hương Thủy, *Lịch sử đấu tranh cách mạng*, 92.

32 Ibid., 96.

33 Telegram No. 1489, April 11, 1947, Ambassador Jefferson Caffery to Department
    of State, Frames 431–432, Reel 3, in Paul Kesaris, ed., *Confidential US State Depart-
    ment Central Files, Indochina Internal Affairs, 1945–1949* (Frederick, MD: Univer-
    sity Publications of America, 1984).

34 Tonnesson, *Vietnam 1946*, 224.

35 Nguyễn Văn Hoa, *Địa chí Thừa Thiên Huế: Phần lịch sử*, 354.

36 File 1035, "Rapport Politique," September 1949, Phủ Thủ Hiến Trung Việt [THTV,
    Records of the Central Vietnam Governing Committee], VNA4. Translation by
    author: "Si les troupes françaises continuent leur politique de pacification par la

terreur, cette situation pourrait devenir un jour irrémédiable et remettre sur le tapis le problème franco-viêtnamien. Le retrait des troupes françaises dans leurs bases semble être le seul remède possible." Note that from April 1949, the Việt Binh Đoàn local forces were folded into a new national Vietnamese army called Vệ Binh Việt Nam and later Quân Đội Quốc Gia Việt Nam. Locally in Huế, both French and Vietnamese continued to call these battalions Việt Binh Đoàn to 1954.

37 Ibid.

38 Ibid.

39 Ellen J. Hammer, *The Struggle for Indochina* (Stanford, CA: Stanford University Press, 1954), 246.

40 For an extensive historical analysis of the Revers Mission and subsequent report see Danielle Domergue-Cloarec, "La mission et le rapport revers," *Guerres mondiales et conflits contemporains* 148 (October 1987): 97–114.

41 Box 3448, Series 10H, Service Historique de la Défense, Vincennes, France (SHD).

42 Here I am indebted to James Scott for his argument that (pre-1945) lowland states encountered resistance—in the terrain and from upland peoples—and therefore expanded mainly in lowland areas. This he terms the "friction of terrain." See Scott, *Art of Not Being Governed*, 21. In correspondence with Scott, we examined a related question: what do states do in flooded or swampy terrain. In Southeast Asia, especially central Vietnam, coastal lowlands and estuaries were subjected to intensive state-funded irrigation and diking projects. However, some lagoons and swamps proved too expensive or difficult to manage; in my work, I have argued that such swampy terrain also produces a kind of ecological and political "friction," and insurgents allied with indigenous dwellers of these areas to build resistance bases, too. See David Biggs, *Quagmire: Nation-Building and Nature in the Mekong Delta* (Seattle: University of Washington Press, 2011).

43 Translation by author: "LA LIBERTÉ EST MA VIE—ELLE EST AUSSI MA FILLE— O INDEPENDENCE! ARABES: Sachez que la guerre sainté est déclarée à la France qui nous opprime. Que celui qui veut combattre pour lÍndépendance sache quíl se battra sous l'égide du nouveau Parti de la Liberté. Ecoutez! Région de CONBAN les combattants du Vietnam ont remporté de gros succès en très peu de tempe. Du 1/11/49 au 10/12/49 ils ont fait 9 opérations. Les pertes one été du côté français prend: 112 tués, 17 blessés, 63 prisonniers. Le matériel récupéré comprend: 1 mortier, 9 mitrailleuses, 7 mitraillettes, 181 fusils anglais et américains, un poste radio portatif etc . . . JE COMBATS POUR MA PATRIE ET POUR L'INDEPENDANCE ET TOI TU TE VENDS—TON AME EST PERDUE."

44 Considering the struggle for sovereignty at the heart of the Indochina War, the position of these *goums*–ethnic Berber and Arabic Moroccan soldiers—reflects the multiple contradictions facing soldiers in the occupied zones. In Morocco in the early 1950s, Moroccan political groups made increasing calls for independence from France. The sultan of Morocco, somewhat like Emperor Bảo Đại in Vietnam, was growing increasingly bold in his advocacy for independence too. Inside Morocco and North Africa, Berber-speaking people navigated ethnic

boundaries not only as colonial French subjects but also as historically indigenous peoples in an increasingly Arab-Islamist state. Berbers were one of the oldest indigenous groups, and much like Vietnamese experiences in the Red River delta, they had fought many wars over centuries against Roman, Arab, and French imperial expansion.

45 Edward L. Bimberg, *The Moroccan Goums: Tribal Warriors in a Modern War* (Westport, CT: Greenwood, 1999).

46 "Reflections sur la Region du Sud de Nam Giao," 1953, Box 3166, Series 10H, SHD. For a more positive description of the Ninth Tabor in Indochina, see Bertrand Bellaigue, *Indochine* (Paris: Editions Publibook, 2009), 95–100.

47 Box 3166, Series 10H, SHD.

48 "Reflections sur le Region au Sud de Nam Giao," October 1952, Box 3166, Series 10H, SHD.

49 File TV310, SHD–Fort de l'Est.

50 Details of the establishment of these camps can be found in File 3378, Series 10H, SHD.

51 For detailed correspondence on clearing activities around Huế, see Boxes 3482 and 3166, Series 10H, SHD.

52 For a classic study including primary US sources on the decision to offer direct military aid and to recognize the ASV, see the source materials collected for the Pentagon Papers: US Relations with the Bao Dai Government, 1947, Folder 11, Box 01, Douglas Pike Collection: Unit 13—The Early History of Vietnam, the Vietnam Center and Archive, Texas Tech University, accessed December 17, 2014, www.vietnam.ttu.edu/virtualarchive/items.php?item=2410111012.

53 American diplomatic historians Mark Atwood Lawrence and Fredrik Logevall provide extensive, compelling treatments on the American entry into the Indochina War. See Mark Atwood Lawrence, *Assuming the Burden: Europe and the American Commitment to War in Vietnam* (Berkeley: University of California Press, 2005); Mark Atwood Lawrence and Fredrik Logevall, eds., *The First Vietnam War: Colonial Conflict and Cold War Crisis* (Cambridge, MA: Harvard University Press, 2007); Logevall, *Embers of War*.

54 Ironically, some of the first pieces of American military equipment sent to Indochina were the radio sets delivered by the OSS to Hồ Chí Minh's guerillas in southern China in 1944–45. See beginning of this chapter. Logevall, *Embers of War*, 284–85.

55 Ibid., 321.

56 Logevall devotes an entire chapter to Graham Greene, illuminating in new ways the interconnected world of spies, diplomats, generals, and journalists who crossed paths on the streets of Saigon. See Logevall, *Embers of War*, 293–310. Bernard Fall, a former *maquisard* with the French resistance and a child of Vienna Jews killed by the Nazis, came to the United States on a Fulbright scholarship in 1951 and a year later took up studies of the Indochina conflict. See Logevall, *Embers of War*, 358–59. His account of a huge but largely unsuccessful French

offensive to clear areas of Highway 1 north of Huế in 1953 gave the name of his account of the French defeat, *Street without Joy*. See Graham Greene, *The Quiet American* (London: William Heinemann, 1955). See also Bernard Fall, *Street without Joy: Indochina at War* (Harrisburg, PA: Stackpole, 1961).

57   Tourane Base Justifications, March 1953, Series 10H3388, SHD.

58   The Indochina War, 1945–1956, An Interdisciplinary Tool, last accessed September 2, 2017, http://indochine.uqam.ca/en/historical-dictionary/288-civil-air-transport-cat.html.

59   February 1952, Commandement des Forces Terrestres du Centre Vietnam, "Directive Particulière à la Zone Nord," Box 3248, Series 10H, SHD.

60   October 1953, Le Chef des Escadrons BONNEFOUS à Monsieur le Général de Division, Box 3248, Series 10H, SHD.

61   Fall, *Street without Joy*, 171.

62   Ibid., 170.

CHAPTER FOUR: RUINS

1   For a party-centered history of Interzone IV drawn especially from party and People's Army records on the 1953–54 period, see Trình Mưu, ed., *Lịch sử kháng chiến chống thực dân Pháp của quân và dân liên khu IV* [History of the resistance against French colonialism by the military and people of Inter-Regional Zone IV] (Hà Nội: NXB Chính Trị Quốc Gia, 2003), 556–80.

2   See Ken MacLean, "Manifest Socialism: The Labor of Representation in the Democratic Republic of Vietnam (1956–1959)," *Journal of Vietnamese Studies* 2, no. 1 (2007): 27–79. See also Edward Miller's in-depth discussion of Diệm's agricultural development centers, *Misalliance: Ngo Dinh Diem, the United States and the Fate of South Vietnam* (Cambridge, MA: Harvard University Press, 2013), 158–84.

3   One of the only biographies of Cẩn is a somewhat popularized police genre account by the People's Police Publishing House describing details of the police unit's atrocities taken from seized police records after 1975. See Công An Nhân Dân, Đoàn *mật vụ của Ngô Đình Cẩn* [The secret police division of Ngô Đình Cẩn] (Hà Nội: NXB Công An Nhân Dân, 1996).

4   Dương Phước Thu, *Tử Ngục chín hầm và những điều ít biết về Ngô Đình Cẩn* (Huế: Thuận Hóa, 2010).

5   Ann L. Stoler, ed., *Imperial Debris: On Ruins and Ruination* (Durham, NC: Duke University Press, 2013), 9.

6   Thomas F. Conlon, "John J. Helble" (Arlington, VA: Foreign Affairs Oral History Project, Association for Diplomatic Studies and Training, 1998), 53–55, last accessed March 10, 2016, http://adst.org/wp-content/uploads/2012/09/Helble-John-J.toc_.pdf.

7   Trình Mưu, *Lịch sử kháng chiến chống thực dân Pháp của quân và dân liên khu IV*, 569–72.

8   Ibid., 571. Translated by author: "Tiếp tục giải quyết tư tưởng, thống nhất nhận định, quán triệt phương châm và đường lối mới của cấp uỷ Trung ương, sửa chữa sai lầm, khuyết điểm. Cán bộ các cấp phải thấy được tình hình miền Nam và Trị Thiên . . . Tổ chức cơ sở đảng phải giữ vững nguyên tắc bảo đảm bí mật và quan hệ chặt chẽ với quần chúng. Việc sắp xếp lại chi bộ, chọn lọc đảng viên phải tiến hành dần dần, có kế hoạch, có trọng điểm, tránh làm chấn động trong đảng. Thường xuyên bồi dưỡng cán bộ để khi cần tăng cường cho địa phương."

9   Ngô Kha, *Lịch sử đảng bộ huyện Nam Đông*, 63–64.

10   November 22, 1955, Director of National Police, Central Vietnam, to General Director of National Police, Saigon, File 1927, Records of Government Delegate to Central Highlands and Central Vietnam (hereafter TNTP), VNA4.

11   August 21, 1954, Letter from Nguyễn Hữu Đính to Director of Forestry, Central Vietnam, File 2837, TNTP, VNA4.

12   August 30, 1954, Province Chief of Thừa Thiên to Lt. Col. Robert Le Bihan, Commander of Huế Sector, File 2837, TNTP, VNA4.

13   Thừa Thiên Province Chief to Central Vietnam Delegate, October 6, 1954, re "Thanh Thủy villagers riot after we apprehend two cadres" [Dân chúng Thanh-Thủy Thượng bạo động tiếp ứng giải vây cho hai cán bộ bị ta bắt], Folder 1949, TNTP, VNA4.

14   Miller provides an excellent thirty-thousand-foot perspective on the Diệm-Hinh struggle in the summer and fall of 1954, drawing largely from Vietnamese, French, and American primary records. Miller, *Misalliance*, 102–6.

15   Special Information Bulletin: August 3, 1954 re: anti-French activities of a company in the Twenty-Fifth Vietnamese Infantry Battalion, File 10H3246, SHD. Translation by author: "Ngo-Dinh-Diem se rendra sous peu en Amérique pour demander l'intervention armée de ce pays contre les Français et les VM. Si Ngo-Dinh-Diem a laissé les Français partager le Viêtnam, c'est parce qu'il espérait une réaction américaine qui se matérialisera par le bombardement atomique de la zone VM. La France réssemble, après le partage du Viêtnam, à une prostituée qui s'offre à tous, même à un lépreux, pour de lárgent. C'est une ennemie perfide qu'il nous faut combattre avant les V.M. qui sont nos compatriotes. Notre devoir à nous, catholiques patriotes, est d'effectuer partout une propagande anti-française. Cette propagande doit insister sur le perte de prestige de la France après la conférence de Genève."

16   Popular seizure of the Gia-Le-Chanh Post, August 5, 1954, File 10H3246, SHD.

17   Worker protest at Phú Bài during American aid delegation visit, September 10, 1054, File 1993, TNTP, VNA4.

18   Activities of the French Army in Central Vietnam, 1954–55, File 1927, TNTP, VNA4.

19   Ibid.

20   Nick Valery, "Difference Engine: Revenge of the Gooney Bird," *Economist*, May 13, 2014.

21 "MAAGV 320.2—Development of US Forces and Equipment for VN Forces in Region," Box 4, Security Classified General Records, 1950–1961, MAAG Vietnam—Adjutant General Division, RG472, NARA-CP.

22 US Army, *Vietnam Studies: Command and Control, 1950–1969* (Washington, DC: GPO, 1991), 7.

23 Ibid., 13–14.

24 September 10, 1956, Monthly Summary Report, Box 8, MAAG-VN, RG472, NARA-CP.

25 January 10, 1956, Central Vietnam Delegate to Lieutenant General of Huế Sector, File 2051, TNTP, VNA4.

26 Hữu Mai, *Ông cố vấn: Hồ sơ một điệp viên* (Hồ Chí Minh City: Văn nghệ, 2002).

27 Dương Phước Thu, *Từ Ngục chín hầm và những điều ít biết về Ngô Đình Cẩn*, 86–88. The party began as a political seminar organized by older brother Nhu, but after July 1954, both Nhu in Sài Gòn and Cẩn in Huế used the Cần Lao Party as a secretive organization for indoctrinating regime loyalists and infiltrating such organizations as the national assembly and the military. Edward Miller's unpublished paper on the Cần Lao remains one of the most informative investigations of this little-studied organization. For his discussion of Cẩn's mobilization of the party network, Edward Miller's unpublished paper remains one of the few English-language sources detailing conflicts between Diệm's two brothers. See "A House Divided: Ngô Đình Nhu, the Cần Lao Party and the Internal Politics of the Diệm Regime," paper presented at the conference The American Experience in Southeast Asia, 1945–1975, US Department of State, Washington, DC, September 30, 2010, esp. pp. 18–20. CIA historian Thomas Ahern's book *CIA and the House of Ngo* (Washington, DC: Center for the Study of Intelligence, 2009) relies on American sources who suggest that by 1957 Cẩn and his allies were in a position to take over the party nationally with help from loyalists in the Mekong Delta (p. 106).

28 Dương Phước Thu, *Từ Ngục chín hầm và những điều ít biết về Ngô Đình Cẩn*, 63–64.

29 Ibid., 153. At the historic monument today, guides show tourists to specific bunkers reserved for Buddhist protesters and students as well as one bunker where the French-Vietnamese manager of the Morin Hotel was taken and held for ransom. The ransom paid, he was released but soon after died from his injuries.

30 Ahern, *CIA and the House of Ngo*, 106.

31 Trullinger, *Village at War*, 75–77.

32 Ibid., 78.

33 "V/v trả trường Giạ Lê Thượng để có chỗ học sinh học," File 2973, TNTP, VNA4.

34 Nguyễn Văn Hoa, *Địa chí Thừa Thiên Huế: Phần Lịch sử*, 401.

35 Letter from the Consul in Huế (Heavner) to the deputy Chief of Mission in Vietnam (Elting), October 15, 1959, in *Foreign Relations of the United States, 1958–1960, Vietnam, Volume 1*, ed. John P. Glennon et al. (Washington DC: GPO, 1986), 244–46.

36 "Kết quả cuộc nghiên-cứu về địa-điểm Dinh Điền Nam-Đông," November 16, 1960, File 14319, RG ĐICH, Vietnam National Archives Center no. 2 (hereafter VNA2).

37 For an in-depth treatment of RVN policies on sedentarization see Salemink, *Ethnography of Vietnam's Central Highlanders*,184–94.

38 Ibid., 51. Translation by author: "Phải biến đổi hoang thành rẫy sắn; nhà nhà, người người, thôn thôn sản xuất, thi đua nhau sản xuất để có cái ăn, nuôi quân đánh giặc."

39 Hickey, *Window on a War*, 71–75.

40 Nguyễn Văn Hoa, *Địa chí Thừa Thiên Huế: Phần lịch sử*, 403.

41 Ngô Kha, *Lịch sử bộ huyện Nam Đông*, 73–74.

42 Nguyễn Văn Hoa, *Địa chí Thừa Thiên Huế: Phần Lịch sử*, 403.

43 Miller, *Misalliance*, 198–202.

44 Lien-Hang T. Nguyen, *Hanoi's War: An International History of the War for Peace in Vietnam* (Chapel Hill: University of North Carolina Press, 2012): 41–47.

45 Ronald H. Spector, *Advice and Support: The Early Years of the United States Army in Vietnam 1941-1960* (New York: Free Press, 1984): 332.

46 Ngô Kha, *Lịch sử đảng bộ huyện Nam Đông*, 106–8.

47 Miller, *Misalliance*, 208–10.

48 November 11, 1960, Province Chief to Government Delegate for Central Highlands and Central Region, File 6077, Phủ Thủ Tướng Record Group (Prime Minister Office, hereafter PTTG), VNA4. Translation by author: "Cuộc hành quân có tính cách thuần tuý quân sự và hoàn toàn nhằm mục đích quân sự: tảo thanh, truy kích địch và khám phá cơ sở của chúng. Không có sự phối hợp với các cơ quan Hành chánh, Công an, và các lực lượng bán quân sự."

49 Nancy Peluso and Peter Vandergeest discuss similar maps developed by American and Thai military and development officials. They targeted "pink areas on the map," especially near national borders, for forest clearing and permanent settlements similar to Nam Đông. These maps, with pie charts and pink zones, and land clearing strategies fit in a broader set of American designs on development and counterinsurgency. See Nancy Peluso and Peter Vandergeest, "Territorialization and State Power in Thailand," *Theory and Society* 24 (1995): 410n129.

50 Trullinger, *Village at War*, 85.

51 Document 303, Memorandum from Robert H. Johnson of the Policy Planning Staff to the Counselor of the Department of State (Rostow), October 16, 1962, *Foreign Relations of the United States, 1961-1963, Volume II, Vietnam, 1962* (Washington: GPO, 1990), 703–6.

52 Nguyễn Tú and Nguyên Triều, *Địa chí Hương Thủy*, 406–7.

53 Nguyễn Văn Hoa, *Địa chí Thừa Thiên Huế: Phần Lịch sử*, 413–14.

54 Helble's accounts of Cẩn are some of the only American comments from the Huế area prior to the coup that toppled his brother's regime in November 1963. Helble's only face-to-face meeting, ironically, occurred as he escorted Cẩn by plane to Sài Gòn where he was taken by South Vietnamese military officers and later

imprisoned. See Thomas F. Conlon, "John J. Helble," Foreign Affairs Oral History Project, Association for Diplomatic Studies and Training, 1998, 53–55, last accessed Thursday, March 10, 2016, http://adst.org/wp-content/uploads/2012/09/Helble-John-J.toc_.pdf.

55 Thomas F. Conlon. "John J. Helble."

56 Nguyễn Văn Hoa, Địa chí Thừa Thiên Huế: Phần lịch sử, 425–26.

57 Hickey, Window on a War, 75.

CHAPTER FIVE: CREATIVE DESTRUCTION

1 US Army, Vietnam Studies, v.

2 Trần Mai Nam, Narrow Strip of Land, 90–91.

3 Samuel Huntington, "The Bases of Accommodation," Foreign Affairs 46 , no. 4 (1968): 642–56.

4 Ibid., 652.

5 Đảng Ủy Ban Chỉ Huy Quân Sự Huyện A Lưới, Lịch sử lực lượng vũ trang nhân dân huyện A Lưới (1945–2010) [History of popular armed forces in A Lưới District] (Hà Nội: NXB Quân Đội Nhân Dân, 2011), 86–89.

6 David Biggs, "Frame DS1050–1006DF129: March 20, 1969," Environmental History 19, no. 2 (2014): 271–80. The resolution of these images varied, but high-resolution stereo images produced from 1968–72 had a comparable digital resolution of about one pixel per meter, equivalent to commercial satellite imagery produced after 2000.

7 Historian David Zierler provides a detailed account of the Kennedy administration's debates as well as efforts by senior American scientists in the late 1960s to force the United States to abandon herbicides. See Zierler, The Invention of Ecocide: Agent Orange, Vietnam and the Scientists Who Changed the Way We Think About the Environment (Athens: University of Georgia Press, 2011).

8 Historical Working Group, "Herbicide Operations in the Republic of Vietnam," Box 8, Historians Background Material Files, MACV Secretary of the Joint Staff (MACJ03), RG472, NARA-CP.

9 Flight records for the first six missions list the type of herbicide as "unknown." The arsenical herbicide Agent Blue was available and used for crop destruction missions throughout the war. In these early tests it was available, possibly in commercial form, as Phytar 560G, produced by the Ansul Company in Wisconsin. Records of these early missions are included in the "Services HERBS Tape—A Record of Helicopter and Ground Spraying Missions, Aborts, Leaks, and Incidents." Special Collections, USDA National Agricultural Library, last accessed December 6, 2016, www.nal.usda.gov/exhibits/speccoll/items/show/1258. For an in-depth discussion of the early testing of herbicides in Vietnam, see also Alvin Young, The History, Use, Disposition and Environmental Fate of Agent Orange (New York: Springer, 2009), 65–69. For the area sprayed, see Historical Working Group, "Herbicide Operations in the Republic of Vietnam," 11–12.

10 Historical Working Group, "Herbicide Operations," 20–21. In their recent studies of the DRV's path to all-out war in 1964, historians Lien-Hang Nguyen and Pierre Asselin both highlight the intense struggles that occured that summer between prowar and coexistence camps in Hà Nội as well as Beijing and Moscow. By the mid-fall, the prowar group had succeeded in convincing a majority of party leaders as well as allies in China and the Soviet Union that it was time to fight. Radio broadcasts alleging chemical war and American confirmations that chemicals had been sprayed certainly helped the prowar cause. The party passed Resolution 9 on January 20, 1964, mobilizing PAVN units for war in the south. See Pierre Asselin, *Hanoi's Road to the Vietnam War, 1954–65* (Berkeley: University of California Press, 2013), 163–67. See also Nguyen, *Hanoi's War*, 62–64.

11 Robert A. Darrow, Report of Trip to Republic of Vietnam, August 15–September 2, 1969. Alvin Young Collection, USDA National Agricultural Library, last accessed July 7, 2017, www.nal.usda.gov/exhibits/speccoll/files/original/f994332e7ad90b c9b846049d846b4639.pdf.

12 The Eighth RRU and surrounding installations is described in a map accompanying documents on the Eighth RRU. See "Phu Bai," Box 23, MACV J3 Historians Working Group Files, RG472, NARA-CP.

13 "US Electronic Espionage: A Memoir," *Ramparts* 11, no. 2 (1972): 50. For a history of the NSA direction-finding operations in Vietnam, see a recently declassified history of the NSA and cryptology during the Cold War. Thomas R. Johnson, *American Cryptology during the Cold War, Book II: Centralization Wins, 1960–1972* (Washington, DC: National Security Agency, 1995), 509–28. The declassified, redacted history is available online at the George Washington University National Security Archive, last accessed December 5, 2016, http://nsarchive.gwu.edu /NSAEBB/NSAEBB260/index.htm.

14 Correspondence dated August 15, 1964, File 21852, PTTG Record Group, VNA2.

15 Correspondence dated November 3, 1964, File 21852, PTTG Record Group, VNA2.

16 Harvey Smith, *Area Handbook for South Vietnam* (Washington, DC: GPO, 1967), 292.

17 April 1965, Về tình hình, biện pháp an ninh, chính trị, quân sự tại Vùng Chiến thuật năm 1965, File 17115, PTTG Record Group, VNA2.

18 Nguyễn Tú and Nguyên Triều, *Địa chí Hương Thủy*, 412.

19 Russel H. Stolfi, *U.S. Marine Corps Civic Action Efforts in Vietnam, March 1965–March 1966* (Washington, DC: Headquarters US Marine Corps, 1968), 17–18.

20 Ibid., 19.

21 Bruce C. Allnutt, *Combined Action Capabilities: The Vietnam Experience* (Washington, DC: Office of Naval Research, 1969), 8.

22 Interview with Paul Ek, January 24, 1966, US Marine Corps History Division Oral History Collection, the Vietnam Center and Archive, Texas Tech University, last accessed January 10, 2017, www.vietnam.ttu.edu/virtualarchive/items.php?item= USMC0046.

23 Ibid., minutes 43:00–46:00.

24   *Congressional Record—Senate* 112 (February 23, 1966) (Washington DC: GPO, 1966), 3888–89. The debate over tax increases and the US$10.7 billion spending bill in 1967 appears in *Congressional Record—Senate* 112 (March 4, 1966) (Washington DC: GPO, 1966), 4930–31.

25   Ibid., 3890.

26   Nguyễn Tú and Nguyên Triều, *Địa chí Hương Thủy*, 416.

27   A Shau was an American spelling of the Vietnamese A Sầu, however it referred to just one of the three special forces bases, the southernmost base. See Plate 4. Also, I use the term "PAVN-PLAF units" because many of the communist large-unit battles involved integrated units with component battalions and companies coming from separate PAVN and PLAF commands.

28   After-Action Report—The Battle for A Shau: A Shau SF Disaster, March 1966, Folder 03, Box 03, Dale W. Andrade Collection, the Vietnam Center and Archive, Texas Tech University, last accessed September 13, 2017, www.vietnam.ttu.edu /virtualarchive/items.php?item=24990303002.

29   Captured Documents (CDEC): Unknown Interrogation Source, Log Number 12-2318-00, 10/28/1966, A Shau, December 24, 1966, Reel 0060, Vietnam Archive Collection, Vietnam Center and Archive, Texas Tech University, last accessed September 13, 2017, https://www.vietnam.ttu.edu/reports/images_cdec.php?img= /images/F0346/0060-1135-000.pdf.

30   Nguyễn Văn Hoa, *Địa chí Thừa Thiên Huế: Phần Lịch sử*, 531.

31   A detailed account of the American actions at Phong Điền is provided in the official US Marines history of the Vietnam War. See Jack Shulimson, *US Marines in Vietnam: An Expanding War, 1966* (Washington, DC: History and Museums Division, Headquarters, US Marine Corps, 1982), 323–26.

32   This highly detailed GIS is publicly available by the US Air Force Research Institute. To access datasets of US bombing missions since World War I, see US Air Force, THOR: Theater History of Operations Reports, last accessed January 18, 2017, http://afri.au.af.mil/thor/index.asp. For an essay describing the dataset, see Sarah Loicano, "Historic Airpower Database Now Online," U.S. Air Force, last accessed January 18, 2017, www.af.mil/News/ArticleDisplay/tabid/223/Article /466817/historic-airpower-database-now-online.aspx.

33   The primary source for strategic bombing in World War II are the many volumes of the US Strategic Bombing Survey published in 1945. Historians Claudia Baldoli and Andrew Knapp cite the figure of two hundred thousand tons of bombs dropped by the US Eight Air Force and the Royal Air Force in 1943. See Claudia Baldoli and Andrew Knapp, *Forgotten Blitzes: France and Italy under Air Attack, 1940-1945* (London: Continuum, 2012), 42.

34   Robert Topmiller's *The Lotus Unleashed: The Buddhist Peace Movement, 1964–66* (Lexington: University Press of Kentucky, 2002), remains one of the few, in-depth English-language studies of the Unified Buddhist Church and the Buddhist protests. In Vietnamese sources, opinions on the Struggle Movement in the diaspora and opinions about the protests are deeply divided among those following

Buddhist organizations and others that accuse the Buddhist leaders of being secretly in coordination with the NLF and North Vietnam. For one of many works exploring the "secrets" of the protests, see Liên Thành, *Biến động miền Trung: những bí mật chưa tiết lộ giai đoạn 1966–1968–1972* [Operations in Central Vietnam: Secrets not et revealed from 1966–1968–1972] (Westminster, CA: Tập san Biệt Động Quân xuất bản, 2008).

35 "Ky Foes Seize Two Radio Stations: Assail US and Military Junta," *Chicago Tribune*, March 23, 1966, 1–2.

36 Topmiller, *Lotus Unleashed*, 75.

37 Ibid., 132.

38 Michael Kelly, *Where We Were in Vietnam: A Comprehensive Guide to the Firebases, Military Installations, and Naval Vessels of the Vietnam War* (Central Point, OR: Hellgate Press, 2002), 5-5.

39 One of the most useful English-language texts on PAVN and PLAF history is historian Merle Pribbenow's excellent translation of the PAVN's official military history. See Merle L. Pribbenow, trans., *Victory in Vietnam: The Official History of the People's Army of Vietnam, 1954–1975* (Lawrence: University of Kansas, 2002), 209–10.

40 The history of the origins of the 101st or Trần Cao Vân Regiment is recorded in Phạm Gia Đức, *Sư đoàn 325: Tập một* [325th Regiment: Volume 1] (Hà Nội: NXB Quân Đội Nhân Dân, 1981), 25–30. The activities at Khe Sanh are detailed in Đảng Bộ Quân Khu 4, *Lịch sử đảng bộ sư đoàn 324 (1955–2010)* (Hà Nội: NXB Quân Đội Nhân Dân, 2012), 140–45.

41 Ibid., 212–13.

42 Nguyễn Văn Giáo, "Lực lượng vũ trang Thừa Thiên Huế trong tổng tiến công và nổi dậy Tết Mậu Thân 1968," in *Cuộc tổng tiến công và nổi dậy Mậu Thân 1968*, by Military History Institute of Vietnam (Hà Nội: NXB Quân Đội Nhân Dân, 1998), 143–52.

43 Ibid., 146–47.

44 Author interview with former PAVN soldier in Huế, July 2009.

45 James Willbanks, *The Tet Offensive: A Concise History* (New York: Columbia University Press, 2008), 46–47.

46 Two of the most succinct histories of the battles in Huế for English-language readers include Willbanks, *Tet Offensive*; and Pribbenow, *Victory in Vietnam*, 216–229.

47 Privately contributed copies of CBS newscasts have been uploaded to Youtube. com. The February 6 segment can be found at www.youtube.com/watch?v=vDyoZ3HSkTE, last accessed January 30, 2017.

48 Willbanks, *Tet Offensive*, 50–52. For Vietnamese civilians in Huế who survived the destruction of the city, personal accounts of the fighting remain a divisive topic for many; discussions of local personal and neighborhood involvement are still largely confined among family and close friends. Some neighbors revealed hidden identities as party members and participated in identifying officials in the

city administration. After the communists retreated, they either fled or exposed themselves to reprisals and detention.

49 Willbanks, *Tet Offensive*, 54.

50 Pham Van Son, *The Viet Cong 'Tet' Offensive (1968)* (Saigon: RVNAF Printing and Publications Center, 1969), 294–96.

51 Pribbenow, *Victory in Vietnam*, 224.

52 This is one of Trịnh Công Sơn's more popular works and is still available in many versions and formats in Vietnam and diasporic communities. For one album, see Trịnh Công Sơn, *A Tribute to Trịnh Công Sơn* (Independence, OR: East Wind Records, 2004). While most of his family left Vietnam, Sơn stayed in Vietnam after 1975. He was sentenced to a reeducation camp, but in the post-1986 liberalization period, he enjoyed a popular resurgence and accolades from the state. The Vietnamese name of the song is "Bài Ca Dành Cho Những Xác Người".

53 Nhã Ca, *Mourning Headband for Hue*, xix–xx.

54 Ibid., 283.

55 Willard Pearson, *The War in the Northern Provinces, 1966–1968* (Washington DC: US Army, 1975), 58–59.

56 Pearson, *War in the Northern Provinces*, 67–68.

57 Trullinger, *Village at War*, 133–34.

58 Ibid., 135.

59 Ibid., 137.

60 First Cavalry Division (Airmobile), Construction of a Firebase, Box 17, Command Historian General Records, Headquarters US Army Vietnam, RG472, NARA-CP.

61 Directorate of Intelligence, Intelligence Memorandum 68–46: Road Construction in the Laotian Panhandle and Adjacent Areas of South Vietnam, 1967–1968, CIA CREST Declassified Documents, Report Number CIA-RDP85T00875R0015002 20048-6, 1–3, last accessed February 3, 2017, www.cia.gov/library/readingroom /document/cia-rdp85t00875r001500220048-6. John Prados describes the oil pipeline in his history of the trails. See John Prados, *The Blood Road: The Ho Chi Minh Trail and the Vietnam War* (New York: Wiley, 1999), 339–40.

62 The communist history of the battle is detailed in Đào Quang Đới, Nguyễn Thống, and Võ Việt Hòa, *Sư đoàn 324* (Hà Nội: NXB Quân Đội Nhân Dân, 1992), 53–55. Thanks to military historian Merle Pribbenow for excerpts.

63 Project CHECO Southeast Asia Report #2—Special Report: A Shau Valley Campaign—December 1968 to May 1969, October 15, 1969, Folder 1306, Box 0008, Vietnam Archive Collection, the Vietnam Center and Archive, Texas Tech University, last accessed February 3, 2017, www.vietnam.ttu.edu/virtualarchive /items.php?item=F031100081306.

64 See "U.S. Troops Abandon Viet Hill, Center of Congressional Storm," *Los Angeles Times*, May 28, 1969, A1, A13; and "Reds Back On Viet Hill; US General Ready To Fight," *Los Angeles Times*, June 18, 1969, A1, A12.

65 Diplomatic historian David Zierler provides an in-depth study of US government

deliberations over use of herbicides as tactical agents in war. See Zierler, *Invention of Ecocide*, 117–18.

66   For a description of domestic American pesticide use in 1968–69, a comprehensive source is the USDA's annual Pesticide Review. For discussion of 2,4,5-T see US Department of Agriculture, *The Pesticide Review: 1968* (Washington, DC: USDA Agricultural Stabilization and Conservation Service, 1969).

67   These missions are detailed in the Tenth Chemical Platoon's Daily Mission Log. Chemical Officer Daily Journal, Box 1, 101st Airborne Division, United States Army Vietnam, RG472, NARA-CP. As with most US military operations, there were manuals that explained procedures for each of these chemical operations. For the manual used by the Tenth Platoon, see Box 1, Tenth Chemical Platoon, Chemical Units, RG472, NARA-CP.

68   Edwin Martini, *Agent Orange: History, Science and the Politics of Uncertainty* (Amherst: University of Massachusetts Press, 2012), 77–83.

69   Herbicide Operations Project 1/2/2/70, Records Pertaining to Herbicide Operations, Assistant Chief of Staff for Operations (G3) Advisor, MACV First Regional Assistance Command, RG472, NARA-CP.

70   Local party histories of these mountainous districts note significant participation in both political and military agendas by the ethnic minorities in the highlands. Many descendants of these highlanders continue to serve in regional and national government posts in the present. For histories of Montagnard participation in Thừa Thiên Huế Province, see Ngô Kha, *Lịch sử đảng bộ huyện Nam Đông*, 48–54; and on ethnic minority participation in the A Sầu Valley, see Đảng Ủy Ban Chỉ Huy Quân Sự Huyện A Lưới, *Lịch sử lực lượng vũ trang nhân dân huyện A Lưới*.

71   Ecologists in particular pointed to picloram in Agent White as a more problematic military herbicide for its persistence. It rendered soils unproductive far longer than Agent Orange. For a detailed study on Agent White, see Leif Fredrickson, "From Ecocide to Eco-ally: Picloram, Herbicidal Warfare, and Invasive Species, 1963–2005," *Global Environment* 7, no. 1 (2014): 172–217. Agent Blue was an arsenical herbicide and used especially for killing rice crops. See US Army, *Field Manual 3-3: Tactical Employment of Herbicides* (Washington, DC: US Army, 1971).

72   Robert A. Darrow, Report of Trip to Republic of Vietnam, August 15,—September 2, 1969, Alvin Young Collection, USDA National Agricultural Library, last accessed July 7, 2017, www.nal.usda.gov/exhibits/speccoll/files/original/f994332e7ad90b c9b846049d846b4639.pdf.

73   Author interview with Mr. Dan, February 2, 2012, Thủy Phương Commune, Thừa Thiên–Huế Province. Also like many other *bộ đội* (infantry) soldiers who fought in these areas, Mr. Dan reported that he could not have more children after he and his wife gave birth to a severely disabled daughter in 1984. He believed that her ailments were directly related to his exposure to dioxin.

74   Trần Mai Nam, *Narrow Strip of Land*, 9–10.

75   Barry Weisberg, *Ecocide in Indochina: The Ecology of War* (New York: Harper and Row, 1970).

76 Kelly, *Where We Were in Vietnam*, 44.

77 Nguyen Duy Hinh, *Lam Sơn 719* (Washington DC: US Army Center for Military History, 1979), 161.

78 Ibid., 117.

79 "Eagle Turnover," January 16, 1972, Box 3, Real Property Management Division: Property Disposal Files, 1972, MACV Headquarters: Construction Directorate, RG472, NARA-CP.

80 Discussion of the terms for exempting Pacific Architects and Engineers' property from the agreement happened after the transfer in late January 1972. See "MACDC14-Update," January 26, 1972, Box 2, Real Property Management Division: Property Disposal Files, 1972, MACV Headquarters: Construction Directorate, RG472, NARA-CP.

81 "Eagle Turnover," January 16, 1972. American military officials in Saigon quickly responded to the bad press, and they scrambled to arrange an additional sale of used equipment to the RVN for an additional US$4 million.

82 NBC News, "Camp Eagle is Handed Over to Vietnamese Army," January 21, 1972, clip 5112474944_s01, www.nbcuniversalarchives.com/nbcuni/clip/5112474944_s01.do.

83 Nguyễn Văn Hoa, *Địa chí Thừa Thiên Huế: Phần lịch sử*, 470–71.

84 Malcolm W. Browne, "Firebase Yielded to Foe a 2nd Time," *New York Times*, July 28, 1972, 1. See also Craig R. Whitney, "Supplies Running Low at Besieged Fire Base near Hue," *New York Times*, April 13, 1972, 16, http://search.proquest.com/docview/119445069?accountid=14521.

85 Cao Van Vien, *The Final Collapse* (Washington DC: US Army Center for Military History, 1985), 34.

86 Ibid., 31. The same back-and-forth exchanges by smaller units is discussed from a communist unit perspective in Nguyễn Văn Hoa, *Địa chí Thừa Thiên Huế: Phần lịch sử*, 473–74.

87 Ibid., 44.

88 Ibid., 484.

89 Ibid., 488.

CHAPTER SIX: POSTWAR

1 Interview with Ông Phương, Hamlet 5, Dạ Lê, January 20, 2012.

2 Paul A. Scipione, "Life in Vietnam," *New York Times*, December 4, 1983.

3 Interview with Ông Phương, Hamlet 5, Dạ Lê, January 20, 2012.

4 Bảo Ninh, *The Sorrow of War*, trans. Martin Secker (New York: Riverhead, 1996), 72–73.

5 There is an especially robust scholarly literature on issues of the Vietnamese diaspora and economic and cultural dimensions of transnational migrations. For her treatment of remittances and the sparking of new commercial enterprises see Ann Marie Leshkowich, "Wandering Ghosts of Late Socialism: Conflict,

Metaphor, and Memory in a Southern Vietnamese Marketplace," *Journal of Asian Studies* 67, no. 1 (2008): 5–41.

6   Interview with Mr. Minh, Dạ Lê, January 18, 2012.

7   Details of the cleanup can be found in Province People's Committee Decree 272, January 26, 2000. More recently, the Vietnamese daily *Pháp Luật VN* returned to the site to investigate alleged cancer clusters around the pollution site. See Thùy Nhung, Nghi vấn thảm họa ung thư từ hầm chứa chất độc CS và kho trữ thuốc trừ sâu, in *Pháp Luật VN*, August 18, 2016.

8   L. Wayne Dwernychuk, H. D. Cau, C. T. Hatfield, T. G. Boivin, T. M. Hung, P. T. Dung, and N. D. Tha, "Dioxin Reservoirs in Southern Vietnam—A Legacy of Agent Orange," *Chemosphere* 47 (2002): 117–37.

9   Ibid., 121.

10   The ecologist, Dr. Phùng Tửu Bôi, is nationally and internationally known for his work in the A Sầu Valley. In 2007 the *New York Times* featured his development of the "green fence" approach to keep village cattle from grazing around the hotspot area. See Christie Aschwanden, "Through the Forest, a Clearer View of the Needs of a People," *New York Times*, September 18, 2007. Environmental activist Susan Hammond also describes elements of the A Shau base as well as the problem of disentangling the Agent Orange disaster narrative from specific sites like A Shau and the nearby commune. See Susan Hammond, "Redefining Agent Orange, Mitigating its Impacts," in *Interactions with a Violent Past: Reading Post-Conflict Landscapes in Cambodia, Laos and Vietnam*, ed. Vatthana Pholsena and Oliver Tappe (Singapore: National University of Singapore Press, 2013), 186–207.

11   Patrick Meyfroidt and Eric F. Lambin, "Forest Transition in Vietnam and Bhutan: Causes and Environmental Impacts," in *Reforesting Landscapes: Linking Pattern And Process*, ed. H. Nagendra and J. Southworth (Dordrecht: Springer, 2010). See also McElwee, *Forests are Gold*, 97.

12   Nguyễn Hữu Đính, "Lâm phần miền nam Việt Nam nói chung, Thừa Thiên Nói Riêng và vai trò trước mắt của rừng rú chúng ta một khi hòa bình được thật sự văn hồi," *Nghiên Cứu Huế* 6 (2008): 7–30.

13   James C. Scott, *Seeing Like a State: How Certain Schemes to Improve the Human Condition Have Failed* (New Haven, CT: Yale University Press, 1998), 201.

SELECTED BIBLIOGRAPHY

Ahern, Thomas. *The CIA and the House of Ngo*. Washington, DC: Center for the Study of Intelligence, 2009.

Allnutt, Bruce C. *Combined Action Capabilities: The Vietnam Experience*. Washington, DC: Office of Naval Research, 1969.

Anderson, James A., and John K. Whitmore, eds. *China's Encounters in the South and Southwest: Reforging the Fiery Frontier over Two Millennia*. Leiden: Brill, 2015.

Asselin, Pierre. *Hanoi's Road to the Vietnam War, 1954–65*. Berkeley: University of California Press, 2013.

Baldoli, Claudia, and Andrew Knapp. *Forgotten Blitzes: France and Italy under Air Attack, 1940–1945*. London: Continuum, 2012.

Bảo Ninh. *The Sorrow of War: A Novel of North Vietnam*. Translated by Frank Palmos. New York: Pantheon, 1995.

Bellaigue, Bertrand. *Indochine*. Paris: Editions Publibook, 2009.

Bennett, Brett M. "The El Dorado of Forestry: The Eucalyptus in India, South Africa, and Thailand, 1850–2000." *International Review of Social History* 56, no. 4 (2010): 27–50.

Bienvenue, R. "Régime de la propriété foncière en Annam." Doctoral thesis, University of Rennes, 1911.

Biggs, David. "Aerial Photography and Colonial Discourse on the Agricultural Crisis in Late-Colonial Indochina, 1930–45." In *Cultivating the Colonies: Colonial States and Their Environmental Legacies*, edited by Christina Folke Ax, Niels Brimnes, Niklas Thode Jensen, and Karen Oslund, 109–32. Athens: Ohio University Press, 2011.

———. "Frame DS1050-1006DF129: March 20, 1969." *Environmental History* 19, no. 2 (2014): 271–80.

———. *Quagmire: Nation-Building and Nature in the Mekong Delta*. Seattle: University of Washington Press, 2010.

Billot, Albert. *L'affaire du Tonkin: Histoire diplomatique de l'établissement de notre protectorat sur l'Annam et de notre conflit avec la Chine, 1882–1885*. Paris: J. Hetzel, 1888.

Bimberg, Edward L. *The Moroccan Goums: Tribal Warriors in a Modern War*. Westport, CT: Greenwood, 1999.

Borri, Christoforo. *An Account of Cochinchina: Containing Many Admirable Rarities and Singularities of that Country.* London: Robert Ashley, 1633.

Braudel, Fernand. *The Mediterranean and the Mediterranean World in the Age of Philip II.* Vol. 1. Berkeley: University of California Press, 1995.

Brenier, Henri. *Essai d'atlas statistique de l'Indochine Française.* Hanoi: Extrême-Orient, 1914.

Brocheux, Pierre. *Histoire du Vietnam contemporain: La nation résiliente.* Paris: Fayard, 2011.

Brocheux, Pierre, and Daniel Hémery. *Indochina: An Ambiguous Colonization, 1858–1954.* Berkeley: University of California Press, 2009.

Brown, Kate. *Plutopia: Nuclear Families, Atomic Cities, and the Great Soviet and American Plutonium Disasters.* New York: Oxford University Press, 2013.

Bùi Thị Tân. *Về hai làng nghề truyền thống: Phú Bài và Hiền Lương* [Regarding two traditional craft villages: Phú Bài and Hiền Lương]. Huế: Thuận Hóa, 1999.

Cadière, Léopold M. "Sauvons Nos Pins!" *Bulletin des amis de Vieux Huế* 3, no. 4: 437–43.

Cadière, Louis. "Documents relatifs à l'époque de Gia-Long." *Bulletin de l'École Française d'Extrême-Orient* 12 (1912): 1–82.

———. "La Pagode Quoc-An: Les divers supérieurs." *Bulletin des amis de Vieux Huế* 2, no. 3 (July 1915): 305–18.

Caillard, Jean-Pierre. *Alexandre Varenne: Une passion républicaine.* Paris: Le cherche midi, 2007.

Cao Van Vien. *The Final Collapse.* Washington, DC: US Army Center for Military History, 1985.

Chaigneau, Michel Đức. *Souvenirs de Hué.* Paris: Imprimerie Impériale, 1867.

Chapuis, Oscar. *The Last Emperors of Vietnam: From Tu Duc to Bao Dai.* Westport, CT: Greenwood, 2000.

Choi Byung Wook. *Southern Vietnam under the Reign of Minh Mạng (1820–1841): Central Policies and Local Response.* Ithaca, NY: Cornell Southeast Asia Program, 2004.

Colin, Armand. "L'évolution de la pensée géographique de Pierre Gourou sur les pays tropicaux (1935–1970)." *Annales de géographie,* no. 498 (March–April 1981): 129–50.

Công An Nhân Dân. *Đoàn mật vụ của Ngô Đình Cẩn* [The secret police division of Ngô Đình Cẩn]. Hà Nội: NXB Công An Nhân Dân, 1996.

Cooke, Nola. "Nguyen Rule in Seventeenth-Century Dang Trong (Cochinchina)." *Journal of Southeast Asian Studies* 29, no. 1 (March 1998): 122–61.

Cosgrove, Denis. *Social Formation and Symbolic Landscape.* Madison: University of Wisconsin Press, 1998.

Đảng bộ huyện Hương Thủy. *Lịch sử lực lượng vũ trang huyện Hương Thủy (1945–2005)* [History of the armed forces of Hương Thủy District (1945–2005)]. Huế: NXB Thuận Hóa, 2008.

Đảng Bộ Quân Khu 4. *Lịch sử đảng bộ sư đoàn 324 (1955–2010)* [History of the party cell, 324th Regiment (1955–2010)]. Hà Nội: NXB Quân Đội Nhân Dân, 2012.

Đảng Ủy Ban Chỉ Huy Quân Sự Huyện A Lưới. *Lịch sử lực lượng vũ trang nhân dân huyện A Lưới (1945–2010)* [History of the people's armed forces of A Luoi District (1945–2010)]. Hà Nội: NXB Quân Đội Nhân Dân, 2011.

Đào Quang Đới, Nguyễn Thống, and Võ Viết Hòa. *Sư đoàn 324*. Hà Nội: NXB Quân Đội Nhân Dân, 1992.

Davis, Bradley Camp. "The Production of Peoples: Imperial Ethnography and the Changing Conception of Uplands Space in Nineteenth-Century Vietnam." *Asia Pacific Journal of Anthropology* 16, no. 4 (2015), 323–42.

Domergue-Cloarec, Danielle. "La mission et le rapport revers." *Guerres mondiales et conflits contemporains* 148 (October 1987): 97–114.

Doumer, Paul. *Situation de l'Indo-Chine (1897–1901)*. Hanoi: Schneider, 1902.

Dror, Olga, and Keith Taylor. *Views of Seventeenth-Century Vietnam: Christoforo Borri on Cochinchina and Samuel Baron on Tonkin*. Ithaca, NY: Cornell Southeast Asia Program, 2006.

Dudley, Marianna. *An Environmental History of the UK Defence Estate, 1945 to the Present*. London: Continuum, 2012.

Duiker, William J. *Ho Chi Minh: A Life*. New York: Hyperion, 2000.

Dương Phước Thu. *Tù Ngục chín hầm và những điều ít biết về Ngô Đình Cẩn* [The Nine Bunkers Prison hell and some little known items regarding Ngô Đình Cẩn]. Huế: Thuận Hóa, 2010.

Dutreuil de Rhins, Jules-Léon. *Le royaume d'Annam et les Annamites*. Paris: E. Plon and Cie, 1879.

Dutton, George. *The Tây Sơn Uprising: Society and Rebellion in Eighteenth-Century Vietnam*. Honolulu: University of Hawaii Press, 2006.

Dwernychuk, L. Wayne, H. D. Cau, C. T. Hatfield, T. G. Boivin, T. M. Hung, P. T. Dung, and N. D. Thai. "Dioxin Reservoirs in Southern Vietnam—A Legacy of Agent Orange." *Chemosphere* 47 (2002): 117–37.

Enloe, Cynthia H. *Bananas, Beaches and Bases: Making Feminist Sense of International Politics*. Berkeley: University of California Press, 1990.

———. *Maneuvers: The International Politics of Militarizing Women's Lives*. Berkeley: University of California Press, 2000.

Fall, Bernard. *Street without Joy: Indochina at War*. Harrisburg, PA: Stackpole, 1961.

———. *Street without Joy: Insurgency in Indochina, 1946–53*. London: Pall Mall Press, 1963.

Farmer, Jared. *Trees in Paradise: A California History*. New York: W. W. Norton, 2013.

Franck, Harry A. *East of Siam: Ramblings in the Five Divisions of French Indo-China*. New York: Century Company, 1926.

Fredrickson, Leif. "From Ecocide to Eco-ally: Picloram, Herbicidal Warfare, and Invasive Species, 1963–2005." *Global Environment* 7, no. 1 (2014): 172–217.

Gallin, L., and Indochine Française. *Le service radiotélégraphique de l'Indochine*. Hanoi: Imprimerie d'Extrême-Orient, 1931.

Gillem, Mark L. *America Town: Building the Outposts of Empire*. Minneapolis: University of Minnesota Press, 2007.

Glennon, John P., and Edward C. Keefer, eds. *Foreign Relations of the United States, 1958–1960, Vietnam*. Vol. 1. Washington, DC: GPO, 1986.

Goldwyn, Adam J., and Renée M. Silverman. "Introduction: Fernand Braudel and the Invention of a Modernist's Mediterranean." In *Mediterranean Modernism: Intercultural Exchange and Aesthetic Development*, edited by Adam J. Goldwyn and Renée M. Silverman, 1–26. New York: Palgrave Macmillan, 2016.

Goscha, Christopher E. "The Borders of Vietnam's Early Wartime Trade with Southern China: A Contemporary Perspective." *Asian Survey* 40, no. 6 (November 2000): 987–1018.

———. *Thailand and the Southeast Asian Networks of the Vietnamese Revolution, 1885–1954*. Richmond, UK: Curzon, 1999.

———. *Vietnam: Un état né de la guerre 1945–1954*. Paris: Armand Colin, 2011.

———. *Vietnam or Indochina? Contesting Concepts of Space in Vietnamese Nationalism (1887–1954)*. Copenhagen: Nordic Institute of Asian Studies, 1995.

Gourou, Pierre. *Les paysans du delta tonkinois; étude de géographie humaine*. Paris: Les éditions d'art et d'histoire, 1936.

Gouvernement Général de l'Indochine. *L'aéronautique militaire de l'Indochine*. Hanoi: Imprimerie d'Extrême-Orient, 1931.

———. *Service géographique de l'Indochine: Son organisation, ses méthodes, ses travaux*. Hanoi: Imprimerie d'Extrême-Orient, 1931.

Greene, Graham. *The Quiet American*. London: William Heinemann, 1955.

Grove, Richard. *Green Imperialism: Colonial Expansion, Tropical Island Edens and the Origins of Environmentalism, 1600–1860*. Cambridge: Cambridge University Press, 2003.

Guibier, Henri. *Situation des forêts de l'Annam*. Saigon: Imprimerie Nouvelle Albert Portail, 1918.

Haffner, Jeanne. *The View from Above: The Science of Social Space*. Boston: MIT Press, 2013.

Hammer, Ellen J. *The Struggle for Indochina*. Stanford, CA: Stanford University Press, 1954.

Hammond, Susan. "Redefining Agent Orange, Mitigating its Impacts." In *Interactions with a Violent Past: Reading Post-Conflict Landscapes in Cambodia, Laos and Vietnam*, edited by Vatthana Pholsena and Oliver Tappe, 186–215. Singapore: National University of Singapore Press, 2013.

Hardy, Andrew. "Eaglewood and the Economic History of Champa and Central Vietnam." In *Champa and the Archaeology of Mỹ Sơn (Vietnam)*, edited by Andrew Hardy, Mauro Cucarzi, and Patrizia Zolese, 107–26. Singapore: National University of Singapore Press, 2009.

Hardy, Dennis. *Utopian England: Community Experiments, 1900–1945*. New York: Routledge, 2012.

Harper, Michael W., Thomas R. Reinhardt, and Barry R. Sude. *Environmental Cleanup* at *Former and Current Military Sites: A Guide to Research*. Alexandria, VA: Office of History and Environmental Division, US Army Corps of Engineers, 2001.

Harvey, David. "Neoliberalism as Creative Destruction." *Annals of the American Academy of Political and Social Science* 610 (March 2007): 22–44.

Hickey, Gerald C. *Window on a War: An Anthropologist in the Vietnam Conflict*. Lubbock: Texas Tech University Press, 2002.

Hồ Trung Tú. *Có 500 năm như thế: Bản Sắc Quảng Nam từ góc nhìn phân kỳ lịch sử*. Đà Nẵng: NXB Đà Nẵng, 2013.

Horowitz, David, and Peter Collier. "U.S. Electronic Espionage: A Memoir." *Ramparts* 11, no. 2 (1972): 35–50.

Hostetler, Laura. *Qing Colonial Enterprise: Ethnography and Cartography in Early Modern China*. Chicago: University of Chicago Press, 2001.

Huard, Lucien. *La guerre illustrée, Chine-Tonkin-Annam, Tome 1: La guerre du Tonkin*. Paris: L. Boulanger, 1886.

Hughes, William Ravenscroft. *New Town: A Proposal in Agricultural, Industrial, Educational, Civic, and Social Reconstruction*. London: J. M. Dent, 1919.

Hùng Sơn and Lê Khai, eds. *Đường Hồ Chí Minh qua Bình Trị Thiên* [The Hồ Chí Minh Trail through Bình Trị Thiên]. Hà Nội: NXB Quân Đội Nhân Dân, 1992.

Huntington, Samuel. "The Bases of Accommodation." *Foreign Affairs* 46, no. 4 (1968): 642–56.

Hữu Mai. *Ông cố vấn: Hồ sơ một điệp viên*. Hồ Chí Minh City: Văn nghệ, 2002.

Ikuhiko, Hata. "The Army's Move into Northern Indochina." In *The Fateful Choice: Japan's Advance into Southeast Asia, 1939–1941*, edited by James William Morley, 155–280. New York: Columbia University Press, 1980.

Indochine Française. *Historique de l'aéronautique d'Indochine*. Hanoi: Imprimerie d'Extrême-Orient, 1931.

Jackson, John Brinckerhoff. *Discovering the Vernacular Landscape*. New Haven: Yale University Press, 1984.

Johnson, Thomas R. *American Cryptology during the Cold War, Book II: Centralization Wins, 1960–1972*. Washington, DC: National Security Agency, 1995.

Kelly, Michael. *Where We Were in Vietnam: A Comprehensive Guide to the Firebases, Military Installations, and Naval Vessels of the Vietnam War*. Central Point, OR: Hellgate Press, 2002.

Klein, Naomi. "Baghdad Year Zero: Pillaging Iraq in Pursuit of a Neocon Utopia." *Harpers*, September 2004: 43–53.

———. *The Shock Doctrine: The Rise of Disaster Capitalism*. New York: Picador, 2007.

Kreis, John F. *Piercing the Fog: Intelligence and Army Air Forces Operations in World War II*. Washington, DC: Air Force History and Museums Program, 1996.

Kwon, Heonik. *Ghosts of War in Vietnam*. Cambridge: Cambridge University Press, 2008.

Lam Thi My Dung. "Sa Huynh Regional and Inter-Regional Interactions in the Thu Bon Valley, Quang Nam Province, Central Vietnam." *Bulletin of the Indo-Pacific Pre-History Association* 29 (2009): 68–75.

Lawrence, Mark Atwood. *Assuming the Burden: Europe and the American Commitment to War in Vietnam.* Berkeley: University of California Press, 2005.

Lawrence, Mark Atwood, and Fredrik Logevall, eds. *The First Vietnam War: Colonial Conflict and Cold War Crisis.* Cambridge, MA: Harvard University Press, 2007.

Lê Vũ Trường Giang. "Sự vận động của làng xã cổ truyền, bản Thuận ước và những dấu ấn văn hóa ở làng Thần Phù." *Tạp Chí Sông Hương* 302 (April 2014).

Lefebvre, Henri. *The Production of Space.* Oxford: Blackwell, 1991.

Leshkowich, Ann Marie. "Wandering Ghosts of Late Socialism: Conflict, Metaphor, and Memory in a Southern Vietnamese Marketplace." *Journal of Asian Studies* 67, no. 1 (2008): 5–41.

Li Tana. *Nguyễn Cochinchina: Southern Vietnam in the Seventeenth and Eighteenth Centuries.* Ithaca, NY: Cornell Southeast Asia Program, 1998.

Liên Thành. *Biến động miền Trung: những bí mật chưa tiết lộ giai đoạn 1966–1968–1972* [Operations in Central Vietnam: Secrets not yet revealed from 1966–1968–1972]. Westminster, CA: Tập san Biệt Động Quân xuất bản, 2008.

Logevall, Fredrik. *Embers of War: The Fall of an Empire and the Making of America's Vietnam.* New York: Random House, 2012.

Marr, David G. *Vietnam: State, War and Revolution (1945–1946).* Berkeley: University of California Press, 2013.

———. *Vietnam 1945: The Quest for Power.* Berkeley: University of California Press, 1995.

Martini, Edwin. *Agent Orange: History, Science and the Politics of Uncertainty.* Amherst, MA: University of Massachusetts Press, 2012.

Maspero, Georges. *The Champa Kingdom.* Bangkok: White Lotus Press, 2002.

Maurer, Maurer. *Combat Squadrons of the Air Force: World War II.* Washington, DC: US Air Force Historical Division, 1969.

McElwee, Pamela D. *Forests Are Gold: Trees, People, and Environmental Rule in Vietnam.* Seattle: University of Washington Press, 2016.

Meyfroidt, Patrick, and Eric F. Lambin. "Forest Transition in Vietnam and Bhutan: Causes And Environmental Impacts." In *Reforesting Landscapes: Linking Pattern and Process,* edited by H. Nagendra and J. Southworth, 315–39. Dordrecht: Springer, 2010.

Miller, Edward. *Misalliance: Ngo Dinh Diem, the United States and the Fate of South Vietnam.* Cambridge, MA: Harvard University Press, 2013.

Ngô Kha, ed. *Lịch sử đảng bộ huyện Nam Đông (1945–2000)* [History of the Party in Nam Dong District (1945–2000)]. Hà Nội: NXB Chính Trị Quốc Gia, 2003.

Nguyễn Đình Đầu. *Chế độ công điền công thổ trong lịch sử khẩn hoang Lập Ấp ở Nam Kỳ Lục Tỉnh.* Hà Nội: Hội Sử Học Việt Nam, 1992.

———. *Nghiên cứu địa bạ triều Nguyễn: Thừa Thiên* [Research on Nguyễn dynasty land registers: Thừa Thiên]. Hồ Chí Minh City: NXB Hồ Chí Minh City, 1997.

Nguyen Duy Hinh. *Lam Sơn 719.* Washington, DC: US Army Center for Military History, 1979.

Nguyễn Hữu Đính. "Lâm phần miền nam Việt Nam nói chung, Thừa Thiên Nói Riêng và vai trò trước mắt của rừng rú chúng ta một khi hòa bình được thật sự văn hồi" [Forest sector in Southern Vietnam generally, Thừa Thiên specifically and the role of our forests in producing a peaceful climate that can be truly sustained]. *Nghiên Cứu Huế* 6 (2008): 7–30.

Nguyễn Hữu Thông, ed. *Katu: Kẻ sống đầu ngọn nước* [Katu: Living at the headwaters]. Huế: NXB Thuận Hóa, 2004.

Nguyễn Khắc Thuần, ed. *Lê Qúy Đôn tuyển tập: Phủ biên tạp lục (phần 1)* [Frontier chronicles (part 1)]. Hà Nội: NXB Giáo Dục, 2007.

Nguyen Kim Dung. "The Sa Huynh Culture in Ancient Regional Trade Networks: A Comparative Study of Ornaments." In *New Perspectives in Southeast Asian and Pacific Prehistory*, edited by Philip J. Piper, Hirofumi Matsumura, and David Bulbeck, 311–32. Canberra: Australia National University Press, 2017.

Nguyen, Lien-Hang T. *Hanoi's War: An International History of the War for Peace in Vietnam*. Chapel Hill: University of North Carolina Press, 2012.

Nguyễn Thế Anh. "The Vietnamization of the Cham Deity Pô Nagar." In *Essays into Vietnamese Pasts*, edited by Keith W. Taylor and John K. Whitmore, 42–50. Ithaca, NY: Cornell University Press, 1995.

Nguyễn Tú and Trie u Nguyên, eds. *Địa chí Hương Thủy*. Huế: Nhà xuaˆt bản Thuận Hóa, 1998.

Nguyễn Văn Giáo. "Lực lượng vũ trang Thừa Thiên Huế trong tổng tiến công và nổi dậy Tết Mậu Thân 1968." In *Cuộc tổng tiến công và nổi dậy Mậu Thân 1968*, by Military History Institute of Vietnam, 143–52. Hà Nội: NXB Quân Đội Nhân Dân, 1998.

Nguyễn Văn Hoa, ed. *Địa chí Thừa Thiên Huế: Phần lịch sử* [Monograph of Thừa Thiên Huế: History]. Hà Nội: Khoa Học Xã Hội, 2005.

Nguyễn Văn Tạo. *Đại Nam nhất thống chí: Thừa Thiên Phủ; Tập Thượng, Trung và Hạ*. Sài Gòn: Bộ Quốc gia Giáo dục, 1963.

Nhã Ca. *Mourning Headband for Hue: An Account of the Battle for Hue, Vietnam, 1968*. Translated by Olga Dror. Bloomington: Indiana University Press, 2014.

Nietzsche, Friedrich. *Thus Spake Zarathustra: A Book for All and None*. Translated by Walter Kaufmann. London: Penguin, 1968.

Nitz, Kikoyo Kurusu. "Japanese Military Policy towards French Indochina During the Second World War: The Road to the 'Meigo Sakusen' (March 9, 1945)." *Journal of Southeast Asian Studies* 14, no. 2 (1983): 328–53.

Paglen, Trevor. *Blank Spots on the Map: The Dark Geography of the Pentagon's Secret World*. New York: Dutton, 2009.

Pearson, Chris. *Mobilizing Nature: The Environmental History of War and Militarization in Modern France*. Manchester: Manchester University Press, 2012.

Pearson, Chris, Peter Coates, and Tim Cole, eds. *Military Landscapes: From Gettysburg to Salisbury Plain*. London: Bloomsbury, 2010.

Pearson, Willard. *The War in the Northern Provinces, 1966–1968*. Washington, DC: US Army, 1975.

Peluso, Nancy, and Peter Vandergeest. "Territorialization and State Power in Thailand." *Theory and Society* 24 (1995): 385–426.

Phạm Gia Đức. *Sư đoàn 325: Tập Một* [325th Regiment: Volume 1]. Hà Nội: NXB Quân Đội Nhân Dân, 1981.

Pham Van Son, ed. *The Viet Cong 'Tet' Offensive (1968)*. Saigon: RVNAF Printing and Publications Center, 1969.

Phan Châu Trinh. *Phan Châu Trinh and His Political Writings*. Edited and translated by Vinh Sinh. Ithaca, NY: Cornell Southeast Asia Program, 2009.

Phan Thi Minh Le. "A Vietnamese Scholar with a Different Path: Huỳnh Thúc Kháng, Publisher of the First Vietnamese Newspaper in Quốc Ngữ in Central Vietnam, *Tieng Dan* (People's Voice)." In *Viêt-Nam Exposé: French Scholarship on Twentieth-Century Vietnamese Society*, edited by Gisele L. Bousquet and Pierre Brocheux, 216–50. Ann Arbor: University of Michigan Press, 2002.

Prados, John. *The Blood Road: The Ho Chi Minh Trail and the Vietnam War*. New York: Wiley, 1999.

Pribbenow, Merle L., trans. *Victory in Vietnam: The Official History of the People's Army of Vietnam, 1954–1975*. Lawrence: University Press of Kansas, 2002.

Binh Chủng Thông Tin Liên Lạc, Quân Đội Nhân Dân Việt Nam. *Lịch sử bộ đội thông tin liên lạc, 1945–1995* [History of military communications, 1945–1995]. Hà Nội: NXB Quân Đội Nhân Dân, 1996.

Reinert, Hugo, and Erik Reinert. "Creative Destruction in Economics: Nietzsche, Sombart, Schumpeter." In *Friedrich Nietzsche (1844–1900)*, edited by Jürgen Backhaus, 55–85. New York: Springer, 2006.

Russell, Edmund, and Richard P. Tucker. *Natural Enemy, Natural Ally: Toward an Environmental History of Warfare*. Corvallis: Oregon State University Press, 2004.

Salemink, Oscar. *The Ethnography of Vietnam's Central Highlanders: A Historical Contextualization, 1850–1990*. Honolulu: University of Hawaii Press, 2003.

Sauer, Carl O. "The Morphology of Landscape." *University of California Publications in Geography* 2, no. 2 (1925): 19–53.

Schumpeter, Joseph. *Capitalism, Socialism and Democracy*. New York: Harper, 1950.

Schwenkel, Christina. *The American War in Contemporary Vietnam: Transnational Remembrance and Representation*. Bloomington: University of Indiana Press, 2009.

Scott, James C. *The Art of Not Being Governed: An Anarchist History of Upland Southeast Asia*. New Haven, CT: Yale University Press, 2009.

———. *Seeing Like a State: How Certain Schemes to Improve the Human Condition Have Failed*. New Haven: Yale University Press, 1998.

Sheppard, Francis. *London: A History*. Oxford: Oxford University Press, 1998.

Shinjiro, Nagaoka. "The Drive into Southern Indochina and Thailand." In *The Fateful Choice: Japan's Advance into Southeast Asia, 1939–1941*, edited by James William Morley, 209–40. New York: Columbia University Press, 1980.

Shulimson, Jack. *U.S. Marines in Vietnam: An Expanding War, 1966*. Washington, DC: History and Museums Division, Headquarters, US Marine Corps, 1982.

Smith, Harvey. *Area Handbook for South Vietnam*. Washington, DC: GPO, 1967.

Smith, Ralph B. "The Japanese Period in Indochina and the Coup of 9 March 1945." *Journal of Southeast Asian Studies* 9, no. 2 (1978): 268–301.

Spector, Ronald H. *Advice and Support: The Early Years of the United States Army in Vietnam 1941–1960*. New York: Free Press, 1984.

———. "Allied Intelligence and Indochina, 1943–1945." *Pacific Historical Review* 51, no. 1 (February 1982): 23–50.

Stanley, Roy M. *World War II Photo Intelligence*. New York: Scribners, 1981.

Stoler, Ann L., ed. *Imperial Debris: On Ruins and Ruination*. Durham, NC: Duke University Press, 2013.

Stolfi, Russel H. *U.S. Marine Corps Civic Action Efforts in Vietnam, March 1965–March 1966*. Washington, DC: Headquarters US Marine Corps, 1968.

Sun Laichen. "Military Technology Transfers from Ming China and the Emergence of Northern Mainland Southeast Asia (c. 1390–1527)." *Journal of Southeast Asian Studies* 34, no. 3 (October 2003): 495–517.

Szonyi, Michael. *Cold War Island: Quemoy on the Front Line*. Cambridge: Cambridge University Press, 2008.

Taylor, Keith W. *The Birth of Vietnam*. Berkeley: University of California Press, 1983.

———. "The Early Kingdoms." In *The Cambridge History of Southeast Asia: Volume 1, Part 1*, edited by Nicholas Tarling, 137–82. Cambridge: Cambridge University Press, 1999.

Thích Đại Sán (Thạch Liêm). *Hải ngoại kỷ sự*. Huế: Viện Đại học Huế—Ủy ban Phiên dịch sử liệu Việt Nam, 1963.

Thomas, Frédéric. *Histoire du régime et des services forestiers français en Indochine de 1862 à 1945: Sociologie des sciences et des pratiques scientifiques coloniales en forêts tropicales*. Hanoi: NXB Thế Giới, 1999.

———. "Protection des forêts et environnementalisme colonial: Indochine, 1860–1945." *Revue d'histoire moderne et contemporaine* 56, no. 4 (2009): 104–36.

Thường Vụ Huyện Ủy Hương Thủy. *Lịch sử đấu tranh cách mạng của đảng bộ và nhân dân huyện* Hương Thủy [A history of the revolutionary struggles of party cells and the people of Hương Thủy District]. Huế: Thuận Hóa, 1994.

Tonneson, Stein. *Vietnam 1946: How the War Began*. Berkeley: University of California Press, 2000.

Topmiller, Robert. *The Lotus Unleashed: The Buddhist Peace Movement, 1964–66*. Lexington: University Press of Kentucky, 2002.

Trần Mai Nam. *The Narrow Strip of Land (The Story of a Journey)*. Hanoi: Foreign Languages Publishing House, 1969.

Trình Mưu, ed. *Lịch sử kháng chiến chống thực dân Pháp của quân và dân liên khu IV* [History of the resistance against French colonialism by the military and people of Interregional Zone IV]. Hà Nội: NXB Chính Trị Quốc Gia, 2003.

Trullinger, James Walker, Jr. *Village at War: An Account of Revolution in Vietnam*. New York: Longman, 1980.

Trương Hữu Quýnh and Đỗ Bang, eds. *Tình hình ruộng đất nông nghiệp và đời sống nông dân dưới triều Nguyễn* [Situation of agricultural land and agricultural livelihood under the Nguyen dynasty]. Huế: Thuận Hóa, 1997.

US Army. *Field Manual 3-3: Tactical Employment of Herbicides.* Washington, DC: US Army, 1971.

———. *Vietnam Studies: Command and Control, 1950–1969.* Washington, DC: GPO, 1991.

US Department of Agriculture. *The Pesticide Review: 1968.* Washington, DC: USDA Agricultural Stabilization and Conservation Service, 1969.

van Schendel, Willem. "Geographies of Knowing, Geographies of Ignorance: Jumping Scale in Southeast Asia." *Environment and Planning D: Society and Space* 20 (2002): 647–68.

Vickery, Michael. "Champa Revised." In *The Cham of Vietnam*, edited by Trần Kỳ Phương and Bruce Lockhart, 363–420. Singapore: National University of Singapore Press, 2011.

———. "A Short History of Champa." In *Champa and the Archaeology of Mỹ Sơn (Vietnam)*, edited by Andrew Hardy, Mauro Cucarzi, and Patrizia Zolese, 45–60. Singapore: National University of Singapore Press, 2009.

Viện Sử Học. *Đại Nam thực lục* [Chronicles of Đại Nam]. Vols. 1 and 6. Hà Nội: Giáo Dục, 2006.

Weisberg, Barry. *Ecocide in Indochina: The Ecology of War.* New York: Harper and Row, 1970.

Wheeler, Charles. "Re-Thinking the Sea in Vietnamese History: Littoral Society and the Integration of Thuận-Quảng, Seventeenth-Eighteenth Centuries." *Journal of Southeast Asian Studies* 37, no. 1 (February 2006): 123–53.

Whitmore, John K. "Cartography in Vietnam." In *The History of Cartography: Volume 2, Book 2*, edited by J. B. Harley and David Woodward, 478–508. Chicago: University of Chicago Press, 1994.

Willbanks, James. *The Tet Offensive: A Concise History.* New York: Columbia University Press, 2008.

Woodside, Alexander. *Vietnam and the Chinese Model: A Comparative Study of Nguyen and Ch'ing Civil Government in the First Half of the Nineteenth Century.* Cambridge, MA: Harvard University Press, 1971.

Young, Alvin. *The History, Use, Disposition and Environmental Fate of Agent Orange.* New York: Springer, 2009.

Yumio Sakurai. "Chế độ lương điền dưới triều Nguyễn." In *Việt Nam Học: Kỷ yếu hội thảo quốc tế lần thứ nhất* [Vietnam Studies: First International Conference proceedings], by National Center for Social Sciences and Humanities, 577–80. Hà Nội: Thế Giới, 2002.

Zierler, David. *The Invention of Ecocide: Agent Orange, Vietnam and the Scientists Who Changed the Way We Think about the Environment.* Athens: University of Georgia Press, 2011.

INDEX

A Sáp River, 173–74, *pl.* 6
A Sấu Valley, 9*fig.*, 13, 18*fig.*, 121, 124–25, 128, 130, 135, 139–42, 166–68, 170, 172–75, 179–81, 228n27, *pl.* 3, *pl.* 4, *pl.* 6. *See also* trails
A Shau airfield. *See* military bases
aerial photography, xii, 16–17, 58–59, 63, 98, 99, 136*fig.*, 204n25, 215n54; archival sources, 16–19; B-26 aircraft, 98; colonial surveys, 58–59; CORONA Program satellite photos, 16, 137–38, 144*fig.*, 162*fig.*, 163*fig.*, 167, 174, 192*fig.*, *pl.* 6; Fairchild K-17 camera, 98; Fairchild K-18 camera, 67, 67*fig.*, 216n69; hills (1952–54), 95*fig.*; in histo ric research, 190–91; Japanese installat ions (1943), 67, 67*fig.*; in *Les paysans du delta tonkinois*, 63; US military dominance (1943–45), 66–67; U-2 high altitude, 136–38, 138*fig.*
aerial platform: Air Vietnam, 112–13; airborne radio directional finding, 140–41; Bạch Mai airfield (Hà Nội), 72; bird's-eye views, 18–19; bombing, Nghệ-Tĩnh Soviets, 63; Civil Air Transport (CAT), 97–98, 111–12; Civil Aviation Service of Indochina (Aéronautique Militaire), 58–59, 60–61, 61*fig.*; colonial airfields, 58–59; colonial surveillance, 63–64; communist advantage (1974), 182; definition, 18–19, 57; firebases, 163–64; vs. ground-based networks, 19; inaccessible airfields (1953), 97–98, 98*fig.*; influence on nationalism, 57–58; Japanese development of, 65–66, 67*fig.*; limitations of, 100–101, 147–51; politics of, 215n55; in tex tbooks, 59; US air cavalry approach, 149–50; US Air Force Air Materiel Areas, 112–13; visibility, 135–37
Agent Orange. *See* chemicals
agricultural development center (dinh điền), 118–20
aircraft: AC-47 Spooky, 150–51; B-52, 133, 148, 150, 168, 174, 180; Breguet, 57; C-47 Skytrain, 111–13, 112*fig.*, 113–14; CH-47 (Chinook), 3, 164*fig.*, 165, 165*fig.*, 171–72; CH-54 (Skytrain), 3, 164; DC-3, 97–98, 98*fig.*, 111–14, 112*fig.*, 148; H-34, 139; Lockheed P-38, 66; UH-1 (Huey), 148–50, 171–72. *See also* helicopters
ancestral altar, 15, 53, 54, 153, 174
ancestral tomb. *See* tombs
Army of the Republic of Vietnam (ARVN) First Division. *See* military units
Associated State of Vietnam (ASV), 89, 92–93, 100, 221n52
August Revolution, 71–74, 80, 117, 126

Bảo Chính Đoàn. *See* military units
Bảo Đại, 71, 73, 77, 81, 88–89, 220n44
Bảo Ninh, 187–89
base closures. *See* demilitarization
base construction. *See* militarization
baselines, environmental and historical, 8–10, 22
Bastogne, firebase. *See* military bases
battles: A Bia (Hamburger Hill, 1969), 168–69, 179; A Shau (1966), 147–50, 228n28; Battle of Rice (1952–54), 91–93; Easter Offensive (1973), 178–80, 179*fig.*; French assault on Thuận An beach (1883), 46; French asault on Thuận An beach (1947), 80–81, 81*fig.*; General Uprising (Đồng Khởi, 1960), 122–23; General Uprising (Đồng Khởi, 1964), 129–31; Hòa Mỹ (1948), 84*fig.*, 85–87; Hòa Mỹ (1963), 128; Nam Đông (1964), 129–31; Nguyễn assault on Thuận An beach (1801), 36; Operation Camargue (1953), 99*fig.*, 99–100; Operation Lam Sơn 719 (1971), 176–77; Tết Offensive (1947), 80; Tết Offensive (1968), 154–58, 229n48; Winter-Spring Offensive (1975), 181–82. *See also* tactical zones (communist)

bombing: colonial era, 58; firebase preparation, 163–64, 164*fig.*, 165*fig.*; saturation bombing, 150–51; US bombing (1965–67), 151*fig.*; US bombing (1968–69), 166, 166*fig.*; US bombing (1973), 179–80, 179*fig.*; US protests in Cambodia, 177; World War II era in Indochina, 73

Borri, Christoforo, 28–29

Browne, Malcom, 180

Buddhists, 27–28, 70, 92–93, 116, 122, 126–29, 152–53, 189, 224n29, 228n34

Bulletin des Amis du Vieux Huế, 55–57

Cadière, Léopold, 55–57

Camp Eagle. *See* military bases

Cần Lao (Workers) Party, 103, 115–18, 120, 123, 126, 128, 131, 145, 224n27

cartography: Dutreuil de Rhins, surveys, 41–45; East Asian, 39, 210n59; feng shui, 83; Geographic Service of Indochina (1927), 58–59

Catholics, 38, 88, 91–93, 103, 109–10, 115, 117

cease-fire (1946), 78

cease-fire (1954), 102–3, 111, 113

cease-fire (1973), xvii, 180–82, 197

Central Coast. *See* coastal plain

Central Vietnam Governing Committee, 87

Cham culture and peoples: Đại Việt, 8, 25–26; defeat by Đại Việt, 1470; hybridization, 26–27; Kalinga, 24; Phạm family, 29–30; rule of central coast, 206n15; Thiên Mụ Pagoda, 21; towers, Phú Diên, 21–22, 22*fig.*

chemical warfare, 140, 170–76, 227n10

chemicals: Agent Blue, 139, 226n9; Agent Orange, 8, 138–40, 170–75, 190, 194, 195, 226n9, 233n10, *pl. 6, pl. 7*; Agent Purple, 139; Agent White, 174, 231n71, *pl. 6*; brush clearing, 93; chemical platoons, 170–72, 172*fig.*; CS (tear gas), xii, 7, 110, 156, 170–72, 187; dioxin, 193–97; flamethrowers, 93; napalm (flame drops), ix, x, xiii, 133, 150–52, 162, 164–68, 170–72, 174, 192; pesticides, 170–71; sniffer missions, 172–73, 191; spray drift, 172–73; tactical herbicides, 93, 138–40, 170–75, *pl. 4*; 2,3,7,8-TCDD (dioxin), 139, 170–75, 193–97, 196*fig.*, 231n73; 2,4,5-T, 139, 170–75

Chennault, Claire, 66, 97

Chinese Nationalist Party (Kuomintang), 64, 70, 75, 77–78, 97, 112

cholera, 37–38, 42

coastal plain, 7, 13, 23–24; ancient conflicts on, 13–15, 23–24; archeology, 22–24; Cham culture, 21–22; colonial ports, 51–52; French occupation (1947–54), 90–92; Ô Châu, 27–29; US Marines on (1965–75), 142–44; Việt Minh activity on, 48–49, 78, 99–100

cốc. *See* highlands

communal house (đình), 21, 31*fig.*, 32–34, 53, 81, 87, 95*fig.*

communists. *See* Vietnamese Communist Party

conflicts: Nguyễn-Trịnh War, 26–27; Save the King, 48–49; Tây Sơn Rebellion, 34–35, 37; World War I, 49, 55–58; World War II, 64–74

CORONA Program. *See* aerial photography

counterinsurgency, 14, 20, 89, 91, 101, 123–26, 145–47, 225n49

"creative destruction," theories of: Hungtington, Samuel, 132–34; Nietzche, Friedrich, 11; Oppenheimer, Robert, 12; Schumpeter, Joseph, 11; "shock doctrine," 12; Sombart, Werner, 11, 202n10

CS (tear gas). *See* chemicals

Dạ Lê Village, 69*fig.*, 88; and Càn Lao Party, 117; chemical hazards, 190–92; female suicide bomber, 147; French military occupation (1947–54), 93; gold week, 78; location, 9*fig.*; postwar remediation, 187–88; public lands, 32–33; restricted zones, 199*fig.*; US military land seizures, 159

Đại Việt, 25–26

deforestation, 33, 56, 213n27

demilitarization: abandoned weapons destruction (1954–56), 102; base-industrial park conversions, 10–11, 193–94, 194*fig.*, 202–3n13; clearing Nam Giao, 115–16; Minh Mạng and cultivation policy, 37–39; policies of the French Left, 61–62; recovering civilian properties, 117; removal of French material, 111–12; removal of US material, 184–87; salvage (1975–); surplus World War I aircraft, 49; US troop withdrawal (1972–73), 3, 4, 177–78, 183–84; *See also* demilitarized zone (DMZ, 1954)

demilitarized zone (DMZ, 1954), 103, 107–8, 122, 129, 130, 136–38, 142, 148, 151–52, 158, 168, 178, 187

Democratic Republic of Vietnam (DRV), 73, 140, 227n10

động. *See* highlands

Đông Sơn Commune, 195–96

Doumer, Paul, 50–52
Dutreuil de Rhins, Jules-Léon, 41–45. *See also* cartography; maps

Eagle Bowl, 3. *See also* military bases
Eastern Wood (Đông Lâm), 31, 31*fig.*, 33, 44, 53
Ek, Paul, 145
elephant grass (*Pennisetum purpureum*), 140
elevational logics: Braudel, Ferdinand, 26–27; ecopolitical boundaries, 13; friction of terrain, 90–92, 220n42; helicopters and, 149–50; Inner Road, 31–32; lowland, midland, highland divisions, 13; upper and lower villages, 30–31, 31*fig.*; zomia, 205n3. *See also* coastal plain; highlands; Highway 1; hills

Fall, Bernard, 15, 96–97, 99–100, 221n56
famine, 34, 64, 72–73, 78, 209n44
fire support bases. *See* military bases
firing range (*champ de tir*), 52–53
559th Transportation Group. *See* military units
forestry: British colonial models, 56–57; colonial department of, 56–57; nurseries, 56, 60, 64, 74, 197, 213n28; plantations, 94; during World War II, 69–70
Franck, Harry, 60–61

Geneva Accords (1954), 102–3
geographic information system (GIS), 18–19, 151*fig.*
Geographic Service of Indochina. *See* cartography
Gia Long, 36–38
Gourou, Pierre, 63, 215n54
Great War. *See* conflicts
Greene, Graham, 96–97, 221n56
Guibier, Henri, 56–57, 64, 73–74, 197

Hải Vân Pass. *See* highlands
Hàm Nghi, Emperor, 48
Heavner, John, 118
Helble, John, 126, 129–30
helicopters, xiii. *See also* aircraft
herbicides. *See* chemicals
Hickey, Gerald, 120, 130
highlands: ARVN military rule (1960–), 123–24; động and cốc, 40–41, 84*fig.*, 210n60; *du thượng* (travel to), 76–77, 81, 85; as frontier, 13, 23–24, 39, 47; Hải Vân Pass, 76*fig.*; location, 9*fig.*; in maps, 39–40, 83–85, 84*fig.*;

mountain passes, 25*fig.*, 26–27; Ngang Pass, 76*fig.*; swidden (*rẫy*), 56–57
Highway 1: as ancestral beachhead, 29–30; Colonial Route No. 1, 60; corvée labor obligations to, 54; First Indochina War, 87–91, *pl.* 1; Geneva Accords, 108; Inner Road, 29–31, 31*fig.*, 39–41, 40*fig.*, 125–26; location, 7, 9*fig.*; in *Street Without Joy*, 15, 96–97
Highway 9. *See* roads
hills: ancient occupants, 13; ecological poverty of, 33–35; colonial military encampments, 52–57; French descriptions (1876–77), 44–45; French occupation post-1954, 108; French reconquest (1947), 77; importance to Việt Minh, 75; Ngự Bình Mountain, 63; photographed, 95*fig.*; postwar reforestation, 196–98. *See also* ruins: Nine Bunkers
Hồ Chí Minh, 48–49, 57, 59, 63, 70, 72–73, 75, 77–79, 103
Hồ Chí Minh Trail. *See* trails
Hoàng Cao Khải, 48, 51–53
Huntington, Samuel, 133–34, 151–52, 154, 156
Huế: citadel, 60, 78, 154, 162, 162*fig.*; colonial tourism, 59–60, 61*fig.*; construction of, 38; destruction, 15, 17, 36–37, 80–82, 152–58; liberation (1945), 73; palace, 36; Phú Xuân, 32–33, 37; Struggle Movement (1963–67), 152–55; symbol of traditionalism, 14. *See also* battles
Hương Thủy District, 39–40, 61*fig.*, 63, 71–72, 82
Huỳnh Thúc Kháng, 62–64

Indochina Communist Party. *See* Vietnamese Communist Party
Inner Road (Đàng Trong). *See* Highway 1
Interzone IV. *See* tactical zones (communist)
iron smelting, 9, 32–33, 59

Jackson, James Brinckerhoff, 13, 203n16. *See also* landscape
Jope, Clifford, 97–98

Katu culture and peoples, 24, 30, 75, 84, 86–88, 118–24, 128–31
Kempeitai, 65
Khải Định, 60–61, 61*fig.*, 70

land reform: colonial concessions, 51–53, 52*fig.*; communist policies (1930s), 63; loss